A Reverend and a Rabbi Talk About the Stories of Genesis is an enjoyable and satisfying book. I had a hard time putting it down. But it is also a challenging read that forced me to think hard about the biblical stories and my own life. I am deeply grateful for a Christian pastor and a Jewish rabbi who have the kind of relationship that can produce this level of honest, confessional, and interactive conversation. Their obvious love of the conversation—and the insights that are gleaned from it—are a gift to all who read.

—*Daniel Vestal*
Director of the Baugh Center for Baptist Leadership
Distinguished University Professor of Baptist Leadership

Mike and Rami present the best that biblical scholarship, pastoral care, interfaith dialogue, and loving friendship can offer. When these two come together, they invite us to a fresh conversation with Genesis with two friends as our guides. We learn where Christian and Jewish traditions converge and gain a deeper understanding of our differences. By learning from them, pastors and teachers are equipped to articulate their beliefs without ignoring the perspective of others. We learn how to dialogue with people of other faith traditions. Our faith in God is challenged, deepened, and strengthened by their study of Genesis.

—*William Shiell*
Senior Pastor
First Baptist Church of Tallahassee, Florida

BEGINNINGS

A REVEREND AND A RABBI
TALK ABOUT THE STORIES OF GENESIS

Smyth & Helwys Publishing, Inc.
6316 Peake Road
Macon, Georgia 31210-3960
1-800-747-3016
©2015 by Rami Shapiro and Michael Smith

Library of Congress Cataloging-in-Publication Data

Smith, Michael, 1954 September 1-
Beginnings : a reverend and a rabbi talk about the stories of Genesis / By Michael Smith and Rami Shapiro.
pages cm
ISBN 978-1-57312-772-1 (pbk. : alk. paper)
1. Bible. Genesis--Criticism, interpretation, etc. I. Shapiro, Rami M. II. Title.
BS1235.52.S6535 2015
222'.1106--dc23

2015001915

BEGINNINGS

A Reverend and a Rabbi Talk About
the Stories of Genesis

Michael Smith *and* **Rami Shapiro**

Also by Rami Shapiro and Michael Smith

Let Us Break Bread Together: A Passover Haggadah for Christians

Mount and Mountain, Volume 1:
A Reverend and a Rabbi Talk About the Ten Commandments

Mount and Mountain, Volume 2:
A Reverend and a Rabbi Talk About the Sermon on the Mount

Dedication

To my dad, Archie Jack Shapiro, whose love of Torah
shaped his life as well as my own. —RS

To E. Glenn Hinson, who taught me the value of
cross-tradition conversation. —MS

Contents

Preface

Rabbi Rami

Stories matter. In fact, when it comes to the creation of personality and civilizations, stories matter more than almost anything else. The stories we tell and the stories we are told create our sense of identity, morality, and group cohesion. We belong to this or that group because of the stories we tell about them and ourselves. We reject this or that group because the stories they tell are perceived as alien and perhaps hostile to our own. There is no aspect of human personhood and community that is not impacted by story. So the study of story is essential to our understanding of humanity, and the study of the stories we tell is essential to our understanding of ourselves.

This is why the book of Genesis is so important to me; it contains some of the most foundational stories that shape me as a person and the two civilizations in which I live: Jewish and Western. And this is why I am so excited about exploring these stories with Mike Smith.

Mike and I are similar enough to make conversation possible—we are both married, middle-class, white male Americans with grown children; we are both card-carrying members of AARP; we share a passion for comic books, science fiction, and movies that fall into either of these genres; and we share a love of God, a deep curiosity about religion, and a passion for sacred text, especially the Bible (though his Bible is larger than mine).

And we are different enough to make conversation interesting—he is a deeply committed Christian; I am a serious Jew. He is a Baptist pastor; I am a Reform rabbi. His doctorate is in church history; mine is in Jewish thought. He believes Jesus is God, the Second Person of the Holy Trinity; I believe Jesus was a rabbi awake to the unity of God, woman, man, and nature but no more (or less!) divine than anyone else. His mother gave away all his comic books while he was away at college; I sold mine around the same time to pay the rent.

I am offering this brief comparison so as to help you understand where we are coming from as we read the great stories of the book of Genesis. This book is not a scholarly exploration of the Bible, but a spiritual conversation between friends who, each in his own way, take the Bible very seriously.

For me the stories of Genesis are myths and parables. Myths and parables are two of the most powerful teaching tools we humans have invented.

They speak to truth without having to be anchored to fact. The truth of Adam and Eve is no less true if you doubt, as I do, the historicity of Adam and Eve. The parable of the flood is no less instructive if you doubt, as I do, the historicity of the flood, the ark, and Noah. And because it doesn't matter that these things be factually true in order to be mythically true, Mike and I are not going to spend time trying to prove or disprove the literal dimension of the Bible. What we will do is peel back and reveal layer after layer of insight and meaning that the two of us believe these stories contain. We will differ as to what we find in these stories, and the difference will trigger a deepening of our dialogue, which in turn will help each of us find even more meanings than we could find on our own.

What is true of us is true of you as well. You are no less a part of this conversation than Mike and I. While you cannot add your voice to the printed text, you can add it to the margins. That is, you can read the story, listen to what we discover in it, and then put this book aside to see what you discover for yourself. You might want to literally jot down your ideas in the margins or keep a separate journal of your ideas as you explore Genesis along with us.

Like our two previous Mount and Mountain volumes (volume 1 covering the Ten Commandments and volume 2 dealing with the Sermon on the Mount), *Beginnings: A Reverend and a Rabbi Talk about the Stories of Genesis* is an edited transcript of a conversation between Mike and myself. Like all conversations between friends, ours had a tendency to ramble. To keep us on track and to help make sure that we respond to one another clearly and cogently, we invited my son, Aaron, to be our first reader. Aaron teaches writing, American Jewish literature, and introduction of Judaism and Jewish civilization at Middle Tennessee State University. He edited both volumes of Mount and Mountain, as well as *Beginnings*, and though his words and textual insights do not appear explicitly in this discussion, they echo throughout.

I am grateful to (and very proud of) Aaron, and I want to thank Mike for blessing me with his friendship and for suggesting that we continue our conversation by focusing on Genesis. I also want to thank the good people at Smyth & Helwys for sharpening the book even further and for their willingness to publish it. While Ecclesiastes wasn't happy about the fact that "to the making of books there is no end," as a person who makes his living doing little else, I am made both happy and humbled by the privilege of sharing my thoughts with you through the pages of this book.

Preface

Michael Smith

Long before I heard of theology, I read the stories of Genesis. For reasons not germane to this book, I learned to read long before I started school. My maternal grandmother gave me a book of Bible stories for children, and many of the stories were drawn from Genesis. Admittedly, the tales had been sanitized. Still, they caught my attention and piqued my curiosity.

Naturally, I did what any inquisitive child might do. I went looking for the real thing. Not long thereafter you might have found me working my way through the King James translation of Genesis.

Looking back, I think this important. I first read Genesis because the stories were great stories. I did not read the text in order to find answers about anything. Frankly, I did not know one could ask questions of stories, and I continue to think one should not first read a story in search of what it might teach. Instead, read and enjoy the story as story.

Rami and I agree that stories shape individuals and civilizations. We cannot begin to understand ourselves and others without reference to our stories.

Rabbi Rami Shapiro is my friend. We enjoy one another's company, have enough in common to enable us to understand one another, are different enough to enlighten or confuse one another from time to time, and share a love for the sacred literature of our religious traditions.

Some years ago we began to hold online conversations about some of our sacred texts. The conversations resulted in two books, one covering the Ten Commandments, the second dealing with the Sermon on the Mount. The volume before you records our conversations on the stories of Genesis.

I stress the term *conversations*. Those who come to any of the three volumes looking for a classic, scholarly exchange of essays will be disappointed. The same is true if the reader expects us to tie up our discussions in neat packages and perhaps harmonize our differences. Instead, I invite you to listen in on our conversation, much as if you were reading a collection of letters between two good friends. Our hope is that you will discover the joy and worth of such conversations and start some of your own.

More and more I am convinced the best hope of making our world a good place in which to live is to learn to hold conversations with one another, conversations in which we seek more to understand than to win, conversations that bind us together not through agreement on all matters but in genuine friendship.

Quite a few years have passed since I first began to read the stories of Genesis. They continue to engage my imagination and inform my walk with God and others. My hope is that our recorded conversations help our readers better love and appropriate the stories.

Editor's Note

Aaron Herschel Shapiro

Bizarrely, when anyone mentions the book of Genesis to me in conversation, I tend to think, but only rarely to say, "Oh yeah, that's the book that proves the Jews invented baseball." The cause of this particular mental tick can be traced pretty much directly to my father, Rabbi Rami Shapiro, who pointed out in a sermon given sometime in my early childhood that the book opens with the immortal words "In the big inning." It's a bad pun, I know. But not when you're five, or six, or seven, or whatever I was. Back then, it was *hilarious*.

It was also, though I could not have known it, rather appropriately rabbinical. It turns out that word games of this sort are, in fact, an essential part of what it means to read Jewishly, which means to read with an eye not toward deciphering a text for its *real* meaning, but toward multiplying and extending its possible meanings. The rabbis have been doing this kind of thing for thousands of years, and they have a very specific set of tools for it, many of which Rabbi Rami (Dad) will share with you in the upcoming pages, but truth be told this style of reading should not be labeled exclusively Jewish; rather, it is simply and deeply and essentially human.

As both Reverend Mike and Rabbi Rami mention in their prefaces, humanity lives by story. It is story that grounds and organizes all the mad data of existence; it is story that shapes our experience and consciousness and that, when told and remembered collectively, fashions our cultures and histories. But storytelling is not a one-shot deal. To remain vital, stories must be retold—not just repeated, but reinvented, reimagined, and reexperienced. They must be *made to mean* again and again both by other storytellers, who recast the stories in new forms, and by readers, who interpret those forms anew with each encounter. Thus, the stories change and grow with us as we change and grow with them. Storytelling, then, is an infinite game, and the way to play is never to stop, never to imagine one has reached the "end" of the tale, the "end" of meaning-making, but to see instead that one is only ever, is always and has always been, just beginning.

And so we arrive back at my father's pun, the point of which has very little to do with baseball and a whole lot to do with the game of meaning-making, of reading and storytelling. Puns, after all, are funny because the meanings they embed are both entirely present and entirely deferred. They are the figure/ground paintings of language, in which a goblet resolves into two faces and the two faces resolve into a goblet over and over again. This, perhaps, is what it means to read not Jewishly, but *sacredly*. To seek in story—and especially in sacred texts—not a decisive, ultimate interpretation, but a renewal of interpretive possibilities: an awakening to the infinite recursion of possible visions. And in this way the beginning really is the "big inning," the moment on which the game of storytelling and meaning-making, of truth-telling, really hinges. For it is at this moment that we either shut down the potential of our stories, demanding some absolute disclosure, or embrace the ambiguity of the text and revel in its multiplicity, in the fantastic range of illuminations it offers to us.

This book, *Beginnings*, along with the other books Mike and Rami have written together as part of the Mount and Mountain series, is an attempt at that kind of reading: the kind that embraces ambiguity and seeks illumination over revelation. Focusing on the text of Genesis, the book records a long-running e-mail conversation between Mike and Rami as they read, explore, interpret, discuss, argue over, reimagine, and rediscover that perennial work. Their conversation, as always, is wild and wandering, but also insightful and enlightening. Most importantly, it is open—both in the sense of being honest and accessible and in the sense of being radically incomplete. Mike and Rami are neither striving toward consensus or synthesis, nor aiming for rhetorical victory. They read, individually and together, listening to each other as they listen to the words of the text in front of them, responding to each other as they respond to the story of creation, of Adam and Eve, Cain and Abel, Noah, Jacob, and Joseph, changing the stories by interpretation as they themselves are changed by story and interpretation. And we read with them, and we too respond and interpret and change. And so the game of storytelling goes on: beginning and beginning and beginning.

Chapter 1

The First Creation

(Genesis 1:1–2:4)

Mike: The longer I live with this text, the more I discern a handful of embedded themes, a number of which play out in various ways in subsequent stories.

God is the star of the story. I can almost hear you saying, "Well, of course. There's no one else around!" Quite true! The world we know takes shape because God intervenes to form it from chaos. By my count, the name God pops up thirty-three times in thirty-five verses. Talk about top billing! As Genesis unfolds, God appears again and again as one who acts to shape or reshape human lives and the emerging story of the world. Other actors step on stage. Often they exhibit improvisational skills of a high order, whether for good or ill. Again and again, though, God works onstage or backstage to keep the story moving along in his chosen, general direction.

God works with what is at hand. The story, insofar as I can tell, does not deal with the theological question of creation from nothing. Instead, God starts with what is already there, an earth that is formless and covered in darkness. A wind from God sweeps over the face of the deep, which is to say God surveys the situation. God then acts to bring order from chaos. Light and darkness, day and night, sky and earth, dry earth and water-covered earth—each is put in its place, and each is given its proper role in the larger life of the world. Nothing is wasted; nothing is declared evil and banished. God makes use of all things in order to do one thing: fashion a world.

God does good work. Over and over again we read, "And God saw that it was good." Light, darkness, land, sea, sky, sun, stars, moon, living creatures, vegetation, humankind—God declares all things and creatures well made. Each fits in its assigned place, each complements all other parts of the creation, each is just what it was and is meant to be. In the homey image chosen by the author of Genesis, the world works well enough that God can take a day off and rest from his labors, thereby establishing the place of rest in the larger scheme of things.

God takes a chance with humankind. Within the framework of the larger work of creation, God fashions humanity in God's image. What does that mean? I think the best clue lies in the work assigned humanity: dominion. Hitherto in the story, God has been the sole, self-conscious actor on stage, the one exercising dominion through the act of ordering the world. Now, God invites another set of actors to the platform. They are amateurs, mind you, yet they are gifted with potential to partner with God, taking up management of the stage he has created, so to speak.

That being said, God takes a risk in endowing humanity with the gifts necessary to exercise dominion: free will, self-awareness, intelligence, the ability to think both concretely and abstractly, curiosity, and the capacity not only to preserve but to the shape the world. Many of the stories that follow will trace how such a grand experiment plays out and what God does in response.

Rami: Whoa! Slow down, brother. You got from light to Shabbat in less than six minutes, when it took God six days! So let me slow you down a bit and take up each of your points in turn.

God is the star of the story. No disagreement here, only a question: Who or what is God? The Hebrew word for "God" in Genesis 1 is *Elohim*, a plural noun coupled with a singular verb. The singular verb lets us know that *Elohim* is one and not many, but why use the plural at all? Why not speak of *El*, God singular, rather than *Elohim*, Gods plural?

Since Judaism is a theologically open system, with rabbis priding ourselves on generating multiple and often mutually conflicting answers to every question, I cannot answer this question definitively, but I will share my favorite answer. It comes from what we call *Gematria*, an ancient system of biblical interpretation based on Hebrew numerology.

Hebrew lacks a separate number system and uses the *aleph-bet* as both letters and numbers. This means that every word of the Bible is both a word and a mathematical sum. Whenever words share a common numerical value, we may treat them as synonyms and can substitute one for the other if the result adds to our understanding of Torah. Clearly, we Jews are not literalists.

The numerical value of *Elohim*, God, is 86 (*Aleph* = 1, *Lamed* = 30, *Hay* = 5, *Yod* = 10, and *Mem* = 40). This is the same numerical value as the word *ha-teva*, nature (*Hay* = 5, *Tet* = 9, *Vet* = 2, *Ayin* = 70). *Elohim* and *ha-teva*, God and nature, are synonymous. *Elohim* is that aspect of the divine operating in, with, through, and as nature. And since nature produces a multiplicity of forms, *Elohim* is plural.

Am I reducing God to nature here? Not at all. Think of God as an ocean and creation as the waves of the ocean. The ocean is greater than the sum of its waves, but the waves are not other than the ocean. Nature is a manifestation of God in time and space the way waves are a manifestation of the ocean in time and space. God includes and transcends creation. So, yes, God is the star of this story, and the God that is revealed is one who manifests in, with, through, and as the natural processes by which the universe emerges.

Before I take up your next points, let me stop and invite you to respond to what I have said so far and see where our conversation takes us.

Mike: Sorry, Rami. I'm accustomed to squeezing a great deal into a twenty-minute time slot. That being said, I want to interact with what you say about God. You pose a great question: "What is God?" The answer you give boils down to panentheism, the idea that God is in the creation and the creation is part of God, though God is more than the creation.

I tend to start with the story and ask two questions: Who is God, and what is God like? The story portrays God as separate from creation, though deeply involved in the work of shaping it and in celebrating the results. God pours himself into the work, much as a great artist invests himself or herself in painting, poetry, or sculpture. God's stamp is on God's work. With regard to humanity, God goes even farther, making male and female in God's own image. Who is God? God is the one apart from all things yet the shaper of all things, deeply involved in all he has made but distinct from all things as well. What is God like? At the very least, God is like an artist, who creates something new from the materials at hand, declares it good, and rests content with beloved creation.

Moving beyond the story to ask questions of particular terms brings me to *Elohim*. I find your description of *Gematria* fascinating, but ultimately the correspondence you find between *Elohim* and *ha-teva* (God and nature) feels like coincidence to me. To be honest, such a feeling may reflect nothing more than my own prejudice against numerology as an interpretive tool. Now that I think about the matter, I am uncomfortable with interpretive frameworks that start with particulars rather than larger stories. For example, I tend to distrust Christian theologies that design theologies on the basis of grammar rather than story.

So what do I make of *Elohim*? I suspect it implies something about the nature of God: God is interactive with God; God is one, yet also a community. In some sense God talks to God's self! The Christian idea of Trinity will grow from such an insight. With regard to the story before us, though, the more important point may be that such a God can hardly help but create a world characterized both by individuality and interconnectedness.

Rami: You and I differ greatly as to the nature of God, and this difference will influence our understanding of the book of Genesis. This is what makes our conversations worth having and this book worth reading. If I wanted to talk with someone who agreed with me on every issue, I'd talk to myself. Well, that isn't 100 percent true since I do talk to myself and often find myself disagreeing with myself. That is what it is to be Jewish: one Jew, two opinions.

So as you correctly said, I am a panentheist. I believe that all (*pan*) life is in (*en*) God (*theos*). Just as the ocean is greater than even the sum of its waves and yet no wave is other than the ocean, so God is greater than the universe, but the universe is not other than God. This is a fairly normative view among Jewish mystics and has been for well over 1,000 years. While I hesitate to call myself a mystic, I do draw my theology from them.

As to your challenge to *Gematria*—that these numeric similarities are mere coincidences—I would say this: if Torah is the actual word of God dictated to Moses on Sinai, these coincidences are not coincidental at all, but deliberate hints woven into the text by God to help us get beyond a literal reading of the text, which we rabbis see as the lowest reading, toward a deeper, more imaginative reading.

Now, I do not believe God dictated Torah, but I still use these hints as catalysts for my imagination. In Judaism, the imagination is the primary tool for biblical interpretation, what we call *midrash*. The entire rabbinic enterprise rests on using our imaginations to find and unpack meanings hidden in the text. We are taught to interpret not only the written word, what we call Black Fire, but the spaces between the words, what we call White Fire. We are taught to "read" not only what is on the page but also what isn't! And not to put too fine a point on it, we even interpret the decorative crowns placed on top of certain letters. We have been doing this for over two millennia, so I hope you will bear with me when I can't help but share some of these imaginative readings with you.

Anyway, so as not to lose the thread of your original four points on Genesis 1, let me go back and pick up the second one: **God works with what is at hand**. Fair enough. The text may or may not imply creation out of nothing. The mainstream rabbinic position is that all creation comes out of nothing, and that nothing, in Hebrew *ain*, is one of the names of God, *Ain Sof*, the infinite No-thing that creates all things. God is no thing in particular and yet manifests as all things in general. Again, the ocean/wave metaphor helps here. All things arise from God, in God. And all things return to God in the end. So yes, God creates with what is at hand, but what is at hand is God. See, you just can't keep a good panentheist down!

Your third point was that **God does good work.** I'm glad we are in agreement that the word *tov*, good, doesn't carry moral implications here. In this context *tov* means "whole," and to be whole is to embrace both one thing and its opposite. God creates night along with day because night and day cannot exist with each other. God creates earth and sky because these also go together. God creates the sea and the shore because . . . you get the idea. Torah isn't saying that creation is good in a moral sense, but that creation is whole. And because it is whole, it is sound, and it is in this sense that it is *tov*, good.

Compare this to Genesis 2:5, in the second creation story, where we are told that the garden was barren because God had yet to create rain and gardeners. In Genesis 2 humans are the servants of creation, tending the garden, but in Genesis 1 we are the recipients of creation; we are an act of pure grace created not to serve, but to have dominion.

Which takes us to your final point: **God takes a chance with humankind.** Fair enough, but why? What do we add to the mix? The answer depends on how we understand the word "dominion," and to answer that we have to know what it means to be "the image of God."

Simply put, being the image of God means that we humans are the way godliness comes into the material world. We Jews derive a working understanding of godliness from our admittedly imaginative reading of Exodus 34:6-7: transcendence; creativity; compassion; grace; patience; trustworthiness; truthfulness; preserving kindness (rather than grudges); forgiving the errors, mistakes, and even sins to which our species is prone; and cleansing ourselves of ignorance, arrogance, anger, and fear.

Having "dominion" over life means that we are to be the bearers of these attributes among the living. When we act godly, we are living up to our potential; when we don't, we aren't. And you are right—God is taking a chance on us, and our record is mixed. But from the Jewish point of view, God continually forgives us our failings and sets us back on track to try again. God—the eternal optimist.

Mike: I want to add a bit to our conversation about the nature of God and *Gematria*. As I've noted in our earlier conversations on the Ten Commandments and the Sermon on the Mount, I regard panentheism as the only potentially viable alternative to Christianity. All of life, indeed all of creation, exists within God. We also agree that God is greater than the universe. Where we differ, I think, is over the question of whether God may also be personal. My tradition attempts (and often fails) to hold together two concepts of God: a God who is wholly other and majestic beyond imagination and a God capable of genuine intimacy. The latter factor prohibits me from embracing panentheism on its own terms, though I believe many of its insights can be incorporated into theism.

Perhaps I am able to do so because I am at heart a Christian mystic. I tend to see the unity of all things in Christ. Therefore, I am drawn to whatever various approaches to life hold in common and suspect creation is so built as to tug us in the direction of unity enriched by endless diversity. The other component to my brand of mysticism is an appreciation for direct experience of the divine, however rare it may be.

That being said, I appreciate your use of *Gematria* as a spark for the imagination. I am sorry I did not understand your intent in the first place. What I might call a baptized imagination, an imagination steeped in faith traditions yet also informed by other resources, is essential to the interpretation of Scripture. Without imagination, our interpretations devolve into pale imitations of the scientific method or repetitions of what others have said. So have at it, Rami, and don't be surprised when I also cheerfully apply informed imagination to the interpretive task!

With regard to **God works with what is at hand**, you write, "All things arise from God, in God. And all things return to God in the end." Where we may differ, I think, is in our vision of what such a return might look like. Correct me if I am wrong (and I may well be!), but panentheism tends to visualize creation as a kind of extension of God, destined to be absorbed by God when all is said and done. I think the Genesis story suggests something rather different—a God who dares create a universe and life forms that exist within the larger reality of God yet which also possess a life or essence of their own as a gift from God. All creatures shall return to God in the end, but they shall do so as themselves. I'm content to allow our difference (assuming we have a difference) on this matter to ride along with our unfolding conversation.

You're correct with regard to *tov*. I see no moral implications in the term as used in Genesis. Each aspect (a term I prefer over "stage") of creation is complete within itself, though fully integrated with all other features of creation, at least in the first creation story (Gen 1:1–2:4).

I love your take on the matter of dominion's meaning: "We humans are the way godliness comes into the material world." God certainly is the eternal optimist. I might add God also is the eternal realist, able and willing to recognize whenever the experiment goes awry and to take steps to address the challenge. But that's the kind of thing best left for discussions of stories yet to come in Genesis!

Rami: I appreciate your fine-tuning of panentheism in a Christian context, Mike. I'm surprised, however, that you didn't quote my cousin, Saul of Tarsus, who spoke of God as that in whom "we live and move and have our being" (Acts 17:28). This is a wonderful definition of panentheism.

Anyway, regarding a personal God, there was a time back in the 1970s and 1980s when I would have cringed at the idea of a personal God or a God with whom I might have an intimate relationship. But that all changed in the 90s when I began to have a series of encounters with God as Mother. Honestly, these shook the very foundation of my nondualist theology. If God is everything, how could God be one thing?

I sought guidance from a number of teachers, and one of them, Andrew Harvey, hit me over the head with a 2x4, saying, "If God is everything, how can God as That not also be God as This?" If God manifests as everything, how can God not also manifest as this "thing"? So I stopped resisting what I was experiencing and allowed the process to continue and ripen of its own accord. It has never gone away.

So where you experience God as Christ, I experience God as *Chochma*, Wisdom (*Sophia* is Greek). You meet God's Son; I meet God's Daughter, Jesus' older sister revealed in Proverbs 8:22. She is the first of God's manifestations and the master builder of creation (Prov 8:30). She is the pattern of life, and she delights in humankind and sends her apostles, all of whom are women, into the world to call humanity to her feast (Prov 9:2-3). She is the earliest expression of what John calls *Logos* in his Gospel. Where Logos becomes flesh in Jesus, Logos remains spirit in Chochma. Where Christians are taught to worship Jesus as Christ, we Jews are taught to plumb Chochma through Torah.

Ultimately, I suspect, Chochma and Jesus are the same truth, though we imagine them in very different ways. These are different personae of the same reality. Both Chochma and Jesus are identified as Logos (in Philo and John, respectively), so I suspect we see what our traditions condition us to see, and if we could get beyond the image, we would discover we are encountering the same Truth. This is why I love the writings of the Christian mystic Jacob Boehme (1575–1624), who wrote so eloquently of *Christos-Sophia*, the Wisdom Christ.

Okay. Onto your thoughts on "returning to God" at death.

You are right that I don't see humans endowed with independent and immortal souls. God breathes consciousness into us at birth (Gen 2:7); we are, in a sense, the exhalation of God. When we die, our final breath is God's inhalation. Judaism speaks of this as the kiss of God, and our return to God is a moment of supreme intimacy and ecstasy. No heaven, no hell, just God breathing out and God breathing in.

Do we return to God as "ourselves"? It depends what we mean by "ourselves." I would say that my ego-ic self is the by-product of the stories I tell and was told and that this self isn't my truest self at all. My truest self is the breath of God, which is God. So I do return as my Self, if not as myself.

This raises all sorts of questions: What happens to my personality? What happens to all my memories? What happens to the "me" I imagine myself to be when I look into a mirror or browse through a family photo album? Honestly, I have no idea. Nor do I care. Physically, my cells regenerate over seven-year cycles, so this body isn't mine. Mentally, I think and feel very differently today than I did in the past, so my mind is no more permanent than my body. Other than the disembodied sense of "I" that embraces old photos as "me" and old ideas as "mine," what am I?

So I take refuge in the notion that "I" am simply a temporary persona worn by God to bring godliness to bear on the world as "Rami" encounters it.

One last comment, and then we can move on if you like. Your notion that God is both the eternal optimist and the eternal realist is fascinating. You said God is "able and willing to recognize whenever the experiment goes awry and to take steps to address the challenge." That is certainly how Genesis portrays God. And I know we are only talking about Genesis, but as a Christian you can't stop there.

God tries to make a perfect world with Adam and Eve. They screw that up, and things get so bad that God wipes the slate clean and starts over with Noah and family. Unfortunately, putting the future into the hands of an alcoholic proves no more wise than putting it into the hands of a guy who can't resist even a piece of fruit. God tries again with Abraham, Moses, and the Jewish people, but that too fails. So God's final effort (unless you are Muslim and can take comfort in Muhammad or you are a Baha'i and can take comfort in Bahá'u'lláh) is to come to earth as Jesus and get himself crucified by the Romans because he realizes that the only way to save humanity is to die himself!

As a Jew, I have no idea what this means, but the story is so compelling that I cannot help but love it. Every God asks people to die for him, but only your God is willing to die for us. Sadly, even your God asks us to kill for him as well, but that is the nature of organized religion. Of course, I don't believe that any god is God, or that any story is the True Story. But as a story, yours is tough to beat.

Yes, I know I have wandered off the beaten path, but you started it.

Mike: Once again, our conversation seems to have led us to find some common ground: the possibility of a God in whom all things dwell yet a God we may experience as personal. I am not trying to minimize our differences, but I believe such shared space is holy ground, space enough to accommodate both of us as we try to bring godliness to bear on the world.

Lest we misunderstand one another on the matter of human nature, I quite agree with your point: I don't believe humans are endowed with independent and immortal souls. Instead, it's best to describe us as creations of God gifted with any number of traits, including an independent identity that may or may not choose to align with the Creator, both now and forever. Heaven and hell, in this framework, become descriptive terms of a condition. To be aligned with or in harmony with God is heaven, and hell is the opposite.

The story of a God willing to die for humanity does grip the imagination, doesn't it? Genesis launches a large story, which read in one fashion leads to the story of Jesus and death. If you're ready, let's return to biblical text and take up the second creation account.

Rami: I was ready to move on to the second creation story, Mike, until I reread your next to last sentence: "Genesis launches a large story, which read in one fashion leads to the story of Jesus and death." Full stop!

First of all, you can't say "which read in one fashion" without also telling me what other fashions are available to us. Certainly, we Jews don't find Jesus anywhere in the Bible. Of course, our Bible, the Hebrew Bible, the TaNaKH (a Hebrew acronym for *Torah*/the Five Books of Moses, *Nevi'im*/Prophets, and *Ketuvim*/Writings) ends long before the birth of Jesus, and while the New Testament is a Jewish literary work, like the Dead Sea Scrolls and the Apocrypha, we Jews don't consider it part of the Bible. But this shouldn't surprise either of us.

Our respective Bibles lead back to our respective religions. The Hebrew Bible is the proof-text that confirms our understanding of ourselves as God's chosen people, the carriers of the one true revelation given at Mount Sinai to the rightful heirs of the promised land. The Christian Bible is the proof-text that confirms your understanding that Christians are God's favorites, that Jesus is God's Son, and that one's salvation is contingent upon one's faith in Jesus as one's personal Lord and Savior. After all, what else would our Bibles say?

Can you imagine Moses endorsing a future Muhammad or Jesus speaking of Lord Krishna as the true incarnation of God? Of course not. Sacred texts are sacred to a people, and the people to whom these texts are sacred are the people who benefit from the notion that they are sacred. Bibles are like advertising campaigns promoting their respective products over and against the products of the competition. So I understand that the Christian Bible leads to Christ, but what do you mean that it also leads to death?

Jesus' death isn't the end of the story. Christianity without the resurrection isn't Christianity, but just another first-century rabbinic movement within Judaism.

Personally, I have no problem with God dying. Jesus's crucifixion is an act of cosmic *seppuku* (Japanese honor suicide) with God choosing to die in response to the shame he feels over the way his creation has turned out. God takes responsibility for his creation and refuses to blame others for the errors of his world. This is a huge step forward in the maturation of God.

In the Noah story God says, "I will blot out from the earth the human beings I have created—people together with animals and creeping things and birds of the air, for I am sorry that I have made them" (Gen 6:7 NRSV). Here, God's will is to blame everyone but himself and the fish. How immature is that?

By the time we get to the Gospels, however, God has grown a bit and is willing to take responsibility for the madness of the world. God can no longer blame others for the insane world he created, so he takes responsibility and commits "suicide by centurion."

I am, as I hope you can tell, being a bit facetious, but only a bit. The death of God as Jesus raises all kinds of fascinating issues, all of which, thankfully, are beyond the scope of our current conversation. But you brought it up. So what do you mean when you say the story ends in death rather than resurrection?

Once you find a way to wiggle off that hook, my friend, let's move on.

Mike: Posting a less than refined sentence to you, my friend, is a bit like scattering chum in shark-infested waters! A clarification is in order.

You wrote, "The story is so compelling that I cannot help but love it. Every God asks people to die for him, but only your God is willing to die for us." I responded, "The story of a God willing to die for humanity does grip the imagination, doesn't it?" What I probably should have written next is this: "Genesis launches a large story, which read in a Christian fashion ends and begins again with the life, death, and resurrection of Jesus." I confess I got caught up in your language (dying God, etc.) and did not take sufficient care in crafting my response.

That being said, you were quite right to pounce. Keep up the good work!

In my next post, I'll take up the second creation story.

The Second Creation and the Garden of Eden

Genesis 2:4–3:24

Mike: Scholars over the past two or so centuries have invested much time identifying and debating the significance of the differences between the creation accounts in Genesis 1 and 2. From where I sit in the early twenty-first century, the concerns seem tied to mindsets dominated by the scientific method as applied to literature. While I find the history of source criticism interesting, at the end of the day we must deal with the text as it exists.

What does that mean in practice with regard to Genesis 1 and 2? I think the author of Genesis was a literary genius, able to gather up various versions of the creation story and blend them into a larger narrative. The author starts with God as star of the story, spins a poetic (almost musical) tale of creation, and ends with the creation of humanity and the blessing of the seventh day. With Genesis 2:4 he picks up the thread of the story, but now the center of attention begins to shift to humanity. The creation, placement, task, and nature of humanity take center stage, and the author feels quite free to play with the order of events in order to drive home the point.

If I'm correct, the author's very freedom tells us not to get caught up in a vain (as in both prideful and futile) effort to reconcile the accounts with geological and biological history as we know it. The author knows nothing of such things and would not care about them if he did. His purpose is to say God brought forth the world and all that dwell therein, including humanity, which God forms from the very stuff of earth. From this point forward, the story will focus on humanity and our interaction with God, the world God made, and one another.

God forms humanity, shaping the dust of the earth into us and breathing the breath of life into us. We are of the earth. So long as we remember this is so and love well the earth, we have the potential to flourish and to help the planet do the same. We are of the earth, but there is something more to us as well: the breath of life, which makes us living beings. Breath of life and image of God (the language from Gen 1) are the same, to my mind. Humans are of the earth but are endowed with something that makes them self-aware, connected to the Creator, and capable of subcreative actions within the context of the larger creation.

What kinds of subcreative work does God have in mind for humanity? Genesis 2 speaks of tending a garden, establishing limits, bestowing names, and needing a partner.

God plants a garden in Eden, a garden God fills with every tree pleasant to the sight and good for food. In addition, God places the tree of life and the tree of the knowledge of good and evil in the garden. Humanity is placed in the garden "to till it and keep it" (2:15 NRSV). Work is part of humanity's lot from the beginning, good work designed to help the garden hold true to its nature and become even more bountiful over time.

Humanity is entrusted with a meaningful task, but God does not transfer ownership of the garden. Humans are stewards with real but derived authority. At the very least, the two trees symbolize the possibilities and limits of humanity. While in the garden, humans may eat from most of the trees, including the tree of life. The tree of life of life is a powerful metaphor for their opportunity to return again and again to the source of life: the God who breathed life into them. But there are limits. They must refrain from eating from the tree of the knowledge of good and evil, yet another metaphor for the temptation faced by all self-aware beings, namely indulgence of the desire to become God unto ourselves and the creation, to claim God's world as our own and to order it as we would without regard for its purpose, for others, or for the God who is its rightful owner.

Bestowing names and the need for a partner go together. Humans do not do well when they live isolated. We must not travel alone for too long. To put it positively, we are made for relationships with others, with whom we may develop bonds of mind and heart and purpose.

The author connects the story of the creation of the animals with God's concern to provide us with the partners we need. In the story, the man is given the authority to name each creature. Naming a creature is an act of power, for the name chosen identifies and frames the nature of the one named. Humanity exercises subcreative power to order the animal kingdom, but while useful and good the work does not turn up the kind of partner we need. Where will God find that kind of partner?

Once again, the author takes a story and weaves it into the larger story. The account of God's intervention, the deep sleep, the purloined rib transformed into a woman, and the resultant potential relationship classically captures our inherent need for one another. We cannot evade the need, nor can we satisfy it by other means: Humans are made for the company of humans. True, later stories will reveal how difficult and dangerous human relationships may be; however, the remedy lies not in abandoning relationships but in redeeming them.

Rami, I hope that's enough to whet your appetite.

Rami: I'm afraid I can't dismiss the notion that the two creation stories in Genesis are just that: two different creation stories. While I agree that we ought not reduce the Bible to science, I cannot agree that abandoning science means that we have to abandon the Documentary Hypothesis and its argument that the Bible is a composite literature written by different people over a long period of time.

Like you, I have no need to reconcile the Bible with geology or biology. I cannot believe the universe was made in six days or that God needed to rest on the seventh. I accept the scientific data that the universe is fourteen billion years old and reject the Jewish calendar's claim that it is only 5,774 years old. Nor can I imagine that a ninety-year-old woman (Gen 18:14) or a virgin (Matt 1:18; Luke 1:26-35) can give birth. This doesn't mean there is no value to these biblical claims—only that their value is metaphoric rather than scientific. When we try to make the Bible jibe with science, we end up with bad science and bad theology.

Separating science from the Bible, however, doesn't eliminate other inconsistencies in the text of Genesis, and these inconsistencies (some of which we will talk about as our conversation progresses) suggest the work of multiple authors with differing ideas over long periods of time. If Genesis was the work of one author and he was the literary genius you claim him to be, he would not have ended Genesis 1 with a rich and fecund earth in which both men and women reside and then picked up in Genesis 2 with a barren earth unable to bring forth life without the help of a man who was created solitary and alone.

Just as I have no need to reconcile science and the Bible, I have no need to reconcile one biblical narrative with another. I believe that the Bible is a composite document and that many (though by no means all) of its authors were both spiritual and literary geniuses, but I have no need for them to speak with one voice, even the voice of the final editor scholars call the Redactor. While he did his best to weave the stories into a coherent narrative, there were elements of each that spoke so strongly to the people with whom they originated that he could do nothing more than splice them together. That's the way, for example, we find two different brothers trying to save Joseph from being murdered: Reuven and Judah. Each brother was the founder of his own tribe, and his tribe told the Joseph story in a way that made his progenitor the hero. Rather than choose one tribe/hero over the other, the Redactor mashed the two together. So when read carefully, we can still hear multiple voices in the final text.

That said, let's move on to the creation story found in Genesis 2. Your overview of the story left me a bit breathless. I can't move that fast through the story. So please bear with me as I take it a bit more slowly.

The author of Genesis 2 places the gardener at the heart of the garden; that is to say, there is no garden until the gardener is formed. I use the term *formed* rather than *made* because the Hebrew Bible does so. In Genesis 1, God made humankind, male and female, simply by commanding their existence. In Genesis 2, however, God formed man, a single male, from the dust of the earth the way you or I might form a snowman. The pun linking the earthling with the earth is found only in Genesis 2, where the earthling, *adam*, is made from *adamah*, the earth. In Genesis 1, the word for earth is *'aretz*, not *adamah*, so the pun never happens.

The point may be that the author of Genesis 1 sees *adam*, humanity (male and female), as different from the earth, where the author of Genesis 2 sees the singular *adam* as being pulled up from the earth and then filled with the breath of God. This breath becomes our consciousness, our capacity to know. And because we are of the earth, the first thing we are expected to know is how to cultivate her.

God provides Adam with no instruction on how to be a gardener; Adam is simply expected to know what to do. And why shouldn't he? In Genesis 2, Adam is the earth made self-conscious for the purpose of cultivating both his lesser self (by obeying the commandment not to eat of the tree of knowledge) and his greater self, the earth. Where Genesis 1 imagines humanity ruling over the earth, Genesis 2 sees us as earth's servants, helping her realize her potential as a being of immense creativity.

Given the wordplay of *adam*/earthling and *adamah*/earth, we humans are speakers for the earth who have lost our connection to her. We are the exhalations of God who have lost contact with the imminent divine and transferred our worship to the extraterrestrial and transcendent. We are the place God and creation meet (dust of the earth and breath of God), and yet we have alienated ourselves from both. We are tragic creatures, and our story in the Bible is a tragedy, albeit a hope-filled one.

Let me stop here for a moment and invite your comments. And then I ask that you walk with me a bit more slowly, taking up some issues raised by the Bible that I deem worthy of careful investigation. Let's begin with the commandment not to eat of the tree of the knowledge of good and evil (Gen 2:17). What do you make of this tree? Why plant it and then not allow Adam to eat from it? What is it about knowing good and evil that leads to death? Or is it merely transgressing God's command that is a capital offense?

I look forward to your insights.

Mike: As per your suggestion, let's slow down a bit and spend some time unpacking the matters you raise and the text.

First, I have no quarrel with your observation that the two creation accounts are different stories with separate origins. The core insight of the Documentary Hypothesis remains valuable: that large portions of the Bible represent various literary traditions and/or authors brought together to form a composite. According to the hypothesis, each tradition exhibits a unique set of theological intentions and insights, a proposition I find enriches interpretation. That being said, I part company with those who seem to believe the final product was produced by editors and is more or less a simple composite. I know of no great work of literature produced by committee. At some point an individual, at least to his or her own mind, finds an overall theme by which to connect and arrange the materials. The result is a work that contains multiple traditions and the work of several authors, all turned to the service of the theme(s) selected by the final author/editor. Genesis, I think, is such a work.

So I expect to find inconsistencies in the text, but I do not find them disconcerting. In the particular case of the two creation accounts' descriptions of God and the work of creation, the differences invite reflection. It is as if the final author/editor is content to let the two portraits stand, perhaps as a subtle reminder that no one image captures God fully. I wonder if the two images might also serve to establish the theme of a God who is both beyond our ken yet intimate. Other matters may come to mind, but my point is the decision to place the two stories side by side may have been quite intentional and in the service of larger purposes.

Frankly, I find this kind of discussion addictive! Lest I ramble, perhaps it's best that I turn back to the other matters you raise.

Start with God's forming the man from the dust of the earth. Personally, I tend to like this image more than the one in which God speaks humanity into existence. I confess, though, that my preference varies with my mood and however I may be experiencing God at a given time. To put it another way, some days I'm into transcendence; other days, I prefer immanence.

The very structure of the two Genesis accounts gives me permission to embrace both possibilities and cautions me against settling for one only. At the risk of tempting us to chase a rabbit, I suspect much of the misery we inflict on others, the world at large, and ourselves begins with opting only for transcendence *or* immanence. Perhaps the different portraits of humanity's origin serve a similar purpose: to remind us to embrace and hold in balance both our earthiness and that of God within us.

As you say, Adam is a gardener, but what a gardener! Made of the stuff of the earth yet filled with the breath of life, he might prove to be the being in which the transcendent and the immanent find earthly expression. Adam's potential is off the scale, though he seems largely unaware of the matter. His success or failure matters not only to himself, but also to God and the rest of the creation we call earth.

Let's turn to the questions you raise about the tree of the knowledge of good and evil. My first response is that I have no certain answer to your questions. That being said, I have some opinions about the tree's role in the story. I do not think planting the tree is a matter of choice. Instead, it (as well as the tree of life) comes with the garden. Any place suitable to serve as the home of a creature such as Adam must include the possibility of life-and-death-dealing decisions. God warns Adam not to eat of the tree of the knowledge of good and evil as one might warn a beloved child: "Yes, it's there. The possibility of all kinds of death is part and parcel of creation as it is. Listen to me! Stay away from the death-dealing fruit. I can't remove it from the garden without unraveling creation itself. I can't give you a sample taste, lest you die. But I can warn you. Trust me; believe me. Leave it alone."

Taken so, the prohibition is about something more than obedience or walling humanity off from something that might make humans more nearly God-like. It roots in God's twin commitment to the good of humanity and the integrity of the world he has created.

I think I'll pause there and wait upon your response and additional insights.

Rami: Once again, we find ourselves in essential agreement. And while I do want to move on to the story, let me say two things about the authorship issue. First, I have no problem with the final editor theory, the Redactor as we call him in academia. Since I have no idea what was in the mind of this person, I have no need to argue over why he did what he did. (I assume in a culture as patriarchal as mine that a woman was not the final editor, though, as Harold Bloom of Yale argues, women writers in King David's court may have authored many of the stories found in Genesis, especially those that show men in less than perfect light.)

I also love your admission that "sometimes you feel like a nut, sometimes you don't." No, wait, that's the advertisement for Almond Joy and Mounds candies. You said, "Some days I'm into transcendence; other days, I prefer immanence." Me too. Ultimately, as Jesus may have said, "The kingdom is within you and around you" (*Gospel of Thomas*, Logia 3), and we have to hold immanence and transcendence together as part of the greater unity that is God.

In Christianity the sign of God's immanence is Jesus, the *Logos* incarnate (John 1:1). In Judaism it is *Shechinah*, the feminine presence of God linked with *Chochmah*, Lady Wisdom, who, like Logos, was present at the moment of creation and may have been, again like Logos, the instrument of creation (Prov 8:22ff). When Jesus says, "I am in my Father, and you are in me, and I am in you" (John 14:20), he is telling us that we are all in the Father, we are all in God, indeed we are all of God the way a branch is of the vine (John 15:5). Which brings me to our story.

Adam (the earthling) is made of *adamah* (the earth) for the purposes of midwifing the planet's innate potential for life. God wisely warns Adam not to eat of the tree of knowledge because Adam isn't ready to know good and evil. He is too immature to grasp the enormity of what the tree can reveal. He has yet to do the hard work of mastering his appetites and desires that is necessary to understanding the deeper wisdom implanted in creation. This is why it is the woman (soon to be named Eve) who is the one who eats of the tree of the knowledge of good and evil.

Let's begin with her birth. For the first time something is "not good" in creation (Gen 2:18). As we suggested earlier, *tov*/good refers to wholeness rather than morality. So to say that Adam is *lo tov*/not good is to say he is not whole. Adam is incomplete, alone, isolated, and alienated. This is important because, as we will see, the same sense of alienation is the reason why Adam is exiled from the garden in chapter 3.

Adam lacks what the NRSV calls "a helper as his partner" (Gen 2:18). The Hebrew is *ayzer k'negdo*. An *ayzer* is indeed a helper, but *k'negdo* means "one who stands against." The role of your intimate life partner is to help you overcome the sense of separateness and alienation that is the root of the "not good."

Before creating woman, God invites Adam to name the animals and, in so doing, to discover that nothing hitherto created can help him overcome his alienation. Something else is needed. Something—indeed someone— who is of the same stature as Adam: bone of his bone, flesh of his flesh (Gen 2:23). This someone is taken from Adam's side, *tzela* (not "rib" as most English translations have it), to say that she is his equal, for only equals can promote each other's spiritual growth.

Chapter 2 ends with the observation that both the man and woman were naked (*arumim*). Chapter 3 opens with the observation that the serpent was the most *arum* of all the beings in the garden. Our English Bibles translate *arum* as "crafty" or "shrewd," but the Hebrew *arum* is simply the singular form of *arumim*, the word "naked" just applied to the man and the woman.

The man, the woman, and the serpent share a common nakedness—not nakedness in the sense of wearing no clothes, though none of them were dressed, but naked in the sense of unvarnished, plain, exposed; naked in the way we say truth is naked. In other words, they were simply who they were, each being true to his, her, or its own nature.

Adam, the woman, and the serpent represent three levels of maturity. Adam is the maturity of the child: driven by primitive desires and dependent on others for survival. The serpent is the maturity of the adolescent: impatient, demanding, rebellious, and eager for an independence for which he is not yet ready. The woman is the maturity of the adult: patient, daring, thoughtful, and driven by the quest for wisdom. Why do I say this? Because the story says this.

Why does the serpent speak to the woman rather than the man? Because the man is the child following the rule set by Dad. God told him (and only him) not to eat of the tree of the knowledge of good and evil, and he's going to do what God said (Gen 2:17), no questions asked. And this is his problem. Adam never asks questions. Adam never inquires beneath the surface of the world he encounters. But spiritual maturation demands inquiry, so the serpent ignores the man and talks to the woman and tells her the secret of the tree: it will open your eyes to *tov* and *rah*, wholeness and alienation, and you will be like God.

Notice he doesn't say she will *become* God, only that she will be *like* God. Isn't this what God intended: to create men and women in God's image and likeness (Gen 1:26)? And yet when they were created, God created them only in God's image, with no mention of likeness (Gen 1:27). Why? Because it is up to us to cultivate the garden within and without. The garden within—the kingdom within, as Jesus might put it—is our capacity to know wholeness; the garden without—the kingdom around us—is our capacity to know separation. What the serpent is telling the woman is that until she knows the unity of whole and part, she cannot fulfill the promise of being the image of God by living the likeness of God through acts of godliness.

What follows are three encounters between the woman and the tree compressed into a single Bible verse with three clauses. The woman, knowing the promise of the tree, goes to investigate the matter for herself. Her first encounter is on the level of appetite, mere hunger. This is the driving emotion of Adam. But the woman controls her hunger, and though she sees the fruit of the tree as "good for food" (Gen 3:6), she doesn't eat it.

Her next encounter is on the level of beauty: she sees that the fruit "was pleasant to the eyes" (Gen 3:6) and was driven to possess it. But the woman masters those desires and doesn't eat of the tree. It is only in her third encounter, when she sees that the tree will "make one wise" (Gen 3:6), that she eats. And then she makes a terrible mistake: she shares the fruit with the man.

The woman had mastered her hungers and desires; wisdom alone is her goal, and wisdom alone is the cause of her eating from the tree of knowledge. Adam, on the other hand, hasn't mastered anything. He is still driven by base hunger. This is why Torah says that the woman "gave also unto her man with her, and he ate" (Gen 3:6). He ate mindlessly, blindly, stupidly. And because he did so, the wisdom he received led him not to wholeness but to a sense of alienation.

With the exception of the woman explaining that it was the serpent who initiated the whole series of events, the woman suddenly and unexpectedly disappears from the story. God calls to Adam alone, asking, "Where are you?" (Gen 3:9; the Hebrew "you" is masculine singular). Adam alone says he was hiding, naked, and afraid.

But what about the woman? We assume she was hiding, naked, and afraid as well, but the Bible doesn't say that. A Jewish tradition teaches that only the man hid, only the man was shamed by his nakedness, only the man was fearful. The woman was wise. She knew what she was doing when she ate from the tree; she did it consciously. She knew it was her role to bring wisdom to the man, and though she did so prematurely, it was her timing in feeding Adam and not her eating from the tree itself that was her mistake.

After the punishments are rendered, Adam names the woman "Eve," *Chavah* in Hebrew, meaning the "living one." Eve has become like the Living One; she has achieved the promise of being the image and likeness of God, and Adam recognizes this and names her as such. Eve is the mother of all the living (Gen 3:20), not biologically but spiritually, for she is the one who will carry wisdom into the world. Adam sees what can be achieved but is far from achieving it, which is why the exile from the garden is necessary.

God says that the man—again the Hebrew is masculine singular, leaving Eve out of the conversation—has become "like one of us," knowing good and evil (Gen 3:22a). But this isn't why the man is exiled. The reason for the exile is to prevent the man from eating from the tree of life, the fruit of which was never forbidden to him (Gen 3:22b). Why is eating from the tree of life suddenly a problem, and why is it only a problem for Adam, since Eve is never mentioned in this at all? Because eating from the tree of life makes one immortal, but does so by freezing one in the state one has achieved when eating.

The state Adam has achieved through his premature eating of the fruit from the tree of knowledge of wholeness and separation is *k'ahchad m'menu*, not "like one of us" but "separated from us; one separated from us." If the Bible had meant to say "like one of us," it would have said *k'echad m'menu*, but it doesn't. It says *k'ahchad*, "separate from, distinct from, other than." Adam's eyes are opened only wide enough to see himself as other than God rather than all the way open to see himself as a unique expression of God.

This is why Adam, and not Eve, is exiled from the garden. The Bible is clear on this in both Hebrew and English; only the man is exiled from the garden. The fact that Eve appears at his side in chapter 4 suggests that she walked out to care for him. Her role hasn't changed. She is to be his *ayzer k'negdo*, the catalyst for his spiritual awakening, and to do that she has to go where he goes so that eventually he can go where she goes: home, back to the garden.

This is the Jewish narrative of exile and return. We return to the garden when we make the whole earth a garden, when we bring holiness to all beings. But if return is the promise, why end the chapter with the cherubim in the east and the flaming sword guarding the "way to the tree of life" (Gen 3:24)?

The Hebrew here is *shomair*, to guard in the sense of "to safeguard" and not necessarily in the sense of "to keep out." The cherubim and the sword will keep Adam out of the garden only until he is ready to return, and when he is ready to return, the flaming sword will light the way to the tree of life.

Again, we Jews don't see this story as the fall of humanity. We see it as the first chapter of the human drama of exile and return. We don't believe that all men are children and all women are wise. Rather, we take the story as parable and see all humanity in exile, trapped in the delusion that we are apart from God, rather than a part of God. And we all need the help and partnership of Lady Wisdom, who calls us to her feast of wisdom that we might eat once again and this time become wise and then, through wisdom, return home (Prov 9:1-6). This is why we are told that Lady Wisdom— *Chochmah/Sophia* in Judaism and *Logos/Christ* in Christianity—is "a tree of life to those who hold her close" (Prov 3:18).

Mike: Never again will I entertain your plaintive protest that I cover too much ground in a single post! You swept through much of Genesis 2 and all of Genesis 3 without pausing for breath! All teasing aside, you set the table quite nicely, providing plenty of food for thought and conversation.

Let's start with the woman. I find your take on *tzela* and *ayzer k'negdo* helpful. It reinforces my sense that the story portrays the woman as the man's full partner, equal in stature, function, and potential. Nothing else in all creation can substitute for a partner able to love yet "stand against" you. We, at our best, keep one another honest! As Genesis 2 ends, the man and the woman need each other in order to live well in the garden, whether the external world of Eden or the garden within themselves.

The flip side of the relationship piece is that we humans do not journey well alone. When we face the complexity of life alone, we often make rash or poor decisions. As you say, the man, woman, and serpent may well be "naked" in the sense that each is simply who or what they are. That being so, the man and woman make a mistake when they go their separate ways on a given day, for they were made to deal together with the garden and dwell in it.

As you can see, my interpretive approach assumes the commands to tend the garden, abstain from eating the fruit of the tree of the knowledge of good and evil, and the like apply both to the man and woman—that is, to all humanity.

The story moves to the encounter between the woman and the serpent. Later Christian tradition, of course, tends to identify the serpent with Satan. The narrative itself does not require us to do so. Let's assume your idea holds true: the serpent is simply being and acting like itself. The serpent is one of the creatures brought before the man to be named and considered as a possible partner. It gets a name, but the serpent (like all the rest of the creatures) is not up to the task of being Adam's partner—that is, humanity's partner. The serpent cannot fulfill the role of the "one who stands against."

Yet the serpent attempts to play such a role. Your idea of the serpent as adolescent interfaces nicely here. The serpent's reach exceeds its grasp. Insofar as the story is concerned (without reference to later theological perspectives), the serpent may well be giving what it considers good advice. Its perspective and wisdom, though, are limited so that even if well intentioned, its counsel is unwise. If we press the adolescent analogy a bit farther, the serpent becomes the teenage friend who says, "Ah, what do they know? C'mon, let's do this. It'll be great!" The serpent steps beyond its station and wisdom. Read in such a fashion, the serpent is not a grand tempter (think Milton) so much as a fool.

As it turns out, even the one formed "to stand against" needs someone to play a similar role in her life. Where you see three encounters between the woman and the tree compressed into a single verse with three clauses, I see a rapid decision made in isolation. Like the serpent, her reach exceeds her grasp. Her wisdom is great, indeed ideally suited to the partnership with the man, but it cannot foresee or imagine the consequences of eating from the tree. She eats, her eyes are opened, and everything changes.

Perhaps it's a matter of translation, but insofar as I can tell, both the man and the woman remain very much a part of the story. The woman offers the fruit to the man, and he eats it. We are not told why she gives him the fruit or why he eats it. Our imaginations are free to roam. I'll select one possibility for the moment: the bond intended for their good becomes the means of their shared catastrophe. Wherever they may go, they will go together.

Both have their eyes opened, though this does not mean they see clearly. In fact, they cannot bear the sight. They sew fig leaves together, the better to hide from whom and what they are and, perhaps, from each other. They no longer trust God, the creation, one another, or themselves. It's a classic snapshot of fear-driven alienation.

Just as they complete their work, they hear God walking in the garden. Both feel the need to hide from the Lord. The presence they once felt at home around now fills them with fright. God addresses the man, and the man's response indicates the degree of alienation between himself and the woman. He speaks of his own fear in the singular "I." When pressed about the matter of the fruit, he speaks of the woman as if he hardly knows her. She is now "the woman." The woman does no better when God confronts her. She points God to the serpent.

We need to take care at this point. This is not simply a tale about our human tendency to shift blame. The man and the woman try to lay down their assigned nature and role in creation. In effect, they say to God, "We failed because you set us up for failure. You put the tree in the garden with us. You made the woman, and look how that has worked out! You made the creature, which then put the idea in the woman's head. Why did you make the snake so crafty?" Both the man and the woman paint themselves as victims rather than stewards of the creation, but they are stewards—stewards with real but defined authority.

God cannot undo what is done without undoing them. Created or formed to be stewards of the earth, companions to one another, and partners with God, they nonetheless must go into exile. Bound together, they share the exile and its hardships. I am enormously attracted to the Jewish tradition you reference and its assignment of the wisdom role to the woman. I think, though, the story itself portrays humanity's inescapable, corporate nature. In some sense, what happens to one happens to all.

God, while constrained by the choices he made in their creation, can adjust the emerging story of creation. What might have been is no longer possible, but another story may yet be written. Animals die for the sake of the humans. The man and woman will die, but their death is postponed. They must leave the garden, but God provides them a world in which to live out their lives. The story will continue, and who can say how it will end?

Rami: I love when you find just the right phrase to clarify my ramblings. Speaking of the relationship between life partners, you said, "We keep each other honest." Yes! That's it exactly.

I want to comment briefly on a couple things. First, regarding the notion of serpent as Satan, in Judaism, Satan is not a rebellious angel, but

God's prosecuting attorney. As we learn in the book of Job, Satan roams the earth, reporting back to God all that he sees (Job 1:7). Satan can do nothing that is not God's will. So if the serpent is Satan, he is acting according to God's plan.

Just to offer a slightly different take, some ancient rabbis, noting that the numerical value of both *serpent* and *messiah* is 358, argue that the serpent is the Messiah in disguise. This is why the serpent was the most *arum*/naked of all creatures: he was the most pure, the most innocent, the most transparent to God's presence within and without. Understanding serpent as Messiah allows us to read the acts of the serpent in a positive light; he was seeking to elevate the consciousness of humanity by opening the eyes of the one-half of humanity that had the potential to master her desires and cravings and realize her unity with God.

I still take issue with the notion that the man and woman "remain very much part of the story." Both in the original Hebrew and in every English translation I know of, after the punishments are announced, the story focuses on the man alone, with every pronoun and accompanying verb being masculine singular. We "remember" Eve being involved, but this is not true to the text itself. But let's not rehash that.

Second, you are right that the story continues, but I wonder if you aren't being a bit disingenuous when you say, "Who can say how it will end?" As a Christian, you know how it ends: with the return of Jesus and the salvation of the faithful. As a Jew, I know how it ends: with the resurrection of the dead (Isa 26:19), the restoration of the people Israel in the land of Israel (Ezek 37:24), with nations hammering their swords into ploughshares (Mic 4:3), and with every human being sitting unafraid beneath her own vine and fig tree (Mic 4:4). These are the promises God gives in our respective traditions.

So we know how the story ends. But do we believe it, and, more importantly, do we act in ways that bring the promise closer to fruition?

But we can't talk about the end of the story without mentioning the dark side of our respective promises. In Judaism, the dark side is the notion that our restoration in the promised land comes at the expense of other people. That is certainly true in the Bible where God sanctions genocide in order to clear the promised land of non-Jews (1 Sam 27:8-9, to cite but one example). And it is also true in the minds of some contemporary Jews who imagine a modern Israel free of Palestinians. I reject both views. God doesn't sanction genocide, and the final promise is not restricted to a chosen few, as the prophet Micah made clear.

As for the dark side of the Christian promise, I invite you to tackle that one yourself. Let me just say that because so many Christians have told me that God's promise for me and my fellow Jews is eternal damnation in the fires of hell, I suspect Christianity's dark side also has to do with exclusivism. Religion is a human invention, and like all such inventions it has the potential for great good as well as great evil.

Mike: You're right. Both our traditions provide endings to the larger story. The Christian tradition actually provides a number of varied endings. Most follow the general outline you suggest. All versions of the great story's ending, though, developed long after the tale of the garden, the man, and the woman assumed its final form. When I write "Who can say how it will end?" I have in mind a specific approach to the Genesis 3 story: trying to read it as a story in its own right, set in a specific context (following Gen 1 and 2). I want to try to read and appreciate the story without imposing later interpretations.

Doing so not only treats the particular story with respect but also opens the possibility of reading subsequent stories with relatively fresh eyes. We cannot escape our interpretive traditions, but we may set them aside for a while by choice. My sense is that we live in a time when both our religious traditions must engage in such an attempt for the sake of God's world.

All of which brings me to the question of the dark side, the teaching embedded in both our traditions that the fulfillment of God's promises to us must come at the expense of others. Exclusivism certainly drives both the proposition and its expression in history. That being said, we need not read exclusivism back into the Genesis stories we have considered to this point. Genesis 1–3, to my mind, challenges the foundations of exclusivism. One God creates one world and a single human species, each one of which is animated by the breath of life and made in the image of God. The exile from the garden, whether read in your fashion or as a result of some kind of fall, does not change the situation. A significant strand within the larger Christian tradition builds on this insight to oppose exclusivism in theory and practice.

Don't worry! I'll be glad to wrestle with the problem of exclusivism when it rears its ugly head in later stories. The matter might arise as we take up the next story in Genesis.

Rami: I was hearing far more than you intended to say, Mike. Thanks for clarifying that. So let's move on and see how able we are to deal with the story of Cain.

Chapter 3

Cain and Abel

Genesis 4:1-16

Mike: The story of Cain and Abel operates at several levels. On the surface, it's the first murder story. Motive, deed, investigation, interrogation, denial, conviction, and punishment—all good murder tales build on such plot elements. We might read it as the first family drama featuring absentee parents, estranged siblings, and the tragedy of murder. Scholars sometimes look to find a story behind the story. They ask if the sad tale captures the conflict between semi-nomads and settled farmers, semi-nomads and city-dwellers and the like.

The story, I think, addresses the nature of human life east of Eden. Eve bears Cain and Abel. Insofar as I can tell, she treats their births as a blessing, the result of a kind of co-labor with God. Her words establish a subtheme: children are a gift from God, regardless of how their lives may play out.

The brothers take up occupations that lead to different lifestyles. Abel becomes a keeper of sheep; Cain takes up farming. Shepherds move around, pitching their tents wherever water and food suitable for sheep may be found. Fields of grain, on the other hand, dictate that a farmer stay put. Their occupations foster the separation of the brothers. Certainly, they have little opportunity to talk with one another, explore one another's thinking, or develop empathy for one another. The general theme of alienation finds specific expression in their relationship.

Both want peace with God. The story does not tell us where they got the idea of offering God a portion of the fruits of their labor, but each man does so. Both bring an offering to God, though they seem to operate from different perspectives on God. Cain brings "an offering" while Abel selects a gift from "the firstlings of his flock, their fat portions." I get the impression Cain's is an *ad hoc* offering, one that entails little faith or risk or perhaps gratitude. Maybe I'm too hard on Cain because of my experience with church people, too many of whom speak of trusting God while making darn sure they have surplus money tucked away before giving a bit of it to God. At any rate, Cain does not bring the first fruits of his harvest, and I suspect this is the key to his problem with God.

Abel, in contrast, selects from among the first born of his flocks and from the healthiest of them. He gives God the first and best of his flock. The implication is that Abel acknowledges the primacy of God in all things.

God accepts Abel's offering but has "no regard" for Cain's. Rather than ask himself hard questions about why this might be so, Cain sinks into an angry sulk. His response reminds me of numerous pastoral encounters with addicts. Some addicts, when confronted with the results of their attitude and behavior, choose to face their own responsibility in the matter. Many, though, opt to blame others. God sees Cain slipping in the latter direction and intervenes to warn him, and I'm paraphrasing here: "You are in trouble, but you can change things for the better. Take care, though, for if you continue down the way you're going, sin will master you" (Gen 4:6-7).

Cain either refuses to heed God's warning or cannot find it within himself to change course. Rather than take responsibility for his perceptions, feelings, and actions with regard to God, Cain turns on his brother. He does not perceive Abel as a human but instead as the cause of his trouble. Cain lures his brother to the relative isolation of the fields and kills him. He commits what appears to be a premeditated murder.

No human confronts Cain about the murder of Abel. Instead, God again speaks to him. God gives Cain an opportunity to confess his crime, but Cain tries to evade the question by posing one of his own: "Am I my brother's keeper?" The question becomes one of the great questions faced by humans and human societies. Cain's implied negative answer finds expression in neglect, racism, slavery, genocide, and every expression of ego-centeredness known to human history. God's implied "Yes" becomes the never-ending counterpoint articulated by many a prophet and, in my tradition, most specifically through the parable of the good Samaritan and Matthew 25:31-46.

God punishes Cain by taking away his livelihood and birth community. Of course, we might argue that Cain wrecks his own world. Either way, he faces exile from the only home and work he has known. Cain the murderer now must live out his life as a fugitive in danger of his life. Cain laments his punishment, but his lament contains no word of regret for his own failure; indeed, it provides no hint that he has any sense of responsibility for his attitudes and deeds. In modern terms, Cain has proven to be a sociopath.

Even so, God acts to inject a bit of grace into Cain's life. God provides him with an undefined mark designed to warn off those who might want to kill him. God promises that should someone murder Cain, God will avenge him. Cain continues his downward spiral. He goes away from the presence of God and settles even farther east of Eden.

Rami, the story seems to me to one that explores the reality, implications, and essential tragedy of alienation. I look forward to reading your take.

Rami: You have given us a great summary of the story, Mike, and I was impressed by how deftly you slipped in a dig at cheap congregants. Now, let me wander a bit.

In Genesis 4:1 we are told that "the man had known Eve his woman, and she conceived and bore Cain." Did you ever wonder when Adam and Eve had sex? The Hebrew euphemism for sexual intercourse is *yadah*, "to know," and is written here in the past-perfect tense, suggesting that Eve became pregnant when she and Adam still lived in the garden.

Why does this matter? First, it satisfies any prurient interests we might have about the sex life of the first couple, but, second, it suggests that Cain, the first murderer, was a product of life in the garden. The garden itself has the capacity to produce evil. This isn't all that surprising since God is the source of all evil; as God tells us in Isaiah, "I form light and create darkness; I create goodness and make evil; I the Ineffable One alone do all these things" (Isa 45:7). Torah seems to be saying that everything from the macrocosmic to the microcosmic is part of the dynamic interplay of opposites as part of a great unity.

Knowing this allows us to avoid the trap of having to explain evil as something separate from both the Creator and the creation. It allows us to own the dark side of life and to work to minimize its impact. This, I will argue later, is what God reveals to Cain after the murder of Abel.

And what shall we make of the word *yadah*, "to know," as a euphemism for sexual intimacy? Knowing is a kind of intimacy. And what is more intimate than sexual union? So I see why knowing and sexual union are linked. In fact, linking knowing with sexual union allows us to set a moral standard for that union. Holy union, sacred union, is that which is an expression of and vehicle for ever deeper knowing, and any sexual encounter that fails to come from and lead to a loving, knowing intimacy is unholy. I'd be interested to hear your take on that.

One last point before I turn it back over to you, and that has to do with the word *ish*, man. While *adam*/earthling (from *adamah*/earth) can refer to both men and women, *ish* can only mean "man." *Isha* is Hebrew for "woman." Our rabbis noted that the word *ish* (*aleph, yod, shin*) is very close to the word *esh*/fire (*aleph, shin*), the only difference being the letter *yod* at the center of *ish*. *Yod* is first letter of God's name YHVH (*yod-hey-vav-hey*) and the first letter of *yadah*, "to know intimately." From this, they taught that man comes to know God and act godly when he burns away the dross of ego. Failing that, men slip from *ish* to *esh* and become raging fires, wantonly consuming life rather than wisely preserving it.

The Hebrew for woman, *isha* (*aleph, shin, hey*), is a bit different. Here, too, we find the word *fire* (*esh: aleph, shin*), but not the letter *yod*. Instead, we have the second and last letters of God's name: *hey*. The *yod*, the "ee" sound on both *ish* and *isha*, is internalized (pronounced but not seen) in women. Just as Eve became wise by mastering her passions rather than succumbing to them (as did Adam), so the divine knowing of which women are capable is a more interior knowing than men normally attain.

The letter *hey* adds a further dimension to *isha*. First, the internalized *yod* coupled with the external *hey* spells *Yah*, God, as in *halleluyah*: praise (*hallelu*) God (*Yah*). So a woman is a more fully actualized expression of God and godliness. But that isn't all. In Hebrew, the letter *hey* often implies direction, movement. Where *ish* is a holy fire, *isha* is a holy fire on a mission. Following the Jewish tradition that only Adam was exiled from the garden while Eve left on her own to guide her man that he might become a holy fire rather than a mindlessly consuming one, the direction toward which woman is leading man is back to the garden. Her route is circuitous because man is a slow learner, but in the end this is her destination.

While moved by this teaching, I take it metaphorically. *Ish* and *isha* are dimensions of our psyche that must intimately know and unite with one another. We are each the *ish* that must beware of becoming *esh*, and we are each the *isha* that can lead us home. The deepest spiritual work is to harness the fire and make it holy and then set its direction back to the garden.

I'll be happy to get back to the story, but first let me invite you share your thoughts on my latest ramblings.

Mike: I am fascinated by your exploration of *yadah*, *ish*, *isha*, and *esh*. Christian scholars do some of the same kind of work when they mine the historical uses and kindred terms of a Greek word or phrase from the

New Testament. Few Christian scholars, to the best of my knowledge, would exercise your interpretive creativity with regard to a consuming fire, holy fire on a mission, and the like. A Christian poet, on the other hand, might do so!

That being said, I agree that *ish* and *isha* may serve as metaphors for dimensions of the human psyche. I would rewrite one of your sentences to read, "The deepest spiritual work is to harness the fire and make it holy so that it drives us into the future alongside and in the wake of God." I do not think we can return to the garden, but I believe we may live toward a God-renewed earth and human society, something akin to yet better even than what God first envisioned.

As for the matter of evil, a monotheist cannot long evade admitting that all things find their ultimate source in God. To my mind, though, God does not create moral evil so much as God fashions a certain kind of world, a world in which human decisions matter. Cain, being human, possesses the power to choose what to make of his humanity. How will he deal with his brother? How will he deal with God? Will he choose the way of humility, or will he try to bend God and the created world to his will? My perspective is that the story in question builds on the preceding stories to teach that God is responsible for creating the world while we are responsible for what we make of it and ourselves.

Rami: Okay, back to the story. You're right, Mike, to remind us that on one level this story reflects an ancient rivalry between farmers (Cain) and herders (Abel). The herders needed unrestricted access to grazing land, and the farmers needed to demarcate their farms and keep the sheep from eating their crops. But as we both know, there is more to the story than this.

In Genesis 4:3 we are told that Cain initiated the idea of making an offering to God. God never asked for this. And while it is only natural that Bible commentators defend Abel, what if things went this way: "And after a time, the harvest ripened and Cain's fields were filled with food. And Cain saw in this bounty the grace of God who had clearly overruled the punishment given his father Adam that would have required the earth to begrudge Cain her bounty" (Gen 3:17-18). So Cain brought the gifts of God back to God as a way of giving thanks. Seeing the action of his brother, Abel, a shepherd unbothered by the punishment set in motion by his father's sin, worried that lest he outdo his brother, God might become angry with him and curse the shepherd's way as he had cursed the farmer's way. So Abel took his choicest lamb and offered it to God. In other words, perhaps Abel's act was fundamentally selfish. When God seemed to reject Cain's offering and accept Abel's, Cain felt betrayed. Cain confronted Abel over this, they struggled, and Abel died. Pure speculation, I know, but since the Bible doesn't tell us why God rejects Cain's gift or what the brothers were fighting about, I may well be on to something.

Moving on to the central message of the story, it seems to me that there are two key verses that require our attention: God says to Cain, "Why are you angry, and why has your countenance fallen? If you do well, will you not be accepted? And if you do not do well, sin is lurking at the door; its desire is for you, but you must master it" (Gen 4:6-7 NRSV). And "Am I my brother's keeper?" (Gen 4:9 NRSV). Let me take up each in turn.

Where is the logic in God's words? It is clear why Cain is angry and depressed: he came to say "thank you" to God—the first human ever to do so—and God rejected him. Really, this isn't Cain's fault but God's. Maybe God didn't know what to do with such an offering and only realized what he needed to do when given a second opportunity by Abel. Maybe what God is saying to Cain in the first half of verse 7 is this, "Look, fella, I'm new at this. Nobody ever gave me anything before. I didn't know what to do. I figured it out by the time your brother came with his gift, so don't be angry or depressed, but try again, give me another chance, and I will accept your gift just like I did your brother's gift."

If this is what God meant to say, Cain didn't get it.

But what about the second half of the verse: "And if you do not do well, sin is lurking at the door; its desire is for you, but you must master it"? This is fascinating. Notice that the sin isn't the action associated with not doing well. It may be not doing well that allows sin to lurk at the door, but the causal deed and sin itself are two different things.

And notice that God says sin desires us rather than we desire sin. It isn't that Cain wants to sin, but that sin has a will of its own and that will is to ensnare us. And then notice that we must master sin, the external force that desires us, not master an internal desire of our own. People aren't yet sinful. It takes us until the story of Noah for that to happen.

Sin here seems to be a free agent, an energy working its own destiny by trying to ensnare human beings. I am partial to this. I sometimes believe that there is a free-floating evil in the world, the *yang* to goodness's *yin*. If good and evil go together, and I think they do, and creation is *tov*/whole, as the Bible says, then it must contain evil as well. We don't bring sin into the world; it has been here all along. We just succumb to it.

In other words, just as Adam was to subdue the earth, Cain learns that we must subdue the evil that resides in the earth as well. How do we do that? I think the "brother's keeper" verse is the answer. We subdue sin when we are the caretakers of person and planet, when we look out for the welfare of others. This is Jesus' telling us to care for the "least of these" in Matthew 25:40, 45.

I have more to say about this story, but let me hear from you first.

Mike: You, my friend, are a city kid. Anyone who grew up on a farm or spent their childhood trying to herd sheep would assume both Cain and Abel worked hard for their respective bounties. The earth yields a harvest, the herd yields lambs, but the farmer and shepherd sweat, freeze, strain muscles and tendons, and lose sleep to make it so.

The two brothers enjoy or endure a level playing field, a world in which knowledge, labor, and a bit of luck are required to produce either a harvest or a growing herd. They are born into such a world. Eden is not ebbing; it is gone.

The story itself treats the brothers in neutral fashion insofar as their childhoods, vocations, and work ethic are concerned. Each brother is gifted with an awareness of God any mystic might envy!

Both bring an offering to God. We're not told why they do so, nor does the story indicate whether either of them is the first to make an offering to God. My strong impression is that they act independently of one another (and one can only wonder how the story might have played out had they talked the matter through together beforehand, in effect acting as one another's keeper).

What's the difference between the offering accepted and the offering rejected? As you note, the tale does not give an explicit answer. To my reader's eye and ear, though, the difference seems to lie in the two men. Both work hard to produce what they have. Perhaps they view the results differently. In the course of my life, I've dealt with three kinds of hard-working persons. The first knows little or nothing of God and simply assumes, "I did this. What I've grown or produced is the result of my brains and hard work. It belongs to me." A second kind of person knows of God and may even want a relationship with God, but he or she might express their view in this way: "I believe in God, and I'm glad God is around, so I throw a bit of my wealth and goods God's way. I'm rather pleased to be able to acknowledge God, especially when things are going well. Of course, I hope to get a thank-you note from God." The third kind of person takes a different tack: "I know all my opportunities are a gift from God, and I work hard to make the most of what God has provided. In acknowledgment that all ultimately comes from God and returns to God, I offer God the first fruits of my labor."

In short, the spirit in which the gift is offered is the core issue. Cain does not do well in that he tends to want to claim his life and labor as his own and makes his offering accordingly. Abel, on the other hand, makes an offering that suggests he believes (or wants to believe) he is a steward of the opportunities God provides. The difference in the two approaches and the kind of world each might build becomes a key theme throughout Scripture.

Cain's perspective makes him vulnerable to sin. Both of us, I think, like the image of sin lurking at the door. We agree the story implies the existence of sin as a kind of power present and at work in the world. Cain is like an adolescent, so caught up in himself and what he wants to do or be, that he cannot see the danger. God graciously warns him, points to an alternative approach, and hopes. Sadly, Cain cannot find the humility to take even God's guidance. Instead, he succumbs to bitterness and rage and kills his brother.

I am inclined to see Cain's story as our story. His opportunities, strong points, struggles, and failures are ours. Abel, on the other hand, is the alternative plot element, the story of what might have been and what still might be, a standing invitation to consider another way from that of Cain.

Rami: Guilty as charged, Mike, I'm a city boy. But that's your fault, not mine. For millennia, Christian authorities forbade Jews from owning land, so I come by my urban bias legitimately. Despite the early Zionist passion for farming, as far as I'm concerned, the mid-sixties television show *Green Acres* could have been a documentary on American farming life. But just because I never milked a cow or sheered a sheep doesn't mean the Bible is saying that Cain is a narcissistic adolescent. I think this is ancient rabbinic bias carried forward by later Christian commentators designed to explain away God's arbitrary preference for Abel over Cain. So let's see if we can go beyond it.

All the Bible says is that both men brought offerings to God, and for no stated reason whatsoever, God preferred Abel's over Cain's and thus set the stage for the world's first homicide. Cain's punishment is banishment: "When you work the ground, it shall no longer yield its bounty to you. You shall become a vagrant and a wanderer on earth" (Gen 4:12). Cain's response to his punishment is intriguing: "Will I be hidden from your face?" (Gen 4:14).

It is important that we translate the Hebrew here literally as "face" rather than "presence" as some English translations render it. Cain complains that he is separated from the "face of the earth" and then worries that he will now be hidden from the "face" of God as well (Gen 4:14). It is the lack of faces that terrifies Cain. To understand the importance of "face," I turn to the Jewish philosopher Emmanuel Levinas (1906–1995). For Levinas, the human face is a gateway to the divine: "The dimension of the divine opens forth from the human face. . . . There is first the very uprightness of the face, its upright exposure, without defense. The skin of the face is that which stays most naked, most destitute. It is the most naked, though with a decent nudity. . . . The face is meaning all by itself. . . . It leads you beyond. . . . The face signifies the Infinite" (*Ethics and Infinity*, trans. Richard A. Cohen [Pittsburgh: Duquesne University Press, 1985], 78, 86–87, 105). To be cut off from the face—the face of the earth, the face of God, and the face of one's fellow human beings—is to be cut off from the deepest levels of being. And this is what Levinas suggests that Cain fears.

Levinas notes that while Cain and Abel speak with one another in the first half of Genesis 4:8, they exchange no words later when they are in the field, the scene of the murder. They didn't speak in the field, Levinas says, because speaking requires speakers to face one another, and had Cain faced Abel, he would have lost his capacity to murder him. So, Levinas argues, Cain attacked Abel from behind and slew him without ever having to see his face. Levinas believes that when we truly face another, we see God and act godly. This is why propagandists always produce posters and cartoons that distort the faces of their enemies. The goal is to erase the humanity of the "other" so the audience at whom the propaganda is aimed can be more easily manipulated into killing or oppressing the "other." If Levinas is right and the face is the signifier of God and God's face is no longer reflected in Cain's face, then Cain's life is indeed in danger. "Whoever meets me will kill me," Cain says (Gen 4:14), because whoever meets him will not see in his face the infinite face of God.

God is moved by Cain's plight and places upon Cain the mark of God "so that none who meet him will kill him" (Gen 4:15). While Torah doesn't tell us what the mark was or where it was placed, following Levinas we might argue that the mark was on Cain's face, and it somehow signified to all who might meet him that Cain was still the image of God, a sacred being worthy of life. The message Torah may be offering us is this: we must live so as to uplift and never degrade or distort the faces of others and do all we can to see the divine reflected in every face, even our own.

We have wandered far from a simple tale of rivalry between shepherds and farmers, and I welcome your comments and/or your decision to move on the next story.

Mike: It seems we must agree to disagree with regard to Cain's and God's roles in the matter of the rejected offering. On the other hand, I resonate with Emmanuel Levinas's take on "face," and I thank you for introducing it. To be cut off from the face of God and others is a working definition of hell. I agree with your suggestion that the story's conclusion calls us to act carefully in our interactions with others so that we see the infinite face of God in their faces.

Chapter 4

The Flood

Genesis 6:1–9:28

Mike: Let's turn to the story of Noah. The story features six acts. Act one describes the overall wickedness of humanity, together with God's intent to destroy it. The second act identifies Noah as the only human God accounts righteous and God's plan to save Noah, his family, animals, and foodstuffs from the coming flood. Act three features the flood itself, which only those in the ark survive. In the fourth act, the flood subsides, Noah and those in the ark emerge, and Noah offers worship to God. In the fifth act, God offers an amended covenant to Noah, which includes a promise never again to destroy all humanity by flood. Finally, the sixth act depicts Noah and his sons establishing a new human society, but Noah's naked drunkenness becomes the occasion for dissension and alienation within the family, portending the continuation of humanity's troubles.

The similarities and differences between the Noah story and other flood stories have long been noted. Some elements found in some of the stories include a god or most of the gods deciding to do away with humanity, a god warning a human of the impending flood and telling him to build an ark and preserve living things, the flood exceeding expectations, and the preservation of humanity and other life. The biblical story includes some of these elements. The narrative, though, features a single God who acts throughout the entire narrative with no reference to other gods.

Genesis 6:1-8 covers act one. Humans multiply; the "sons of God" take human daughters as wives and produce children who become the heroes of legend. God responds by reducing the human lifespan to 120 years. The Lord looks into the hearts of women and men only to find them bent toward evil, and God regrets having made humanity and even other living things. The image is that of a disappointed creator/artist who is ready to blot out his previous work. Whether God will try again or leave the earth barren is open to question, at least for a moment. Act one takes a turn with verse 8, where

Noah is introduced as the one who finds favor in God's eyes. The God who stands ready to destroy all living things must now deal with the fact of one righteous person's existence. If we're hearing or reading the story for the first time, we're left wondering, "Now what will God do?"

Major themes emerge: the growing alienation of humanity from God and God's designs, God's response or responses, and the potentially crucial role of even one righteous person. Such themes will play out in the remainder of the story and emerge again and again throughout the Scriptures.

Rami: Nicely put, Mike. We should also note that the Noah story is a composite of two separate Jewish flood narratives. In one God is called *Elohim* (God), and in the other God is called *YHVH* (Lord). In the YHVH version God acts because of the wickedness of humankind (Gen 6:5). In the Elohim version it is the entire earth that is corrupt (Gen 6:12). In the YHVH version Noah is told to take seven pairs of clean animals and one pair of unclean animals into the ark (Gen 7:2). In the Elohim version God tells Noah to bring just one pair of each animal, clean and unclean (Gen 7:9). In the Yahweh version the flood lasts forty days and forty nights (Gen 6:12). In the Elohim version the flood lasts 150 days (Gen 7:24). In the Yahweh version Noah sends out a raven to see if the flood has receded (Gen 8:7). In the Elohim version he twice sends out a dove (Gen 8:8, 12). But as interesting as this may be in an academic setting, it doesn't move me. Let me set out a few things that interest me about this story and invite you to jump in and comment.

For example, what was it about creation that made it go bad? It can't be a matter of human free will since God says the earth itself was corrupt and "all flesh had corrupted its ways upon the earth" (Gen 6:12). God "blotted out every living thing that was on the face of the ground, human beings and animals and creeping things and birds of the air; they were blotted out from the earth" (Gen 7:23 NRSV) because they were corrupt. Do alligators, cows, and hummingbirds have free will such that they can be corrupted? Further, if all life was corrupted, mustn't there have been a design flaw—a corrupting influence or potential for corruption—in creation itself, and if this is so, mustn't that flaw, that influence or potential, originate with the designer?

And then there is the issue of Noah's silence. The man says nothing throughout the entire ordeal! God tells him about the coming destruction of all life, and Noah doesn't say a thing. Compare this to Abraham, who risks his life to save the people of Sodom and Gomorrah (Gen 18:23).

Confronted with a far greater act of destruction, Noah is mute. And he is the best of his generation!

And then there is the issue of Noah's drunkenness. Noah, we learn, is a farmer, so in a sense he corrects for Cain, the farmer-gone-bad. But Noah is also the first person to plant a vineyard and get drunk. Does he do this as a way of dealing with survivor's guilt? It takes a couple years to produce grapes that can be turned into wine. Are we to imagine that Noah is tormented all this time? Is drunkenness Noah's way of self-medicating?

And finally, why, when at last Noah opens his mouth to speak, can he only curse his son Ham's children (Gen 9:25)? If he's angry with Ham, why take it out on Ham's kids?

There is something very wrong with Noah. He is passive in the face of God and aggressive with his grandchildren. He takes no responsibility for his drunkenness or nakedness. Can his anger be an expression of self-loathing? Does he hate himself for allowing God to destroy the world without even a modicum of resistance? I don't know if these questions bother you like they do me. But I would like to hear what you have to say.

Mike: You raise classic issues, the kinds of questions that trouble (and have troubled) many. I know of no universally accepted answers, but I'll be glad to share my perspective.

Start with the matter of what's gone wrong with creation. If I understand correctly, you posit a design flaw rooted in the designer, which is another way of saying good and evil find their deepest origins in God. You also eliminate human free will as the source of the earth's corruption. God, in such a line of reasoning, becomes the issue, even the problem.

I take theodicy seriously, but I think the storyteller assumes a different perspective, one rooted in the earlier stories of Genesis. God creates or shapes humanity in God's image and charges us to serve as God's stewards of the earth. A steward possesses delegated yet real authority, and the steward's actions affect directly that over which he or she reigns, from the smallest farm to the world itself. The free will of a steward matters. I think it likely the story works from such an assumption. As humanity moves farther away from alignment with the Creator and the Creator's purposes, its heart and actions drag all of creation with it.

Such a perspective feels strange to the modern mind, which still tends to look for direct cause-and-effect answers. On the other hand, we now know we live in a universe in which determinism does not exist in a strict sense at the quantum level: particles separated by any distance may directly affect one another, and all conceivable time lines may develop. The moment we glance at a particle, we affect its position or velocity, and we can't even measure both aspects at the same time! Given the nature of the universe, is it really so hard to imagine that the inclination of human hearts and the actions of human hands may distort the earth itself?

Stewards, to return to the earlier image, can make or wreck that over which they exercise stewardship. Our storyteller intuits the reality of the mystery of the inescapable connectedness of all things. The mystic in me resonates with such a view. For better or worse, humanity occupies a key position in the natural world and exercises far more influence on the course of the world's development than we may wish to accept.

How, then, does the story depict God? God evolves over the course of the narrative. Here we find no distant, unchanging deity, but instead a God who moves through a series of decisions. The first decision is to sit in judgment of humanity and all living things and wipe the slate clean. The second decision finds God confronted with the reality that one person's heart still inclines to God. God's life gets more complicated. What is God to do with this person? The third decision finds God changing his plan so as to preserve Noah, his family, animals, and plants, and give them a fresh start. The fourth decision may be the most remarkable: God chooses to lay aside the option of destruction in favor of binding himself to remain engaged with humanity. Here, perhaps, we see the first hint of what later writers will call *hesed*, God's enduring love.

Noah is interesting, isn't he? I certainly think your take on Noah is reasonable. He is flawed, deeply so, in the ways you describe. If I were looking to create a hero figure, Noah probably would not be my favored model! Scripture writers, on the other hand, delight in flawed central characters. Why? Perhaps the writers are realists, at least from their perspective. It is as if they say, "Here is humanity as it is. Even the righteous, those more or less aligned with God, are broken. God works with them anyway. Get used to it!"

Personally, I tend to see such a dynamic at work in history. Take the case of John D. Rockefeller and the Rockefeller Foundation. Would you allow that the Rockefeller Foundation has proven a boon to the world through its leadership in medicine? The foundation essentially created standards for medical education, the modern research hospital, and the public health system. These are good things. Yet the man who launched the foundation took almost no interest in its work. We must admit his genius in creating the modern corporation, but he also ran competitors out of business and "bought" politicians. John D. Rockefeller, by all accounts, was a deeply religious man. None of us, though, would have wished to be numbered among his enemies. I mention all this to drive home one point: all persons are filled with contradictions, and even those through whom the world receives a blessing are subject to dysfunction, self-delusion, and outright sin.

As you put it, "There is something very wrong with Noah." Noah as dysfunctional hero, as the anti-hero who does some heroic task anyway, seems believable to me. He is the first of many to come.

Rami: You're right that I, along with God in Isaiah 45:7, root evil as well as good in God, but I don't consider it a design flaw, despite what I implied earlier. If God is infinite, God must include and transcend all things. I'm not saying that God is good or evil—only that good and evil are inescapable given the infinite nature of God. Just as we can't have fronts without backs, so we can't have good without evil.

In the eighteenth-century Jewish mystical text *Tanya*, Rabbi Schneur Zalman of Liady says that an infinite God has to manifest a complete spectrum of possibilities. With regard to people, he says God *has* to allow for the saint and the psychopath. And neither the saint nor the psychopath has any choice to be other than who she or he is. So, Rabbi Zalman says, God doesn't punish the psychopath or reward the saint. The rest of us are *baynonim*, "inbetweeners," people with the capacity to do both good and evil, and the responsibility to choose between them.

I find this idea compelling, and it leads me to the notion of functional free will. That is, we have to make decisions, but whether or not we could decide other than we do is up for debate. This is where you're right to bring in the quantum dimension.

There is some debate over whether quantum fluctuations are actually random or only seem random to us because we cannot, given Heisenberg's Uncertainty Principle, gather enough data to predict those fluctuations. If the fluctuations are predictable—that is, if God can predict them—then there is no free will. If they are not predictable even by God, then there is free will, and God is as surprised by reality as we are. I don't know how we might ever solve that one.

As for your idea that human action can distort the optimal functioning of nature—absolutely! This is what global warming is all about. The more alien to this planet we humans imagine ourselves to be, the more difficult it is for us to work in harmony with nature. The more we realize the truth of Genesis 2:7—that humans are the earth made self-conscious—the easier it is for us to work with nature for the mutual benefit of all creation.

Sadly, we usually side with Genesis 1:27 and imagine we are other than the earth and hence insist we are free to manipulate nature without consequences. There are always consequences. Unfortunately, it may take until you and I, living as we do in Tennessee, suddenly find ourselves with oceanfront property before the majority of Americans are willing to do something about climate change.

As for John D. Rockefeller, I am tempted to say, "Judge not, lest ye be judged" (Matt 7:1), but that's your book not mine. Nevertheless, your point is well taken. We are all flawed. And, as you noted, Rockefeller was a deeply religious man, though not a deeply compassionate one. This is one thing (among many, many others) that saddens me regarding religion: you can be very religious and heartless at the same time. Something is wrong with that. Religion ought to make us more compassionate and just, but most often it simply excuses cruelty and injustice as long as the cruel and unjust keep the coffers of the religions filled. Or is that politics?

Mike: Functional free will seems to be potential common ground for us. The concept, to my mind, leaves ample room for personal and corporate responsibility without the need to try to resolve the unresolvable!

Before we move on, I want to pose another question: What did Noah get right? It seems only fair to ask such a question since we've spent time exploring what might have been wrong with Noah or his actions.

Noah quietly swims against the stream. The story draws a sharp contrast between Noah and the larger culture. We're not given specifics, but Noah's heart tilts toward God rather than self. If the story was set in our era, Noah might be the person who simply goes about his daily work, prays, helps others when he can, and resists the cult of self-centeredness. Such a life, while not overtly heroic, packs considerable value.

He obeys God. Noah does not comprehend the magnitude of the coming catastrophe (and who would?). The commandment to build an ark for his family and selected life forms pushes his imagination to its limit. The work fills his days and consumes his resources. We've assumed he said nothing to his neighbors, but I now wonder if we're correct. Can we really believe his neighbors say nothing to him as they watch the boat being built? Is it really conceivable that he says nothing to them about why he labors so? In any case, the act of constructing the ship and gathering its occupants is an act of obedience grounded in considerable faith.

He brought some others with him through the deluge. True, they're all family, but it's a major feat nonetheless. We have to imagine the experience, for the storyteller opts for a lean approach to the narrative. When I try to fill in the blanks, I am rather staggered by Noah's performance in persuading the family to go along, holding them together (not to mention all the other creatures on the boat) throughout the ordeal, and settling them into life afterward. At the end of the story, Noah breaks. The strain proves more than his mind and heart can take. Still, his charges are alive rather than dead, and he has fulfilled the core of his mission: build a boat, take your family and a collection of other life into it, survive the coming storm, and start over.

Rami: Okay, I get it; maybe I'm being too harsh on Noah. He did make future life possible, after all. But how hard was it to get his family on the ark? While the Bible is silent on the matter, here's how I imagine it went:

"Hey, hon, listen to this! God dropped by, and we won a forty-day cruise, all expenses paid! Wanna go with the kids?"

"Absolutely! Oh, but what about the dogs? Who's gonna care for them?"

"Got it covered; you'll see."

"Okay, so where do we depart from?"

"That's the coolest thing. We leave from here; no need to walk hundreds of miles to port."

"From here? How's the boat going to get here? We're landlocked."

"It's an ark, actually, and I'm gonna build it myself. God told me how."

"Really? The way he told you how to build the barn out back? The one I had to have my uncle Beryl come up from Babel to fix?"

"Look, I can do this."

"Well, we could use a vacation. Okay, but I'm warning you, Noah, this trip better be so cool that our neighbors die from jealousy, or you will never hear the end of it."

"Yeah, like I said, got it covered."

On a more serious note, your question "What did Noah get right" is a good one. He did what he was told, and because he did, life continued. That's nothing to sneeze at. But I wonder if it's really an act of faith. Faith makes sense if we have no corroboration for what we believe, but God spoke to Noah directly. Faith had nothing to do with it. This was an act of obedience, not faith.

But maybe we are missing the point. Think of other prophets who were asked to do outrageous things. For example, Ezekiel is commanded to eat a manure sandwich (Ezek 4:12), and Jeremiah is commanded to wear an ox yoke (Jer 28:10). These acts were designed to get people thinking, to get them to open to the prophet's message, and maybe even to get them to move toward repentance.

So what if building an ark was supposed to spark conversation? Maybe God hoped that as folks walked by and saw Noah building his ark, they might ask him what was going on, and Noah would have a chance to tell them what God was planning to do and encourage them to repent and beg God for forgiveness. But no one was curious, and Noah stayed silent.

Maybe the entire story is a condemnation of human complacency. Maybe the message is this: when you see someone acting strange, check it out!

But if this is the message, we aren't getting it. We stay complacent as the glaciers melt, the seas rise, the planet burns, the oceans are poisoned, and millions if not billions of humans suffer needlessly under the boot of economic, social, political, and religious injustice. For all we know, there are prophets among us acting strange to get us thinking, and we walk by oblivious to the truth with our noses buried in Facebook.

In any case, I'm not building anything odd, but if you are Mike, let me know. I might have a few questions.

Mike: Before we take up the next story, I want to spend a little time on the matters of faith and hope.

How God speaks to Noah is a matter of conjecture. Is there an audible voice, or does Noah sense the presence and direction of God in his heart and mind? I suspect narrative convention drives the description. Regardless of how we choose to answer the question, I don't see that hearing God's voice directly takes faith out of the equation. Faith, I think, is best understood as trust. Each act of obedience requires some kind of decision, and all decisions require an act of trust. Perhaps those long experienced in such faith find any given decision requires only a "little" act of trust, but my experience suggests new situations or demands call for more. Noah, though long attuned to God, faces the all too human challenge of decision. Choosing to obey God requires a decision to trust God yet again, which is the heart of faith.

Your remarks on prophets, outrageous actions designed to prompt reflection and repentance, and our complacency prompt me to turn to the matter of hope. Are there those among us acting out prophetic roles? I have little doubt this is so. Are most of us missing their messages? I think so. On bitter days, I find myself tempted by despair when I consider the very examples you raise. Yet the biblical narratives suggest someone or some relatively small number of persons are paying attention and working hard to counter humanity's self-destructive tendencies. Both of us know individuals and organizations dedicated to rescuing the environment. If we took the time, we could find and list examples of how their efforts slow the degradation of the environment and, in some cases, reverse it.

With regard to human suffering, it's easy to despair. The more I learn of human trafficking, child soldiers, and other such evils, the more I feel tempted to surrender hope for humanity. Yet I know individuals and groups who, sometimes at great risk, expose atrocities to public view, work to rescue victims and give them new lives, and challenge the social/political/economic structures that sustain such evils.

The Noah story may well condemn human complacency, but I think it is meant to instill hope, a hope rooted in the active presence of God and in the minority (even of one) among us, who see more clearly than most and try to do something good for God's creation and creatures.

Rami: Hope is important in Judaism. Our national anthem is *HaTikvah*, "The Hope," and we have hoped for a messiah for millennia, though every time we got one (Jesus was not our first or our last), we rejected him. Maybe we love hope more than the fulfillment of hope. But as with many things Jewish, it is our humor that reveals our nature most powerfully:

A rabbi, a minister, a priest, and an imam are summoned to heaven. "I'm sorry to tell you this," God says, "but despite promises to the contrary, I plan to flood the world once again, and this time I will leave no survivors. The flood will commence in thirty minutes. Return to your peoples, and prepare them for the end."

The minister and priest returned, called their people to their churches, explained the situation, and urged them to accept Jesus and pray for forgiveness.

The imam returned, called his people to the mosque, explained the situation, and urged them to surrender fully to Allah and pray for forgiveness.

The rabbi returned, called his people to the synagogue, explained the situation, and said, "We have thirty minutes to learn how to live under water."

Torah says, "Thou shalt never explain a joke" (Exod 20:24), and our rabbis taught, "If a joke needs explaining, rewrite the joke," so I think I should just leave this as it is. While I, too, Mike, have days of despair, in the end I choose to learn how to live under water.

Chapter 5

The Tower of Babel

Genesis 11:1-9

Mike: Sermons and lessons based on the tower of Babel story rarely crossed my path during my boyhood and adolescence. On those rare occasions, the interpretation generally went as follows: Humankind migrates east in the aftermath of Noah's time until they reach the land of Shinar. They share a common language, and once settled in Shinar they discover the craft of brick making. Soon, ambition takes hold, and they choose to build the first city, complete with a tall tower, one that reaches into the heavens. God intervenes. Coming among them, he confuses their language, spawning multiple tongues and sowing confusion among the people. As a result, the people separate from one another and scatter about the earth, launching a process that results in various language groups, tribes, and nations.

Generally, those who outline and interpret the story in this fashion point to pride as the sin that wrecks the city- and tower-building project. I suspect linking the story to one of the classic deadly sins appeals to orderly, theologically inclined minds.

The longer I live with the story, the less I believe such an interpretation does it justice. I prefer to try to understand the story in light of the place it occupies between the Noah and Abraham narratives. Following the flood, God's new covenant requires humanity to multiply and fill the earth. They head east, but the tower story implies they do so as a pack. They do not scatter and fill the earth. Instead, they arrive in Shinar, pick a spot, and start to build a city. In the midst of the city, they begin to raise a tall tower. Perhaps they want to establish a sentry point from which to see and prepare for any approaching catastrophe, or maybe they hope to build a kind of permanent ark in which a portion of the people might take shelter in the event of another flood. They resist scattering over the face of the earth, and the city is both the symbol and the actualized means of their resistance.

Why? Fear, not pride, is at work. They are afraid to fulfill the covenant's requirement to populate the earth, which requires that they break into separated groups. Sure, they have God's promise that they will not be destroyed by a universal flood, but who knows what else God might do or what dangers lurk in the larger world? Fear overwhelms them. As always, fear promises safety through an alternative to God's strategy for humanity and the planet. The alternative, or course, requires that they refuse to trust God.

Under such an interpretation, God acts to yank them back on course. If God does not do so, who knows what other foolish schemes the people may devise? Left to their own devices, their fear will lead them deeper into disobedience and faithlessness and toward a ruin of their own making.

God gives them another chance to honor the covenant by confusing their language or speech. The story itself does not state the precise nature of the confusion: multiple languages, dialects of the shared language so varied that they render communication impossible, or words losing all structure so that they become nonsense in the ears of each hearer. The results, though, are clear: The building of the city grinds to a halt. The fear-driven strategy is stymied. The people scatter as a result of God's action.

My approach treats God's response as a grace-filled rescue of the people rather than a punishment. God is not afraid of the tower builders. Instead, God acts to save them from themselves and restore to them the possibility of honoring the covenant.

Of course, I may be dead wrong, Rami. Perhaps the pride-centered interpretation is correct, or maybe you have a third or fourth alternative to suggest.

Rami: Who knew I was a Baptist preacher? But the fact is you and I read this story in much the same way. Amen. But what kind of rabbi would I be if I only had one take on a Bible story? So here is another. I look forward to your reaction to it.

First let me say what I suspect we both agree upon: that the story of Babel was originally told to answer the question of why people speak different languages and live in far-flung places. If we are all descendants of Adam and Eve, why don't we all speak Hebrew like they did? It's a good question, and the story of Babel isn't a bad answer as such answers go. But let's see what else we might find in this story.

The people migrated to the plain (some say valley) of Shinar and decide to build a town and a ziggurat, a stepped pyramid for the worship of God. In verse 5 we are told that God came down from heaven to see what the humans had done, and verse 6 makes it clear that God is unhappy with what he finds. But why? What is it that troubles God?

This was not the first city ever created. Cain had already become a "city builder" (Gen 4:17), so it wasn't the town that bothered God. Was it the ziggurat? God never prescribed how he was to be worshiped—indeed, as we have already seen, that lack of specificity led to the murder of Abel by his brother Cain—and neither had God proscribed the building of a ziggurat. And though the ziggurat was to reach the "heavens," this only means "sky" and in no way suggests the humans were storming the heavens to topple God. If it isn't the building that bothered God, what's left? Only one thing: the fact that the people spoke a single language.

The Hebrew here is *safat echat* (one language) and *d'varim achadim* (uniform words) (Gen 11:1). *Safat echat* means that all the people spoke a single language, presumably Hebrew. But why does Torah add *d'varim achadim*? What does this phrase add to our understanding that the first phrase leaves out? *D'varim achadim* implies that the meanings of the words were singular and fixed. In other words (pun intended), people could not think for themselves. Look at verse 3: the people speak only in the first-person plural. There is no possibility of anyone questioning the idea of building a town and a ziggurat. And when it comes to the actual building, no one is allowed to opt out.

In Shinar, there seems to have been no wood or stone, which is why the people had to bake bricks and why the Bible tells us the bricks were used as substitutes for stone (Gen 11:3). The people are commanded twice to "give" what they have that it can be melted down and turned into bricks (vv. 3, 4). Again, there was no thought that anyone could disagree.

Compare this to the building of the tabernacle. Here, too, the people are to give what they have to be used in the making of the tabernacle, but there is a huge difference. In Shinar the people are *commanded* to give; in Sinai they are *asked* to give. God says to Moses, "Tell the children of Israel to collect a donation for me; from everyone *whose heart is so moved* to contribute you shall raise my funds" (Exod 25:1-2). God, at least in this case, is championing the power of the individual as individual, whereas in Babel there is no individuality at all. And the root problem is the flattening of language.

I can't read the story of Babel without thinking of George Orwell's novel *1984*. Here's a snippet of conversation between the protagonist Winston and Syme, who works on the dictionary of Newspeak, the official language of the state. It is Syme who is speaking:

Don't you see that the whole aim of Newspeak is to narrow the range of thought? In the end we shall make thoughtcrime literally impossible, because there will be no words in which to express it. Every concept that can ever be needed will be expressed by exactly one word, with its meaning rigidly defined and all its subsidiary meanings rubbed out and forgotten. (*1984* [New York: Penguin, 1983] 46)

The people of Babel are speaking Newspeak, and it is this centralized control of language, this deadening of language and hence the deadening of thought, that troubles God. How do we know this for certain? If the town troubled God, he would have destroyed the town. If it were the ziggurat that bothered him, God would have toppled the pyramid. But God goes after the language because it is the language that bothers him. And what troubles God about the language is that words allow only one meaning (*d'varim achadim*), and because they do, human creativity is lost.

Mike: Thank you for bringing up *safat echat* and *d'varim achadim*. Your interpretation is persuasive. We agree.

Keeping Newspeak in mind, let's revisit the matter of the particular city found in the story. Driven by fear, the people fashion a reduced language that locks down individuality, diversity, and freedom of action. The city they build turns out to be a kind of enclave or ghetto of their own making in which everyone must look and sound alike, march to the same beat, and invest themselves in the same endeavors.

Sounds a lot like the Christian fundamentalist mindset and resultant lifestyle to me! Mind you, such a mindset may embrace a range of formal theologies and political philosophies. Always, though, it creates groups devoted to tight control of language and behavior, parodies of community in which people are bound together in fear rather than love and trust. Such groups sometimes become militant and seek to conquer those outside their walls. Often, though, they hunker inside the walls, afraid of the outside world(s), convinced they can be safe only so long as they maintain their version of purity.

You're right. God is not against cities per se, but God is against the kind of false community represented by the city built in Shinar.

What kind of community might God desire? With regard to individuals, I agree with your insight: God wants to free the poet in each of us so that language functions as a gift rather than a tool of tyranny. Such persons fashion community by choice, and the community they build is blessed by the gifts of each individual.

The mystic in me resonates with your vision of the language of silence. In the meantime, though, I choose to work toward community so grounded in trust and love that it welcomes the diversity inherent in God's general creation and humanity. In such a community, we inevitably must often ask one another, "Now what do you mean by that?"

Rami: Not just Christian fundamentalists, but fundamentalists of all stripes.

As Karen Armstrong convincingly demonstrates in her book *The Battle for God*, fundamentalism is not the reclamation of an ancient and authentic faith, but a fear-filled parody of faith concocted in the present to protect believers from the encroachment of the future.

I believe in both timeless truth and evolutionary applications of that truth. That is to say, when the prophet Micah tells us that what God requires of humanity is justice, compassion, and humility (6:8; especially humility when it comes to "your God"), I think he is speaking timeless truth. You can't do better than justice, compassion, and humility. But you can do justice, compassion, and humility better, and doing them better is what I mean by evolutionary application.

Over time we broaden our understanding of these timeless principles and apply them in more and more inclusive and effective ways. What fundamentalists do is freeze the application in a particular form, either one drawn from the past or one invented in the present and projected back into the past, and then claim that this is the one true understanding and application of these timeless principles. The problem isn't with the principles but with our understanding and application of them.

I believe we humans are on the verge of a great leap forward in spiritual awareness, one that will allow us to embrace and apply in new and more cogent ways the timeless principles of justice, compassion, and humility. Fundamentalists of all kinds fear this happening and will do whatever they can to prevent it from happening. They may win out. And if they do, our species may die out. Or not; look how well cockroaches have done! We may not die out but merely be surpassed by the next species called to justice, compassion, and humility and capable of achieving it better than us. That is the genius of evolution: change happens whether the Neanderthals like it or not.

Chapter 6

The Call of Abram

Genesis 12:1-9

Mike: In Genesis 1–11, God works with creation, then humans, and then a rescued remnant of humanity. Starting with 12:1, the narrative focuses on God's purposeful selection of a particular family through whom to create a new kind of human community. Christian theologians, preachers, and teachers historically have been fascinated by the story of Abram's call. I confess the tale long ago caught my attention and sparked my imagination.

For example, while Abram may well have known ancestral stories about the God who spoke to Noah and the like, I often wonder just how he perceived "the Lord" who spoke to him. Did he think of such a God as one among any number of gods or wonder why this God spoke to him but not his brother? Was he startled when God actually spoke to him, regardless of the manner in which the message was conveyed? My hunch is that Abram honored any number of gods, as did his neighbors. Such would have made good business and relational sense. Now, though, one of the gods speaks to him, and this unexpected turn of events raises new possibilities.

Abram and Sarai have no children. Both are well past childbearing years. His particular family line faces extinction; their story is about to come to an end. In the world as it is, Abram is trapped in such a present and future. God intervenes to create a possible new future featuring a new land, numerous descendants, a great name, and the potential to prove a blessing to all peoples. Abram, though, must choose to leave Haran and his kindred and journey with God if he wants God's promise to evolve from words alone into historical reality. The themes of promise and journey are joined at the hip and remain so to this day.

Gift and responsibility are linked too. The land, descendants, and the great name are gifts from God, things Abram could not create for himself.

A new life, starting at the improbable age of seventy-five, is offered. Yet the language of the promise precludes Abram saying, "This is great. I've got it made. We're set for life, and my descendants are as well." God calls Abram and those who come after him to redefine greatness in terms of being a blessing to all the other families of the earth. To be selected or chosen by God is not so much a privilege as it is a responsibility, one that in time will lead some to deep reflection on love, faithfulness, and servanthood.

Abram must live into the promise. The little phrase translated "so Abram went, as the LORD told him" captures the matter nicely. God's promise does not come fully realized. Abram has to gather his family, servants, and goods and go on the road. Bringing the promise to pass requires walking toward it one step at a time. When he arrives, he finds others settled in the land, Canaanites who have been there for some time. God appears to Abram at Shechem to declare this is the land he means to give Abram's offspring. I can imagine Abram thinking, "Maybe. But at the moment I don't have any offspring, and all the good real estate appears to be taken." Perhaps Abram begins to understand that he has entered into a long-term process.

Nonetheless, he builds altars to the Lord and invokes the name of the Lord. Having started on the road with God, he chooses to continue. Altar building is a rather public way of declaring this is so. The narrative ends with Abram continuing to journey on in stages, which may be taken literally but also as a metaphor for how the longer tale is going to play out.

Rami: This is one of the most important passages of the entire Torah, not simply because it marks the call of Abram, but because it sets forth the mission of my people, and perhaps all people who follow the Abrahamic path: Jews, Christians, Muslims, and Baha'is.

Before I get to the mission, however, let me address your question about Abram and Sarai themselves. There are dozens and dozens of rabbinic *midrashim* (extrabiblical tales about biblical characters and stories) that seek to answer the question you raise (i.e., "Why Abram?"). They all come down to this: while it is true that Abram was raised in a family of idol makers and polytheists, from his youth he intuited the truth of monotheism, the belief in only one God.

Here is but one classic example:

Abram's father had to leave town on a business trip and left Abram in charge of the family idol store. People would enter the shop to purchase a god, and Abram would ridicule them and drive them out.

Abram would ask, "How old are you?" Some would answer "fifty," others "sixty." Abram would then say, "How sad that a person of sixty wants to bow down to a one-day-old god." Disgusted, the customer would leave without buying anything.

Once, a woman came in to the shop carrying a basket of bread that she asked Abram to feed to the gods. When she left, Abram took a hammer and smashed all the gods but one and placed the hammer in the hands of this last remaining idol.

Upon returning to the shop and seeing the mess, his father demanded to know what happened. Abram told his father about the woman. "Each god demanded to be fed first, Father," Abram explained, "and then this one with the hammer used the hammer to smash the competition."

"Do you think your father is a fool? These idols have no minds!"

"Listen to yourself," Abram said. "They have no power at all! So if they have no minds and no power, why worship idols in the first place?" (*Gen. Rab.* 38:13)

Was Abram a monotheist from his youth? I doubt it. But neither was he a nobody, randomly chosen to found a new people and a new faith.

The Hebrew *Avram* means High (*ram*) Father (*av*), suggesting that Abram was already a shaman or spiritual leader when he felt called by God. Similarly, *Sarai* (and *Sarah*, the name of Abram's wife, was actually a title, meaning "my princess" or "my woman of high rank." Sarai is often associated with oak trees, especially the Groves of Mamre, and may have been the leader of a goddess community.

My point is that "Abram" and "Sarai" may be titles given to a priest and priestess who sought to lead the people toward a new understanding of God. Of course, this assumes that they are actual historical figures, which is by no means certain. But this doesn't matter to me. I don't read Torah as history, but as historical fiction. Torah is a fictional narrative set in and drawing from a moment in history; its purpose is to teach us about the nature of life and how best to live it, rather than to chronicle actual historical events. Torah is more parable than history book.

I read Torah as revelation, a peeling back of the veil that keeps me from seeing things as they really are. Read this way, Torah is about me and my life, rather than about Abram and Sarai and their lives. When God calls to Abram, I hear God calling to me through Abram. And it is because I read Torah so personally that this call is so important to me.

I want to go into the actual text of the call, but before I do, let me pause for a moment and invite you to jump in.

Mike: Christian thinkers regard the call of Abram as crucial to defining the Christian way. For example, it's quite common for us to view Abram's story as a faith paradigm. Abram and Sarai's interactions with God, journey, challenges, failure, and victories portray the realities of a life of faith, by which we mean a life in which we learn to trust God. I'll probably have more to say on the matter when we turn back to the matter of call and mission. In the meantime, I love the particular rabbinic tale you chose to share, not least because of its use of humor to drive home a point.

I did not mean to imply Abram was "a nobody randomly chosen by God to found a new people." The text of the story before us, along with the subsequent accounts, depicts Abram as a substantial figure. Christian commentators, to the best of my knowledge, generally see him as the leader of a powerful clan who possesses considerable means in the form of herd animals, servants, and the like. His very status makes his lack of children quite tragic at several levels. God's promise speaks to the situation, offering a previously unthinkable new start.

You read Torah more as parable than history. I tend to see the Abram narratives as stories grounded in history but refined by long use to serve the purpose of answering core questions: What is God doing? What is the purpose or mission of God's people? How does one live into the life of faith? When you write of reading Torah as revelation, so that it is about you and your life, I hear echoes of the Bible study method Christians call *Lectio Divinia*. It's but one of many ways of dealing with the Scriptures, but many of us find it useful. We slow down, savor the words and flow of a given Scripture passage, reflect and pray, and listen with the inner ear for what the text might say about God and us.

I look forward to hearing what you have to say about the text of the call.

Rami: God's call to Abram begins with an interesting Hebrew idiom, *lech lecha*. *Lech* means "to walk" or "to go," and *lecha* means "toward yourself." God calls Abram to move toward his truer self—I would say his "divine" self (i.e., the self that is the image of God; Gen 1:26-27). While the story clearly makes this an outer journey, the Hebrew links it to an inner quest as well: Abram's way in the world is to lead him to his true nature as a manifestation of God and a vehicle for godliness, or what is called here "being a blessing."

This quest requires Abram and Sarai to leave their land, their clan, and their parents' house. The ancient rabbis noted that the order here is the inverse of what Abram and Sarai would actually experience. Practically speaking, they would leave their parents first, then journey beyond their clan, and finally cross the borders of their homeland and enter a foreign land. So, ever on the lookout for meaning-rich anomalies in Torah, our rabbis asked, "Why does Torah put this 'backward'?"

Their answer is psychological: it is easier to leave our geographic setting than it is to leave our cultural conditioning and easier to leave our cultural conditioning than it is to leave the conditioning imprinted upon us by our parents. Torah is saying that the call of God gets progressively more difficult.

Abram and Sarai—and by extension you and I—cannot reach the promised land (more on that in a moment) until we first free ourselves from the conditioning of nationality, ethnicity, and parental bias. I would add to these other forms of conditioning as well: race, gender, class, religion, etc. God is calling us to a state of nakedness (*arum*), the state Adam and Eve were in before eating from the tree of knowledge, a state of being without labels, a state of simplicity and purity that is unconditioned and radically free. Think of St. Paul's notion: "There is neither Jew nor Greek, there is neither slave nor free, there is neither male nor female, for you are all one in Christ Jesus" (Gal 3:28). If we want to reach the land God intends for us to inhabit, we must shed the labels that define and confine us.

After calling Abram and Sarai to radical freedom, God says they are to go "to the land that I will show you" (Gen 12:1). The key here is the future tense: "will show you." Not only are Abram and Sarai stripped of all they used to know (the conditioning of their culture, tribe, and parents); they have no idea where they are going.

We are called to free ourselves of the past and step into the present without any preconceived notion of where we are going. Indeed, without our past conditioning we cannot project our future "landing" and are forced to abandon all our fantasies in order to embrace the reality with which we are presented (present-ed!). In other words, God's promised "land" is wherever we happen to find ourselves in the present moment if we are free from the labels and conditions that blind us from seeing it as such.

While Abram and Sarai are called to free themselves from nationality, ethnicity, and parental bias (at the very least), their descendants, both biological and spiritual, have created new idols of these very conditions. We have yet to reach the promised land—that state of freedom that allows us to be a blessing—because we continue to cast new idols to which we enslave ourselves, surrendering our freedom and capacity for free thought.

The final verse of the call tells us the "why" of this journey: to be a blessing (Gen 12:3). Genesis 12:2 tells us that Abram and Sarai will be blessed and become a great nation, but the catalyst for this is not who they are but how they will live: as "a blessing to all the families of the earth." All the families—human and otherwise! They (and we) are to live in such a way as to promote the thriving of life.

With this in mind, we can better understand the verse dealing with blessing and cursing. God says, "I will bless those who bless you, and I will curse those who curse you" (Gen 12:3). Those who bless us are those who align themselves with the task of being a blessing to all the families of the earth. These are blessed; these thrive. Those who curse us are those who curse the task of seeing to the thriving of others, and they will not thrive and perhaps not survive. Abram and Sarai—again you and I—are called to be vehicles of blessing, catalysts for the thriving of those who work toward the thriving of others. This is the call of the divine to all human beings, and one that very few of us take seriously.

Despite the call to free ourselves of our conditioning, despite the challenge to be a blessing to all the families of the earth, despite the revelation that there are no labels in Christ Jesus, we cling to our conditioning and club each other to death because of our labels. We are being called to something else, something far more radical and free than most of us can imagine, let alone embody. The call of God may simply be too much for humanity, but I still trust it is the right call to follow.

Mike: I think our perspectives on the story have much in common, Rami. That being the case, I want to build on some of the matters you raise.

Your take on *lech lecha* (to walk toward yourself) reminds me of the quest theme's frequent role in literature. The hero is called to go on a journey. He or she must leave behind the familiar and travel toward a place or encounter. I can't think of a major quest story in which the road proves easy or straight. Along the way, the hero surrenders or loses all kinds of things: treasures, burdens, loved ones, perspectives, and the like. The journey is not all about loss, however, for the hero usually makes unexpected friends along the way, discovers her or his real self (for better and worse), achieves some kind of victory (though not always the one envisioned at the start of the trip), and blesses the world in some fashion.

Thinking about your comments on leaving cultural conditioning, stepping into the present, and being a blessing through blessing all others,

I'm struck by how much work is required to follow the call. God speaks a promise: "Leave the place you know, go where I show you to go, accept the place I give you, embrace the offspring I provide, become a blessing to all humanity." On the surface, it sounds like a simple proposition. Pack up, head out, follow the directions, arrive, settle down in the land I've prepared for you, and reap the benefits that will come to you and to others through you. In modern terms, it sounds almost like being offered a furnished home with a good job in a new community—provided you're willing to relocate! If only you will move, everything will be made ready for your arrival.

That's not how God-inspired quests work, is it? Abram and Sarai soon discover the land already has established inhabitants. There is no free space waiting for them to claim as their own. Large portions of the promise appear to be on hold or still in the making. God is with them, but they must pitch in to try to fashion the promised life with the materials God provides.

In *The Silmarillion*, J. R. R. Tolkien spins the story of the world's creation. God shares a music theme with the assembled angels and invites them to make music before him. They do so, though their own agendas creep in, and God must intervene to introduce new subthemes. At the end of the performance, they see a vision in the midst of the void, a world shaped by the music. The vision vanishes, and the angels protest. God speaks a word, and the vision becomes a real place. Many of the angels feel drawn or called to enter into the new world, and God grants their desire, stipulating only that once they come into the place called Middle-earth, they must abide there until its end. The affected angels make the move. But when they arrive, they are astounded to discover the "promised" world is quite unfinished. They must now labor to shape the new home toward the vision.

God calls, we respond, but always—insofar as I know from history, story, and experience—we do not find a world already made for us so much as we find ourselves laboring with God to bring the world envisioned into being. Is it too much for us? I don't know. Like you, I trust it's the right call into which to pour one's life.

Rami: I'm amazed at how you manage to work Tolkien into our discussions. As one who continually gets lost in Middle-earth, I am humbled by your ability to bring its wisdom to the Middle East.

I agree, of course, that one can read the Abram/Abraham story as a hero's journey and wish that more commentators on Genesis would develop a reading of the story along those lines. Sadly, Joseph Campbell, who literally wrote the book on quest narratives in human cultures, had such negative feelings toward Judaism (and maybe Jews as well) that he tended to dismiss the tales of the Hebrew Bible—a great loss to all of us who love both Campbell and the Hebrew Bible.

You are also correct that the historical aspect of the narrative leads our heroes into troubles that the psychospiritual reading does not. On the spiritual level, I think it is true that if we would continually empty ourselves of our conditioning, we might stay open to the presence of God and the possibilities of godliness, but on the historical (and hence socioeconomic-political-military) level, Abram and Sarai find themselves confronting a world not at all interested in being a blessing. Sadly, this is what happens to the Hebrews as well. In fact, it happens to all of us—which brings me back to J. R. R. Tolkien and your reference to *The Silmarillion.*

What Tolkien describes in his creation story is the process of evolution: there is a mutation—God's new theme—which is then followed by innovation around that mutation and then repetition of the innovation. Repetition goes nowhere, so God introduces a new mutant theme, and the process continues. This is the roll of God in process theology: God is creativity, continually keeping the world from devolving or stagnating. God is the opposite of entropy, which is why the world is never finished.

Judaism describes humanity as God's partner in creation and understands the Jews as a central catalyst to that partnership. I'm not so chauvinistic as to make the latter claim, but I do see humanity as a means by which creativity enters the world, especially the world of culture. I do believe God calls us moment to moment. The call is the moment itself. In each moment we are called to free ourselves from the conditions of the past that we might engage the present freely, and in so doing act in such a way as to be blessings and birth further blessings in the world. For us, this is a very this-worldly process. We rarely talk about the afterlife, being far too busy trying to make this life fulfill its promise.

Chapter 7

Abram, Sarai, and Pharaoh

Genesis 12:10-20

Mike: The storyline takes a turn when famine strikes. Abram goes to Egypt to live as a resident alien. Before they reach the border crossing, Abram starts to worry that the Egyptians might kill him in order to take his wife Sarai for their own. He tells her to pretend to be his sister. Sarai goes along with the plan. Eventually, Pharaoh's officials notice her and claim her for his harem. In exchange, Pharaoh showers Abram with sheep, oxen, donkeys, slaves, and camels.

The plan goes awry when God acts and afflicts the house of Pharaoh with plagues. Somehow, Pharaoh discerns that his house is under threat because Sarai is actually the wife of Abram. Pharaoh chides Abram for his deception, returns Sarai, and forces Abram to leave Egypt.

I'll be quite interested to hear your take on the story. In the meantime, I offer the following thoughts.

Insofar as I can remember, this is the first mention of Egypt in Genesis. Given subsequent stories, I imagine those listening to the story in later eras flinched when they heard, "So Abram went down into Egypt." "Egypt" functions almost as code for a place where God's people get hemmed in or enslaved literally and spiritually. I can hear listeners thinking, "Don't go there, Abram. That's not a good idea."

Egypt, though, also fills another role in the biblical narrative: a place of refuge in time of famine and trouble. There, with a bit of luck or for the right funding, an outsider finds a kind of welcome and food enough to survive. Even as late as the New Testament Gospels, Joseph is said to have fled to Egypt with the young Jesus in order to avoid Herod's slaughter of the innocents.

Egypt, in the story before us, seems surprisingly neutral. It is what it is: a kingdom set apart by history and policy from the other peoples, possessed of a relatively advanced civilization that can ride out famine times better than most other cultures and, within limits, provide a safe refuge for "aliens."

In this particular case, Abram creates his own problems. Whereas before he journeyed to and in the land God showed him, he now follows custom and goes down to Egypt in a time of crisis. He displays considerable courage and trust when he chooses to leave his home city and journey with God, but now he grows afraid on the border of Egypt and starts to spin his own plans for his safety. This will not be the last time he or Sarai adopts such a strategy, and it always leads to problems.

At first Abram's ploy works well for all involved (with the possible exception of Sarai). Pharaoh is happy, and he gives generous gifts to the supposed brother of Sarai. It looks as if Abram may have found a "promised land" after all, one rich in sheep, oxen, donkeys, camels, and slaves. He seems well on his way to becoming an Egyptian, or at least the head of a favored alien people among the Egyptians.

God uses Pharaoh, to whom Abram now looks for security, to shake things up. When God's plagues strike his household, Pharaoh pays attention, discerns what is afoot, and acts to rectify the situation. Strangely enough, Pharaoh is more attuned to God than Abram. Pharaoh forces Abram back on the road, where God will continue to challenge and mold him. For the moment, the promise and the journey survive.

We no doubt will name and explore a number of themes suggested by the story, but I want to pause at this point and hear what you have to say.

Rami: Honestly, Mike, I don't have a whole lot to say about this story. I like your homiletic spin, however, and agree that "the promise and the journey survive," but I find nothing of import in these tales and yield to your concern with them.

On the other hand, maybe this story foreshadows the emergence of the darker side of Abram's character. Not only does he twice prostitute his wife, once to Pharaoh in Genesis 12 and again to Abimelech in Genesis 20, but he also risks the lives of Hagar and Ishmael (Gen 21:9-13) and plots to murder his other son, Isaac, in an act of human sacrifice (Gen 22). So, again, we have Torah embracing a hero who is far from perfect.

As for the role Egypt plays in Torah, I agree with you that there is nothing intrinsically evil about it. Most of the time Egypt is a place of refuge, and even the Egyptians' great crime, the enslavement of the Hebrews, is mere turnabout given the prior enslavement of the Egyptians enacted under the auspices of the Hebrew Joseph.

Mike: Like you, I once found little useful in the story. My opinion changed over the past twenty years or so, mostly as I thought more carefully about structure, humanity, and culture.

Let's start with structure. Genesis 12:1-9 and 12:10-20 combine to paint the first portrait of Abram, who will become Abraham. They establish a pattern we see repeated over the course of the Abram tales. Abram trusts God enough to journey with God on the basis of a call and a promise, yet Abram finds it almost impossible to trust God with specific, challenging situations. You aptly point to the Abimelech story in Genesis 20, in which Abram faces a similar danger and repeats the strategy of putting Sarai at risk. The storyteller uses this two-fold pattern quite consciously, I think. We cannot know what the storyteller had in mind, but to my way of thinking, the structure brings Abram to life and makes him a believable character. Abram is "everyone" who must deal with life as it is and the living God.

Which brings me to humanity: I see Abram's complete story as a kind of biblical case study, the first epic-length account of the challenges of a genuine interface between God and an individual. The previous Genesis stories are snapshots compared to the Abram narrative. You note the story may reveal something about the darker side of Abram's character, and I do not disagree. I tend to describe the matter in a different way. I would say the two stories in Genesis 12 establish Abram's humanity, that fascinating and frustrating mix of spiritual intuition, cultural and personal habits of thought, intention, carelessness, courage, and fear that are found in all of us. The ancient Greeks gave us the hero with a tragic flaw, but the Genesis author surpasses their accomplishment in Abram, the hero who is but a human yet in whom lies the hope of humanity.

Abram does not live in a vacuum. He is the product of a culture, which ingrained in him certain ways of seeing life, conducting business, dealing with powerful people, and charting his course. Both of us believe Abram was a substantial person before he set out on his journey. Such persons usually are skilled in the ways of their home culture, successful at using it to advance or protect themselves and those they love.

The long story of Abram's journey with God may be read in any number of ways, but one approach I find useful is to note how many of the accounts feature Abram confronting a dangerous or befuddling situation and deciding how to handle it. More often than not, his first impulse is to do what he knows how to do, what culture has taught him, and it is this impulse that he must overcome, or that God must intervene to help him overcome. Clearly, God is at work to habituate Abram to a new way of seeing and living life, but such change does not come easy!

Does the cultural question offer any possible insights on the story of Abram, Sarai, and Pharaoh? I'll throw a possibility on the table. Suppose this is not a story about sex but about power and the conventions of the day. For example, throughout history rulers have often taken family hostages in order to ensure the good behavior of powerful resident aliens, allies, and such. I wonder if we might be dealing with something similar here. When a considerable clan or tribe arrived on the borders of Egypt, might their entry into the land have required that they send hostages to Pharaoh's court as a pledge of their good behavior? Normally, in such situations, one's sons, daughters, or siblings would have been taken. Abram had no such hostages to offer. Only Sarai was on hand, so to protect their lives and gain entrance into the refuge of Egypt, Abram used deception to become eligible to participate in the established cultural game of hostage taking.

Of course, it may be that an entirely different culturally driven game was in play. My point is not tied to a specific cultural structure. I only stress how difficult it is for any of us to imagine playing any game other than those we've absorbed or been taught by our cultures. Abram is not exempt. Still, God is determined to birth and fashion a new culture, a new game, and Abram and Sarai are the ones selected by God to launch the endeavor. Thus, God uses someone (Pharaoh) on the edges of the new game to force the main players to follow the new rules. It will not be the last time God intervenes through other humans, beings, or creatures to help Abram find his way.

Rami: I can see you don't want to let this story go without some comment from me, and since you bring up the cultural element, let me start with that.

Your notion that this story could reflect a power play motivated by fear of an alien tribe coming into one's land is an intriguing one. It would certainly explain the story. The question we would have to ask is whether or not Abram and company was a large enough group to cause Pharaoh to fear their entry into Egypt. Nothing in the previous verses, however, suggests that they are. It is only after they leave Egypt, taking the gifts of Pharaoh with them, that Torah says, "Abram was very wealthy in herds, silver, and in gold" (Gen 13:1).

If we stick with the notion that the story is about sex rather than fear of an intruding stranger, I would offer this insight: Jewish commentators on this story often speak of the danger married women faced when entering Egypt with their husbands. According to tradition, married women traveling with their husbands were in more danger than single women entering with their brothers. The custom (according to Jewish commentators, and not according to Egyptian records) was for the Egyptians to murder the husband, rape the wife, and then kill her as well. But if the woman was not married, the custom was to shower the brother with gifts in the hope that he would give his sister to her suitor out of gratitude. Knowing this, Abram may have used the strategy he did to protect Sarai as well as himself. This would explain why Abram adopts the same strategy vis-à-vis the Philistines (assuming he believed Philistine custom to be the same as Egyptian custom), as well as why his son Isaac takes the same tack with the Pharaoh of his day. In short, it may be the rational thing to do.

Further support for this reading can be found in the order of Pharaoh's gifts to Abram. Pharaoh sent Abram "sheep and oxen and he-asses and menservants and maidservants and she-asses and camels" (Gen 12:16). Asses were considered beasts of burden and were not as valuable as servants, so one would expect Pharaoh to send servants before asses—or, if he is going to start with asses, to send male and female donkeys together. The chaotic way the gifts are given suggests to some that Pharaoh is just tossing whatever he had on hand at Abram: one day a sheep, the next day an ox, then a male donkey, then a man-servant, etc., hoping that at some point Abram would find something he wanted and give Sarai in exchange. Abram accepted each day's gift, for to refuse would have meant the end of the bargaining and, since Abram had not yet given Sarai to Pharaoh, Abram's certain death.

Now let me comment briefly on the "trust in God" alternative. True, Abram could have relied on God to provide food and not gone into Egypt, but that isn't the normative path in Judaism. We don't test God this way. We are taught that God created humanity with the capacity to figure things out for ourselves and only intervenes if and when we make a mess of things.

Look at what God says to Moses when the Hebrew people are trapped between the Reed (or Red) Sea and the Egyptian army. Facing certain death at the hands of the Egyptians, Moses says to the Israelites, "YHVH will make war for you, and you shall remain silent" (Exod 14:14). But God says to

Moses, "Why do you call out to me? Speak to the Children of Israel and let them journey forth [into the sea]" (Exod 14:15). This is shocking! God has rescued the people from slavery, and now when they turn to God for help once again, God says, "What are you bothering me for? Just keep marching into the sea."

Of course, God does save the people with the parting of the waters, but only after the people make the first move on their own. According to rabbinic lore, Nachshon ben Aminadav, Aaron's brother-in-law, preferring death by drowning to being dragged back into Egyptian slavery, marched into the sea on his own. He waded out until the water was at his throat, and only then did the sea recede before him. The point is that faith in God does not mean waiting on God to save you. You have to act, like Nachshon, even when such action seems hopeless. In fact, in Yiddish there is a phrase "to be a Nachshon," meaning to be a bold initiator of action. We should all be so bold.

Chapter 8

Hagar and Ishmael

Genesis 16:1-16

Mike: Learning to trust God's promise gets harder the longer Sarai and Abram wait on its fulfillment. Sarai takes matters into her own hands by asking Abram to father a child with her slave Hagar. As far as I know, Sarai acts well within the custom of the period. Her proposal would have seemed sensible and normal in her cultural context.

Their age no doubt engenders urgency, but something else may be in play as well. Sarai says, "You see that the LORD has prevented me from bearing children; go unto my slave girl; it may be that I shall obtain children by her" (v. 2). Sarai assumes her barrenness results from an act of God. Perhaps she see this as a punishment, but it seems more likely that Sarai thinks the two of them misunderstood God's intent and are making its fulfillment far more difficult than it need be by waiting for her aged body to conceive and bear a child. After all, there's a perfectly normal, tried and tested means of producing an heir in their circumstances. Why not use it?

I find the phrase "And Abram listened to the voice of Sarai" (v. 2) intriguing. One way to read the stories of Abram and Sarai, their immediate descendants, and the later people of God revolves around a question: "To whom will we listen?" Both individuals and peoples tend to listen to the speaker they know best, namely their birth culture. Our modern culture speaks with many voices, most of them loud and insistent, some quiet but persistent. Modern culture streams a rather constant set of messages: watch out for number one; wealth ensures security; faith is alright provided it stays in its place; some kinds of humans are "in," and others are "out"; might makes right; and the like. Listening to the voice of our birth culture is the human norm, whether it speaks wisely or foolishly, with knowledge or in ignorance.

Starting with Abram and Sarai, God sets out to create a culture that listens for and to God's voice. Such listening, over time, may shape a people who differ in significant ways from those of surrounding cultures. Abram and Sarai find it hard to hear and act upon what God says, so time after time they fall back into the ways of their birth culture. Sarai's attempt to reinterpret the message of God in a way that fits the cultural norm establishes a pattern we find throughout history: the tendency of religious persons and institutions to clothe established viewpoints and practices in the language of faith. My own spiritual forebears, Baptist Christians in the southern United States, once insisted that God spoke in favor of slavery, Jim Crow, and segregation. Abram and Sarai represent us as they try to cope with God by squeezing God into their existing worldview.

The strategy works for a time. Hagar conceives. It appears Sarai has solved the problem of how to help God fulfill God's promise. But human nature intervenes. Hagar, at least from Sarai's perspective, becomes haughty. The two clash. Sarai insists Abram solve the problem, but Abram refuses responsibility and reminds Sarai she has the power to do as she pleases with her slave. Sarai mistreats Hagar, and Hagar runs away. Perhaps Sarai hoped her abuse of Hagar would lead to such a result. Thus, Sarai and Abram's attempt to fashion the promise's fulfillment leads only to disappointment, strife, and pain for all involved.

At this point, the angel of the Lord finds Hagar near a spring and speaks to her. Two elements of the conversation stand out. First, God does not restrict conversation to the "chosen." He speaks to the slave, the Egyptian woman, the one who has no place or voice. Second, God names the child in her womb and declares he and his descendants will be given a role in the story God is writing. The God dealing with Abram, Sarai, and Hagar cannot be constrained by tribal or social boundaries. God cares, in some fashion, for all persons.

Later biblical narratives and the history of Judaism and Christianity demonstrate that we usually prefer a more circumscribed God. Stories such as that of Hagar and Ishmael lay the groundwork for those who challenge such presumptions.

Rami: I think you're tapping into something very important here, Mike: What do we do when the promise of God remains unfulfilled?

It's all well and good to say, "We must wait upon the word of the Lord to be fulfilled in his time," but is there a moment when the long wait leads us to wonder, "Was there ever a promise at all, or are we simply deluded?"

One can read Sarai's actions in this story as a desperate attempt to salvage the promise of God by interpreting it in the light of her current situation. Sarai is seventy-five years old. The chances of her having a child are nil. So Sarai is reduced to two options: wait or act. She chooses to act.

Your take on this seems to be critical: she should have kept the faith and waited. Perhaps I'm wrong to read you this way, and please correct me if this is the case. But whether or not I read you properly, let me say that Sarai's acting is quintessentially Jewish.

Again let me bring up Nachshon at the Reed Sea. Moses calls to God to save the people, and God says, "Why are you looking to me to save you? Save yourselves!" (Exod 14:15). And then Nachshon marches into the sea to what must have seemed to him and the rest a certain death. But better to drown free than to die a slave, so he acted.

Jews act. When exiled by Rome in the year 70 CE, the Jews trusted God to return them to the promised land. Almost 2,000 years later, Theodore Herzl (1860–1904), a secular Jew for whom waiting on God is an absurdity, acts, and Zionism is born. At the heart of at least one strand of Judaism is the notion that God's promises are only fulfilled through human action. As a Christian, a member of a faith who has waited for the fulfillment of Christ's return to earth longer than we Jews waited for the fulfillment of our return to Israel, I can understand your penchant for waiting, but I just wanted to put in a good word for acting.

In any case, you are right; things do not go well for Hagar. Sarai is jealous of her pregnant servant and worried, lest this young woman supplant her in Abram's affections. She abuses Hagar, perhaps, as you suggest, to force her to leave or, perhaps more wickedly, to cause her to miscarry.

To escape Sarai's abuse, Hagar flees into the wilderness, and there she meets four angels. The number four is gleaned from the way the Hebrew text is written. Every time an angel speaks to Hagar, Torah says, "An angel of YHVH said to her" (Gen 16:7, 9, 10, 11). God never speaks directly to Hagar, but as we shall see, Hagar hears God's words in their proclamations.

The first angel asks her, essentially, "What's your plan?" Hagar has no plan and is simply running away. The second angel tells her to return to Sarai and submit to whatever cruelty she will unleash. A third angel makes her a promise, echoing that which God made to Abram: Hagar will be the mother of a great people (Gen 16:10; cf. Gen 12:2). And then the fourth angel says that Hagar will conceive, give birth to a boy, and name him Ishmael, "man of God" (Gen 16:11).

I can't read this passage without hearing a foreshadowing of Isaiah 7:14, where the prophet says an *almah*, a young woman (the Greek Bible uses "virgin"), will give birth to a son and will name him *Emmanuel*, "God is with us." And I cannot make this connection without expecting you to make one more and see in this eighth-century BCE prophecy a foretelling of the birth of Jesus almost a thousand years later when the angel Gabriel says to the virgin Mary, "You will be with child and give birth to a son, and you are to name him Jesus" (Luke 1:32).

So yet again, promises are made. At least Hagar knows she is already pregnant, whereas Sarai and Mary—the one elderly and barren, the other young and virginal—have to wait and see what will come to pass.

Hagar hears the voice of God in these angels and gives God a new name of her own choosing—"the God who sees," perhaps meaning the God who sees the plight of the oppressed.

As you say, Mike, it is important to note that Torah does not restrict God's encounters with humanity to Jews. According to Rashi (1040–1104), perhaps our most famous Torah commentator, Hagar was an Egyptian princess, the daughter of Pharaoh. When her father returned Sarai to Abram, Hagar begged her father to let her go with Sarai, seeing in Sarai's faith something greater than her own.

The irony, as you point out, is that these hints of universalism found throughout Genesis are lost on so many who seek to restrict God to their religious community alone.

Mike: Before leaving Hagar's story for a time, I want to explore the matter of waiting and action a bit more.

I can see where I might come across as critical of Sarai, but such is not my intent. Actually, I feel a sense of empathy or kinship with her and with anyone caught in the time between God's promise made and God's promise fulfilled. Isn't that where most people of faith live most of the time?

You write that Sarai is reduced to two options: to wait or to act. I see her quandary in different terms. She faces a choice between actions: to take control of the situation herself or to continue to go about daily life and see what God might do with it. Either option is an action. Sarai selects the first option. To my mind, her choice comes across as quintessentially human.

We all act. The question always before us is whether or not we act wisely within our limits. I'll risk an analogy. I believe God intends us to function as God's partners in the creation, from the larger scale of ecology to the personal scale of our individual lives. We are junior partners, not equal partners, with God. God listens to our input, but God sets direction, policy, and calendar. Our subcreative gifts are best employed in implementing God's vision. Limited by our finitude, we simply cannot see the big picture God sees. We forget this sometimes and try to shift direction, reframe policy, or alter the calendar to suit our limited vision. Trouble ensues, whether the tensions and dangers of the Hagar and Sarai story, the quandaries of Zionism, or the tragedies and absurdities associated with Christians attempting to hasten the return of Christ.

Rami: Okay, I think we are on the same page here. What I'm calling "waiting," you are calling "seeing what God might do."

Your notion that humanity is God's junior partner in creation is a Jewish one as well, but it is one that I find troubling. I don't believe in a self-conscious God who has a plan for us and for all creation. God, for me, is the process of unfolding creativity in which you and I arise, live, and have our being, to paraphrase St. Paul. If anything, we humans are the way God becomes self-aware in our tiny speck of the universe. That is what "partnership" means to me. We are God's antennae, the way God feels out the unfolding creation. This is as close as I can get to your notion that "God listens to our input."

I'm also curious as to what you mean when you say God sees the big picture. I am not convinced that God knows the future. In fact, for God's sake I hope God doesn't know the future. Just imagine an infinite and all-knowing mind for whom the future is already present. What could be more boring than this? Without surprise, life becomes a long stretch of tedium.

There is a Jewish saying: "Why did God create humanity? Because God loves stories." We are constantly surprising God; we are God's uncertainty principle. In the Hagar story, Abram and Hagar give birth to Ishmael, who is the progenitor of the Arab peoples and the entire new narrative of Islam. We humans are part of what keeps God from being bored. Of course, I'm speaking metaphorically.

The fact that we humans act from our limited perspective isn't a design flaw. How else can we act? How else can we choose? It is what we have to work with, and working with it is what it is to be human. The choice is to act on our limited knowledge or to wait (which I agree is an action in and of itself) until we know more. Since we can never know enough, all our actions are contingent on our own limited knowing or perhaps unlimited ignorance. Acting without knowing is heroic, I think, though sometimes also stupid.

Last thought: your linking of Zionism and hastening the return of Christ. As I mentioned earlier, there were and are those Orthodox Jews who feel we should have passed on the secular Zionism of Herzl and waited on the messianic Zionism of God. If we had done this, the State of Israel would not exist, since neither your Messiah nor mine has made an appearance of late.

Now, some might argue that without Israel, the world and world Jewry might be better off. There is no way to know, and I refuse to speculate. But this line of thought reminds me of a wonderful Yiddish tale by I. L. Peretz called *Bontshe Shvayg*, written in 1894. Briefly put, Bontshe Shvayg is a Jew, recently deceased, who "made no impression" while living on earth but whose arrival in heaven is heralded. Bontshe is celebrated as a saint, and his life of inaction and passivity in the face of injustice is reframed as one of absolute faith in God. At the end of the story, the judge and angels say to Bontshe, "All heaven belongs to you. Ask for anything you wish; you can choose what you like."

The expectation is that Bontshe will choose to end injustice and establish peace on earth. Instead, he asks that each morning, he be granted a fresh roll with butter. God and his angels "hung their heads in shame" while the devil laughed.

Mike: The Yiddish story *Bontshe Shvayg* is a wonderful little tale, which I think drives home three points. First, passivity in the face of injustice is never enough. Second, passivity alone says nothing about the character or motivations of the one practicing it. Third, if we practice only passivity in the face of injustice, injustice prevails to our shame.

Sarai and Abram do not face a justice issue per se. Instead, God calls them to believe the unbelievable and to learn to act accordingly. Mind you, learning to do so is one of the ways in which persons may become able to envision remedies for injustice and believe it's possible to implement them, even if their culture cannot see what they see. Abram and Sarai, though, are dealing with another matter: learning to live by faith rather than by sight. And it's not easy!

I want to nuance one matter: I do not believe in simply waiting to see what God will do, but I do believe in going about daily life and looking to see what God might do with it. Things you might not believe possible sometimes happen as a result. For example, I grew up in the era of the civil rights movement. The rural community where I lived accepted school integration without much overt resistance, but otherwise continued long-established patterns of thought and behavior. We practiced a quiet racism, the kind that kept everyone in their assigned places yet also provided for a degree of compassionate interaction between races in times of personal crisis.

I read widely as a young teenager and reached the conclusion that racism and segregation were wrong in the eyes of God. School integration opened the opportunity to develop friendships across racial lines, and I did so. I wish I could claim it was part of some grand strategy to challenge racism, but the truth of the matter is that I simply fell into conversations, which led to shared activities (from something as simple as sitting together at lunch to choosing one another for teams in gym), and so fashioned friendships.

One day, I invited one of my friends to attend morning worship with me at my church. He agreed. As you might imagine, our all-white, mostly racist congregation was taken aback. Because of their regard for me, they did not say anything, but I felt a chill in the air. I can't claim to have sparked a drastic change in the church. Forty or so additional years passed before meaningful integration took place.

But I had changed, not so much by taking matters consciously into my own hands as by simply living into the opportunities and tasks of each day. Looking back, I tend to see God at work in the mundane to take me to a place neither my family nor faith community could envision at the time.

So I wonder how the story of Abram and Sarai might have played out had both chosen to live into the promise by going about their daily lives and waiting to see what God might do with them. They chose another way, a wholly understandable way. I do not condemn them for doing so, though I sometimes wish they had made a different decision.

Turning to a different matter, I need to clarify my take on God, our partnership with God, and the future. I would not so much say that God knows the future as God inhabits all possible time and space and so can deal with all possible futures. The choices we make unleash such futures, which is a testament to our God-given powers of creativity and decision. While I love your metaphor of a God who values surprise, I would say rather that God delights in diversity. Taking up your other metaphor of a God who loves stories, I tend to think God interacts with all the stories our choices instigate but that God might well prefer some stories to others.

Okay, I feel as if I am starting to wander, perhaps even to chase rabbits (and great fun it is too). You bring out my innate love of speculation and gentle debate!

Rami: Honestly, Mike, I'm surprised this little story has generated so much conversation between us, but I'm grateful that it has since it's raising issues that you and I haven't spoken about before.

I'm struck by your notion that God calls us to "believe the unbelievable." I won't dispute the claim since it may be your experience, but I will admit it isn't mine. If faith is "believing the unbelievable" and religion is the institutionalizing of such beliefs, is there any rational reason for getting involved with religion at all? And if unbelievability is not a hedge against faith but the foundation of it, how can I decide which unbelievable faith claims are worthy of my belief?

The virgin birth is no more or less unbelievable to me than Sarah giving birth in her eighties, and the resurrection of Jesus is no more or less unbelievable to me than God dictating Torah to Moses or the Quran to Mohammad. So how do I choose what to believe? If religion requires that I believe in these things, I would have to abandon religion altogether. If, on the other hand, these claims are part of a mythic narrative that contains insights into humanity and our relationship with the larger reality "in which we live and move and have our being" (to borrow again from St. Paul), I can find value in each of them.

I find the notion of believing the unbelievable oxymoronic; if it is unbelievable, how can I believe it? Writing about the resurrection of Jesus, Tertullian (160–225) said, *certum est, quia impossibile*: "It is certain, because impossible." But there is no logic in this. Impossibility isn't proof of certainty, but its opposite. Tertullian, of course, is talking about the capacity of God to do anything regardless of the logic or the laws of nature, but even if I found this convincing, how do I decide which impossible thing is certain—Krishna appearing to Arjuna as a charioteer, God appearing to us as Jesus, Elijah being lifted bodily into heaven, Mohammad flying to Jerusalem on a winged horse and then climbing up to meet God in heaven? What about Joseph Smith's Golden Plates or L. Ron Hubbard's Xenu the Space Emperor? Where does it end? Impossibility alone tells me nothing about truth.

Of course, you might argue, as my son Aaron does, that faith requires the suspension of disbelief, and in so doing the absurd becomes believable. Hence, Tertullian's other famous statement, *credo quia absurdum est*: "I believe because it is absurd." But this doesn't help me at all, for my question remains: where does believing in absurdity end? It is absurd to believe the earth is at most 10,000 years old. Should I dismiss all scientific evidence to the contrary and simply affirm this absurdity and call it faith?

Aaron argues that faith is about entering into the story as it presents itself to us. What may be absurd when looked at through the lens of science and reason is not absurd when looked at through the lens of the story itself. So Harry Potter is as real as Abraham, Sarah, and Hagar. I can accept this as far as it goes, but I am looking for something more than the reduction of religion to story. But maybe there is nothing more. And if this is true, then I can accept as true not only the miracles of our respective Bibles, but those of the Hindus, Buddhists, Mormons, and Scientologists as well. There is no end to absurdities and impossibilities and no way to choose among them. If I believe any because it is absurd, I must believe all because they are absurd and equally so.

As for your thoughtful and moving comments on racism, let me simply note what both of us know: there were/are lots of people on the side of segregation who believed segregation was/is God's will. It is my experience that people who believe in God most often believe that God is on their side; otherwise, they would change sides. So taking refuge in God is no guarantee that one is taking refuge in morality; we create God in our image to excuse and sanction our desires.

Let me also respond to your notion that "God inhabits all possible time and space." The important word for me here is *possible*. Does all possible time include the future that is as yet unknown to us, and if it does, is the future known to God? If God inhabits the future, doesn't God know the future, and isn't God then robbed of surprise? And if God inhabits the future, does that mean the future already exists, and if that is so, what does that say about determinism versus free will?

Lastly, I'm not sure that God "delighting in diversity" is the same as knowing or not knowing the future. And while I agree that God "delights," God delights only in the way a rose bush "delights" in blossoming roses. I suspect you mean something far closer to what we humans experience as delight, but that requires a belief in a self-conscious and willful God that I just do not share with you. As for diversity, since I believe that the universe with all its diversity is the blossoming of God in time and space, I would agree with your association with God and diversity.

I imagine that we could go on and on about this, and I am more than happy to do so—after all, this kind of conversation is at the heart of our friendship—but it may be time to move on to our next story. Your call.

Chapter 9

The Three Visitors

Genesis 18:1-15

Mike: The unfolding story may drive us back to the question of believing the unbelievable. In the meantime, let's take up the next tale—the story of the three visitors.

Abraham and Sarah (named anew in Gen 17:5, 15) camp at Mamre. As Abraham rests during the midday heat, three men appear nearby. Abraham runs to them, greets them, and offers them hospitality. They accept, and Abraham rushes off to give Sarah detailed instructions for a meal. When the meal is ready, Abraham serves it to his guests.

Their conversation turns to Sarah when one of the three asks, "Where is Sarah?" "There, in the tent," responds Abraham. One of the three men makes a promise: "I will surely return to you in due season, and your wife Sarah shall have a son." Sarah is eavesdropping at the tent entrance. She knows she no longer has the ability to conceive and bear children. When she hears the man's promise, she laughs quietly and thinks to herself, "After I have grown old and my husband is old, shall I have pleasure?" Clearly, in her mind—to use a current phrase—the answer is, "I don't think so!"

In response, "the LORD" (presumably one of the visitors) insists that nothing is impossible with God, that he will return at the right time, and that Sarah shall bear a son. Sarah denies she laughed, but "the LORD" is not fooled.

Now we return to the question of believing the impossible. Regardless of how you or I feel or think about the general matter, in the story Abraham and Sarah are called to act as if God will fulfill the impossible promise of a son. Sarah, at least, cannot believe. She knows the realities of reproduction! I like to think she laughed quietly, perhaps a little bitterly to herself at the foolishness of the males sitting under the shade, eating and drinking, and making impossible promises about the female body. Going farther, perhaps Sarah has had enough of Abraham's God, who promises much but delivers little. I find the little phrase "So Sarah laughed" one of the most moving and thought-provoking in all of the Scriptures.

The story poses a question that crops up in one way or another throughout the Bible: "Is anything too wonderful for the Lord?" To put it more bluntly, "Is anything impossible with God?" Theologians, philosophers, and even Baptist pastors are tempted to treat the question in relation to hypothetical scenarios. Insofar as I know, the Scriptures always attach it to particular situations, such as the promise of a son for Sarah and Abraham. Will their lives be shaped around the promise or in accordance with what everyone thinks is possible?

We've dialogued around the question of faith in earlier conversations. One way to frame a definition of faith might go something like this: Faith is the decision to believe God can and will do as God promises and to shape one's life accordingly.

Rami: To get at the Jewish reading of this story, we have to parse the text carefully. Genesis 18:1 tells us that God "appeared" to Abraham. Jewish tradition holds that this appearance took place three days after Abraham carried out God's command regarding circumcision and demonstrates that God visits the sick, a trait that we too are to practice.

In the next verse, we are told that Abraham "lifted his eyes and saw" three men approaching his camp. You are right to say that these "men" turn out to be angels but, according to Judaism, wrong to think that God was among them. Our rabbis teach that when Abraham ran to greet the "men," he was actually leaving God behind! The teaching here is that "hospitality toward travellers is more important than receiving God" (Talmud, *Shabbat* 127a).

Of course, if I were Christian, I would focus on the sentence where Abraham addresses the three "men" in the singular. While Jews argue that he was addressing the leader of the three, a Trinitarian Christian might say that he saw the three—Father, Son, and Holy Spirit—as one. I appreciate your decision not to read the Trinity into Torah, but somebody ought to, so it might as well be me.

Back on Jewish soil, we have a tradition regarding the tree under which the "men" sought shade. According to our rabbis, this was no ordinary tree, but a truth tree, which reads the character of those who sat beneath it. If the visitors were honorable, the tree would bend toward them and provide them with shade. If not, it would bend away from them and let them sit in the hot sun. So instructing the "men" to sit beneath the tree was Abraham's way of checking them out. You can't be too careful.

This is why Abraham at first only offers the "men" a "morsel of bread," but after he sees the tree shade them, he orders Sarah to bake fresh bread and runs to choose a calf, which he then turns over to "the youth" to prepare. Who is this youth? Torah doesn't say, but the only youth that matters to Abraham thus far would be Ishmael, who is around thirteen when this event takes place. So it makes sense to imagine that just as Abraham has his wife bake the bread, he has his son prepare the meat.

The rabbis had a problem when Torah says that Abraham took cream and milk and set it before the men along with the meat Ishmael had prepared. Eating dairy and meat together is a serious violation of *kashrut*, Jewish dietary laws. While it is true that kosher laws would only come through Moses, our rabbis could not imagine Abraham violating them. The way around this was to imagine that while his guests waited for the calf to cook, they dipped their bread in cream and milk. When the meat was served, the dairy was gone, and hence no law was broken.

After the "men" eat (or appear to eat, since angels don't actually eat), they inquire as to the whereabouts of Sarah. When told she is in the tent, one of the angels, Michael, according to the rabbis, tells Abraham that Sarah will give birth to a son. The absurdity of a ninety-year-old woman giving birth causes Sarah to laugh. It is at this point that God, presumably still hanging out by the tent, objects to Sarah's laughter. Sarah denies having laughed, but God knows better.

I agree with you that we could reprise our discussion of believing the impossible, but there is little point in our doing so. So let me offer another take on Sarah's laughter. Sarah's laughter is spontaneous and, as some rabbis teach, an expression of joy. What the NRSV translates as "pleasure" is the Hebrew word *edna*, "delicate skin." The thought of having the skin of youth in the midst of old age is what causes her to laugh—with joy.

Your question "Will their lives be shaped around the promise or in accordance with what everyone thinks is possible?" is a good one, especially if we personalize it this way: "Shall I shape my life around the promise or in accordance with what everyone thinks is possible?" What is the promise? For Jews it is the promise that a day will come when people "shall beat their swords into plowshares and their spears into pruning hooks. Nation shall not take up sword against nation; they shall never again know war; and all people shall sit under their grapevines or fig trees, and none shall be afraid"

(Mic 4:3-4). For Christians it may be the promise of Jesus' return. In either case, do we live by the promise or not?

Living by the promise means living with hope, a kind of hope that, as Sarah demonstrates when she laughs, is filled with joy. Living by the promise means living with optimism. Living by the promise means never giving into despair. Even if the promise is never fulfilled, living with hope and optimism rather than hopelessness and despair may be worth the suspension of our disbelief.

Mike: Rami, I don't recall labeling the visitors as angels in my earlier remarks, settling instead for the terms "men" and "guests." The visitors are mysterious figures in the story, and I am content to leave them so. All I can say with certainty is that one of them speaks God's word to Abraham and Sarah.

That said, I love the interpretive traditions you mention: God cares for the sick, hospitality to strangers trumps staying close to God, and the truth tree. While I do not find such matters in the story itself, I think they prompt the kind of reflection useful to forming a God-honoring life.

As for rabbinic teachers who have a problem with Abraham serving cream and milk along with the meat, I appreciate the effort of imagination required to conform the story to the demands of Jewish dietary laws. However, when Christian interpreters attempt to find ways to make an ancient story accord with later developments in Christian theology, I grow uneasy. For example, many Christians tend to see the three men as the Trinity. I understand the impulse, but I choose not to follow their lead. The very mystery surrounding the three guests serves as a reminder that we do not and never shall know all there is to know about the nature or ways of God.

I agree that the long-term promise of God is captured, at least in part, by the dream of a day when people "shall beat their swords into plowshares and their spears into pruning hooks. Nation shall not take up sword against nation; they shall never again know war; and all people shall sit under their grapevines and fig trees" (Mic 4:3-4). That, though, is not the promise at stake in the story before us. Here, the promise is not cosmic or even world-wide. Instead, it is quite particular: an elderly, childless couple will be given a son by God.

That specificity delivers the power and charm of the story. I think many of us can embrace the hope that God (or, in your case, humanity) will bring peace to all at some point in history. We find it much more challenging to accept that God might do something in the near future that defies the norm.

We've batted around the matter of belief. If memory serves, you often associate belief with choosing to believe in a set of content that cannot be proven. Without disparaging belief, you note that belief systems are a variety of circular reasoning. Quite so! They are provable only within their set of postulates or assumptions.

However, I don't think Abraham and Sarah (and by extension we) are challenged to accept a belief system. Instead, God seeks to introduce them to a life grounded in faith, a life in which one relaxes and rests in God, floats in God as one might float in water. Isaac, when he arrives, is a living sign that such a life is possible.

Rami: I think we've taken this story as far as we can, Mike, and I look forward to moving on to the story of Sodom. Before we do so, however, let me simply say that the rabbinic approach to reading Torah is rooted in what literary scholar and critic Harold Bloom calls "strong misreading." As I understand this notion, one reads not to understand the writer or the writer's time, but to see what, if anything, the reader can do with what is written to enhance her understanding of her own life and time. Bloom says that any text that yields only a single meaning is a weak and soon forgotten text, and that the great literatures of the world are those that can be reread and in a sense reinvented in each generation. This is certainly how the rabbis understood Torah.

I was taught this in two ways. First, if Torah is the word of God, one cannot expect God to be limited to the niceties of Hebrew grammar or the historical verities of one historical period. Torah must transcend time, place, grammar, and language itself, which is why the rabbis were willing to interpret sections of Torah out of context, read meaning into the shapes of the letters themselves, and even substitute numbers for letters and find in Torah insights that only a numerological "reading" could yield.

Second, since the Hebrew text of Torah lacks punctuation and vowels, it is up to the reader to supply these. The text itself, comprising consonants only, is gibberish unless and until the reader breathes vowels and pauses into the text. Torah is meaningful only when read aloud by a living reader. And since the reader is free to breathe any vowels she or he wishes, the meanings can and do change.

One quick example: In Leviticus 19:18 we read *V'ahavta l'rayecha k'mochha*, "Love your neighbor as yourself." Rabbi Nachman of Breslov (1772–1810) "strongly misread" the text as *V'ahavta l'rahecha k'mocha*, "Love your capacity for wickedness as a part of yourself." The Hebrew text lends itself to both readings, and the fact that the first is conventional doesn't render the second any less accurate or holy.

So while I understand and share your concern about reading "an ancient story in accord with later developments in Christian theology" and while I know my teachers would draw the line when trying to read Christian theology into Jewish texts, their line is arbitrary. Theoretically, there is no limit to what one may discover in Torah.

The best defense against strong misreading isn't to do away with misreading altogether (not that you suggested that), but to realize that any reading of any Scripture is going to tell us more about the reader than the Scripture itself.

Mike: Before we move on, I want to comment on the matter of a "strong misreading" of Torah, or any other Scripture for that matter. I strongly agree that any text yielding only a single meaning is weak and apt to fade into obscurity. The history of Christian biblical interpretation by scholars, poets, mystics, clergy, and laypersons suggests each generation and individual reader will find varied meanings in a great text. Your two examples capture some of the reasons this is the case.

I often use a phrase when talking with others about a given biblical text: "The longer I live with the text, the more I see." What do I see: layers of meaning at the corporate and individual levels, connections of all kinds (other Scriptures, history, literature, the arts, personal experience or the experience of others, etc.), decision points, the nature of God and humanity. I dislike Bloom's phrase "strong misreading," mostly because I think it unintentionally encourages some to willfully misuse texts or seek novelty for the sake of novelty. I prefer to speak of immersing oneself in the text or, more dramatically, of plunging into the text without benefit of lifeline or life preserver. Cease trying to control where the text may take you or what it may do with you. Don't be afraid to drown in the text. Go with the currents to see what beach they may cast you upon.

Still, you jump into a given patch of water, the text as it is. Try to savor your moment or hours there at least as much as the rest of the journey. Embrace, experience, and learn from the entry point, even as you remain open to what may come next. Such an approach to a text requires humility, and I suspect it teaches humility as well.

Alright, I'm ready. Respond as you wish to my ramblings. Once I hear from you, we'll move on to the story of Sodom and Gomorrah.

Rami: Well said, Mike. I especially like your reference to humility. We all need more of that, especially those of us who dare to plunge into the ocean of sacred texts in search of meaning. On to Sodom!

Chapter 10

The Destruction of Sodom and Gomorrah

Genesis 18:16–19:29

Mike: The story of the destruction of Sodom and Gomorrah is divided into three scenes: 18:16-33; 19:1-11; 19:12-29. The first scene features a conversation between God and Abraham. Scene two tells the tale of the two angels, Lot, and the mob outside Lot's door. Scene three tells of Lot's reluctant flight from Sodom and the destruction of the city.

Many a commentator and a large segment of the Christian community read the accounts with reference to one concern: homosexuality. I find the actual story considerably more complicated and layered.

To start with, the story is tied to the ongoing theme of God's effort to forge a covenant community. Humanity proves quite resistant to God's dream. For the most part, people continue what is by now a familiar pattern: they found and nurture communities in which self-centeredness determines all things, as opposed to love of God or neighbor. Even as God works to launch a new community through Abraham and Sarah, God continues to monitor the situation elsewhere, including the towns of Sodom and Gomorrah.

In the first scene, God reveals to Abraham that a great outcry has gone up against the two cities because of their grave sin. God does not define the specifics of their sin. Some of the prophets, though, spoke to the matter. Isaiah's opening words to Judah and Jerusalem compare them to Sodom and Gomorrah (Isa 1:10). The prophet tells the people God cares nothing for their burnt offerings and solemn assemblies and prayers. If the people of Judah and Jerusalem wish to please God, they must cease to do evil, learn to do good, seek justice, rescue the oppressed, defend the orphan, and plead for the widow (Isa 1:16-17). Isaiah clearly implies Sodom and Gomorrah did the opposite. Ezekiel takes a similar approach. He defines the sin of Sodom as pride, excess of food, no concern for the poor and needy, haughtiness, and other abominations (Ezek 16:49-50).

Protestant Christians traditionally claim we wish to use Scripture to interpret Scripture. When we apply such an approach to the Sodom and Gomorrah story, we broaden our understanding of the depravity of the two cities. They are sick communities in which the rich and powerful oppress the weak rather than help them, those strong enough to gratify desire do so without regard for the humanity of others, and violence of all kinds is routine. The two towns' version of community stands in direct opposition to God's vision for human community.

God tells Abraham he intends to judge Sodom and Gomorrah, and Abraham immediately sees that God plans to destroy them. With great care, Abraham challenges God's intent: "Will you indeed sweep away the righteous with the wicked?" The theme of God's chosen acting as God's challenger emerges as Abraham works God through a series of possibilities. If as many as fifty, forty-five, and so on down to ten righteous people live in the cities, will God not spare the inhabitants for the sake of the righteous minority? God concedes Abraham's point and promises to spare the cities should as few as ten righteous people be found in them. The Lord then goes on his way, and Abraham returns to his own place.

Meanwhile, the Lord's two companions, now called angels, make their way to Sodom. Rami, before I move to the next two scenes, I want to pause and hear what you have to say.

Rami: For Jews, the real sin of Sodom and Gomorrah is, as you noted, injustice. This is why Abraham's challenge to God is so powerful: "Should the Judge of all the world not do justly?" (Gen 18:25). Abraham is saying that justice trumps God and that God is about to commit the very sin of injustice that God condemns the people of Sodom for committing. But wait! There's more.

In 18:24 Abraham challenges God to forgive the city *l'mah-ahn ha-tzadikim*, "for the sake of the righteous." *L'mah-ahn* ("for the sake of") doesn't mean that God should spare the city in order to spare the righteous, but that God should spare the city because the righteous are working to save it and need more time. For the sake of their mission rather than their lives, the city should be spared.

How do we know the righteous are trying to save Sodom? Because they live "in the midst of the city" (Gen 18:26), which, we are taught, means that they are actively involved in the life of the city, trying to get people to "turn from evil and do good" (Ps 34:14). Abraham is saying to God, "If you destroy the city, you are destroying the very *raison d'etre* of the righteous" (yes, Abraham spoke French; who knew?). As long as there are people working for justice, the city, no matter how sinful, must be spared. The question is, "How many people are necessary for this task to succeed?"

Abraham argues ten, and God agrees. Abraham stopped at ten because he assumed there were ten righteous people in Sodom already: Lot, his wife, his four daughters, and their husbands. Abraham stopped at ten because he thought he had secured the safety of Sodom. As it turns out, however, Lot's sons-in-law didn't measure up, and the city was lost. Interestingly, God learns from Abraham's miscalculation. When trying to determine the fate of Jerusalem, God commands the prophet Jeremiah to walk through the city and to find even one righteous person there; for the sake of that one, God's mercy will prevail (Jer 5:1).

This should feed right into the Christian story with Jesus being the lone righteous human working to redeem humanity and God sparing us for the sake of Jesus' mission. Sadly, many Christians (and Jews) seem to prefer Noah's God to Abraham's and revel in the slaughter and damnation of the innocent along with the guilty. Help me understand this.

Mike: With regard to the role of the righteous minority, a long tradition in Christianity teaches that God holds off acts of judgment for the sake of what might happen through the work of the righteous. As you note, it ties into the theme of God sparing us for the sake of Jesus' mission. Mind you, it's not the only tradition in the tapestry of Christian thought, but it's one with which I strongly concur.

You, though, are correct. Too many Christians in any given era fixate on a narrow vision of God's justice and how it works. Quite a number have never directly heard or read an alternative vision. The leaders to whom they look warn them that alternatives are of the devil, dangerous to the soul, and guaranteed to lead to their exclusion from the group. I can't speak with reference to Judaism, but often it seems to me that the history of Christianity can be written around the theme of the ongoing tension between those who would draft Jesus in defense of their fear, hate, and prejudice and those who find in Jesus the courage to love and minister to the world through sacrificial service to others in God's name.

The story of the apostle Peter is illustrative. Peter finds it difficult to shake the deeply rooted notion that the world is divided into the clean and unclean (including people). His vision on the rooftop, experience in the home of a Roman military commander, and confrontation with Paul shift him toward love, ministry, self-sacrificing service, and a kind of inclusiveness he never dreamed possible. When all is said and done, Peter must decide between the universal love and mission he now believes are embodied in Christ and the teachings embedded in *some* of the Scriptures and traditions on which he was weaned. At considerable risk and pain, he opts for the Jonah tradition.

Your question about why so many Christians are obsessed with homosexuality requires several answers. First, the current "culture wars" certainly fuel the obsession at both ends of the spectrum of Christian opinion. Daily news articles, blogs, political campaigns, fundraisers who use the issue to increase gifts and the like cannot help but fix attention on the subject.

Second, fewer Christians obsess about homosexuality (or any other single aspect of human orientation or behavior) than one might think. Most, in my experience, focus on daily life and have varying degrees of commitment to worship, helping ministries, various ways of making disciples, and the like.

Third, many Christians want to take the Bible seriously, yet they are poorly equipped to grapple with its languages, cultural contexts, history of interpretation, and complexity. Fearful of misinterpreting a text, they often opt for what feels like the simplest application, lest they somehow dishonor God. Any era characterized by vigorous debate in society or the church challenges such an approach to Scripture. Christians sometimes retreat into their default position, whatever it may be.

Finally, the political structure of the United States poses special challenges. The Bill of Rights mandates a society in which individuals are free to live their lives without being restrained or directed by government-backed religion. At the same time, the documents provide for the free exercise of religion in such a society. Tensions are inevitable. I have not conducted a formal study, but I have found many Christians in the South cannot imagine a world in which church and state might take different roads with regard to whatever issue is in dispute.

Dragging us back to the story at hand, any number of Christians, therefore, read the Sodom and Gomorrah account in light of all of the above. They find it difficult to imagine the sin of the cities to be systemic rather than sharply focused on one matter.

We're dealing with human nature wrapped in human culture(s), Rami. I can, with effort and study, comprehend in part why persons make the choices they make. My calling, as you appreciate, is to love (*agape*) them and to seek to help them make better decisions, even if the only way to do so entails suffering on my part.

Rami: There are times, Mike, when your insight, humility, and honesty leave me speechless. This was one of those times. I hope our readers learn as much from us as I do from you.

Okay, the speechless moment has passed, so let me comment briefly, and then you can move us on to the rest of the story.

Jews, and Judaism too, wrestle with the issue of universal versus particular. There was a time when I thought we had to choose between the two. When I was young, the choice was particularism over universalism. As I got older, it was universalism over particularism. Today, it is universalism through particularism.

We spoke earlier of Genesis 12, where Abram and Sarai are called by God to establish a people who will become a blessing to *all the families of the earth*. This is, as I understand it, the mission of the Jewish people: to live in such a way as to be a blessing to all the families of the earth, human and otherwise. Judaism is the particular way Jews live out this call. It isn't Judaism for Judaism's sake, but Judaism as a way of being a blessing.

Take keeping kosher, for example. As a Christian there is no reason for you to keep kosher, but as a serious Jew, I cannot ignore it. Wrestling with the kosher code and shaping all my consumption around its central ethic of compassion and economic justice is central to my being a Jew.

But my keeping kosher isn't for my benefit; rather, it is for the benefit of others. How so? Kosher obligates me to treat animals with compassion, to treat workers justly, and to avoid wanton destruction (*bal tashchit*) in the process of producing the goods I consume. Keeping kosher benefits animals, humans, and nature as a whole. Thus, the particulars of Judaism are made to serve the cause of universal justice.

Today, however, globalization has put the fear of God into many particularists. That is to say, they are so fearful of losing their particularism to a homogenized universalism that they imagine a God who condones imposing their particularism on others. It's not a misplaced fear, but it is a misguided response.

It is true that universalism can strip away the uniqueness of a religion to the detriment of that religion and the world at large. Indeed, the things that make a religion unique are often the things that spark its greatest creativity. To abandon these in search of some kind of spiritual Esperanto embracing all religions as if they were one and the same is to kill religious creativity. However, to defend particularism for its own sake rather than as a means to benefit others, and to do so through intimidation, violence, and murder, is not only wrong; it's evil.

Mike: Turning back to the text, Genesis 19:1-11 covers the story of the two angels, Lot, and the threatening mob. The angels arrive in the evening to find Lot sitting in the gateway of Sodom. I'll be interested to hear what you make of it, but what strikes me is that Lot is playing the part of an elder, a leader of the city as it were. If so, he—along with others—is responsible in some measure for dispensing justice and settling disputes. Lot, the alien or immigrant, has risen rapidly in society. My guess adds meaning to 19:9, when the mob outside Lot's door cries, "This fellow came here as an alien, and he would play the judge! Now we will deal worse with him than with them." Sodom's social breakdown includes a substantial dose of anti-alien sentiment.

What prompts Lot to rise, greet the visitors, and address them as "lords"? Perhaps nothing more than the hospitality duties of an elder sitting at the gate are in play. On the other hand, Lot may sense their identity and purpose, making his invitation almost an attempt to thwart their mission and send them on their way out of the city the following morning. I find this interpretation attractive, not least because it accords with Lot's character. He wants the settled life, potential wealth, and honors available in the city. Lot seems to have attained these in some measure. The angels are a threat not only to Sodom but also to Lot's chosen life. He attempts to manage the situation without appearing to do so.

The angels refuse his invitation. They want to spend the night in the town square. Maybe they wish to assess the city, and what better way than to observe the population in action through the night? Lot, though, wants to keep the city population and the angels away from each other, so he presses his invitation, and they finally accept his hospitality.

After a meal and as they prepare to sleep, a large mob gathers outside Lot's door. The NRSV translation suggests the crowd consists of every man in the city—perhaps a not too subtle way of suggesting there are no righteous men to be found in the city at large. The mob demands that Lot bring his guests out so that they "may know them." To put it another way, the mob intends to subject the visitors to gang rape.

This is important. Rape is a crime of violence and stands apart from questions related to human sexuality. Gang rape is the product of dehumanized and dehumanizing cultures. Think of war crimes, cults, and the like. The passage, it seems to me, has nothing to do with sexuality and everything to do with a society gone mad.

Lot continues to try to play the role of a community leader or judge. He actually steps outside his door and attempts to reason with the mob. In order to protect his honor as a judge and as host of the men, he offers to turn his two virgin daughters over to the mob. Lot clearly has no doubt the crowd intends to do violence to someone. He attempts to provide substitute victims.

The mob rejects the offer and storms his house. Lot's effort to assume the role of judge or elder in the city angers them, all of them. Their deeper intent now becomes clear: they want to rape, torture, and kill everyone associated with Lot. We can assume they want to do the same to all "uppity" aliens in their midst. The men of the city intend to drive all aliens from Sodom or kill those who attempt to stay.

Sodom, then, is like South Africa during apartheid, the American South under Jim Crow, Nazi Germany, and all cultures in human history that turn in on themselves and become not a blessing but a bane to the outsider. Lot is a tragic character, the outsider who tries to become an insider by playing by the insider's rules. He deludes himself into believing Sodom offers something he must have, something better than what Abraham possesses. Even when the city turns on him and reveals its true feelings and intent toward him and those like him, Lot tries to go on with the game.

The angels pull Lot back into the house and blind all those threatening his house. One gets the impression that Lot would have stood there attempting to preserve his illusions until he died at the hands of the mob.

Rami: I agree, Mike, that it certainly seems that Lot has quickly risen to a position of power in Sodom. Only the city leaders "sit at the gate." Given his status, should we not also give him some responsibility for the quality of life in Sodom? While those who storm his home clearly oppose his leadership, as a leader he cannot escape the moral climate over which he presides.

You mentioned earlier that many Christians are prone to imagining the sin of Sodom to be that of homosexuality, and that is an easy conclusion to draw when we translate the Hebrew *anshe-Sodom* as "the men of Sodom." If Torah were not gender biased—that is to say, if Torah didn't use the term "men" to refer to all humans and not just male humans—I would agree that this is homosexual rape. But Hebrew, like English, is prone to using masculine nouns to reference males and females together, so I think that what we have here is a case of the translation driving the interpretation.

A more accurate translation would be the one you used, that is, "the people of the city" and the "people of Sodom" rather than the "men of the city" and the "men of Sodom." This is supported a moment later when we are told that "*all* the people" (*kol ha-am*) surrounded Lot's house (Gen 19:4). Thus, the Hebrew original provides support for the understanding that the sin of Sodom is injustice rather than homosexuality.

Further support for this understanding comes from Lot's seeming willingness to have his daughters raped by the crowd. If homosexual rape was the key to Sodom's depravity, why would Lot think offering his daughters to the crowd would have any impact whatsoever?

But did he really intend to offer up his daughters? I don't think so. I think we have to read the story of Lot's confronting the injustice of the people of Sodom in tandem with Abraham's confronting the injustice of God.

First, like Abraham, Lot is no coward. Lot confronted the people of Sodom alone in front of his house, having closed the door behind him allowing him no escape (Gen 19:6). Second, again like his uncle, Lot spoke justice to power (Gen 19:7). Third, just as Abraham was willing to use the existence of ten righteous people within Sodom to shame God into changing his mind, Lot is willing to use his two virgin daughters to shame the people into changing their minds. Rather than imagining Lot sacrificing his daughters to the madness of the crowd, think of him as saying to the people of Sodom, "Is your wickedness so great that you would rape two innocent young girls? Far be it from you to do such a thing!"

While I don't want to excuse Lot when it comes to the breakdown of morality in Sodom, I do want to commend him for his moral courage in standing up to it. I don't think he meant to sacrifice his daughters, but to shame the people. Nor am I convinced, as you suggest, that he is defending

THE DESTRUCTION OF SODOM AND GOMORRAH

his illusions. Rather, it was justice that drove him to this act of resistance, and this is what makes him part of Abraham's family.

Mike: Your remarks on the translation of *anshe-Sodom* make sense to me, Rami. Christian translators face similar issues when dealing with the New Testament. I agree with your translation. The translation "all the people" emphasizes the breadth and depth of Sodom's fall into chronic injustice and the violence that accompanies it.

We probably are not going to reach agreement with regard to Lot. Part of the beauty and richness of a story is its potential to call forth varied, even opposite, interpretations. Still, I want to elaborate a bit on my perspective on Lot.

Lot certainly remains a part of Abraham's family. His story illustrates the dangers to a member of the family who opts to live a compartmentalized life, a life in which one tries to keep God and daily life separated from one another. Lot manages to hold such a life together until the day the angels arrive. Whereas you see Lot speaking truth to power while standing in the doorway, I see Lot desperately trying to maintain separation between the worlds of Sodom and Abraham. He will pay any price to do so, up to and including the sacrifice of his daughters. Abraham is following a path (more or less) that will lead toward increasing integration of his daily life and the God he is coming to know. Lot tries to manage his life in such a way as to reap the benefits of being part of two realities without allowing them to meet.

While I think my perspective plays fair with the broad storyline, it is also grounded in forty years of pastoral ministry. I constantly deal with women and men who lose themselves by trying to compartmentalize their lives. When their lives start to collapse, such folks often go to extraordinary lengths to preserve that failed strategy. It never works. In my experience, either they face reality and start the hard work of integrating their lives, or they fall into despair and spiral toward catastrophe.

Which brings me to the third scene in the story: Genesis 19:12-29. The angels urge Lot to gather his entire family and immediately leave the city, lest they be caught up in its destruction. When Lot conveys the message to his sons-in-law, they assume he is joking, and Lot does not press the issue. They all go to bed!

Even in the morning, Lot fails to mobilize his family. If I follow your interpretation of the story, Lot does so as an act of moral challenge to God.

From my perspective, Lot continues to practice a form of denial: "Perhaps if I refuse to go, the promised destruction will not come to pass, the angels will give up, and I can get back to my life." The story, though, implies Lot and his family will die if they remain in the city, regardless of whether Lot can bring himself to admit it. Lot's denial cannot stymie reality.

God's mercy toward the family of Abraham continues. The Lord's angels take hold of Lot, his wife, and his daughters and drag them out of the city. They even grant Lot's request to spare a minor town called Zoar so that he might take refuge there. Lot and his family flee. Destruction falls on Sodom and Gomorrah. Lot's wife looks back and becomes a pillar of salt. The main story ends the next morning with Abraham looking down on the destruction and an assertion that the Lord overthrew the cities in which Lot had settled.

Verses 30-36 serve as a postscript, illustrating the devolution of Lot and his family. Lot leaves Zoar and moves up into the hills, to the very locale he rejected while in conversation with the angels. His daughters, who lost their husbands in the destruction of the city, conspire to get him drunk so that each in turn might become pregnant by him. Their sons become the ancestors of Israel's enemies: the Moabites and the Ammonites. The tragedy of Lot is complete. Lot, who tried to take his existence into his own hands and fashion it after his own design and who by his actions rejected the way of Abraham, destroys his life.

Rami: For me the capacity of Torah to yield varied and even opposing views is its genius. It is Torah's ability to yield new meanings that keeps me coming back to her day after day. And that is why studying it with you is so enriching; you come up with meanings I would miss entirely. Your take on the rest of the story is solid, and I have no real disagreements with it. Let me only focus on Lot's wife becoming a pillar of salt.

Lot doesn't want to leave Sodom, and the angels have to drag him, his wife, and his daughters outside the city (Gen 19:16). You seem to suggest these are his married daughters, but the Jewish view is that his married daughters stayed with their husbands and died in Sodom. These are the unmarried virgin daughters whom Lot was willing to toss to the crowd to be raped (Gen 19:8).

The angels tell them all to flee. The warning not to look back, however, is given to Lot alone, as the masculine singular Hebrew makes clear. This places in doubt the notion that turning Mrs. Lot into a pillar of salt was punishment for her looking back at the destruction of Sodom. How can she be punished for something she was not prohibited from doing?

As they race from the city toward Zoar, Lot's wife stops running, turns around, and observes the destruction of Sodom. How could she not? Her married daughters are still in the city! According to the rabbinic commentators, this was an act of maternal love: she turned back in hopes of seeing her other daughters racing after them to safety. So why, then, is she turned into a pillar of salt?

This is not a punishment, and Torah never calls her transformation a punishment. Torah only says she looked back and became salt. One key to understanding why this happens is to ask another, slightly different question: not why was Lot's wife turned into a pillar of salt, but why *salt* specifically?

According to *Pirke de Rabbi Eliezer*, a collection of midrash (biblical commentary) from the eighth century CE, Lot's wife's name was *Idit* ("choicest"). She was a very special woman, who stood out among the people of Sodom for her compassion. It was compassion for her daughters, and perhaps for all the citizens of Sodom, that moved her to look back. Rabbi Eliezer further suggests that Idit's transformation is also the result of her compassion. As she looked back toward the city, Idit saw that she could do nothing to save her daughters or any other person in the city, but she thought that perhaps she could do something to save the city's other creatures.

Sodom was a city surrounded by rich farmland (Gen 13:10-12), and Lot settled there with his herds of cattle. Now that the city was ruined and no people were left in it, what would become of the cows and their calves? While Idit could do nothing to save her daughters, she could do something to save the mother cows and their children, and that something was to become a pillar of salt. The cows could not survive without salt, and so Idit became salt for them.

According to the midrash, Lot's cows came to Idit daily and licked her salt until she was almost gone. Then, each night, God would "heal" Idit so that on the morrow she might again feed the cattle and their calves (*Pirke de Rabbi Eliezer*, 60 a/b). Idit's compassion for her daughters is transformed into a more universal compassion, and she herself becomes not a symbol of God's wrath, but of God's mercy, of renewal in the wake of destruction. This isn't a punishment, but an act of sacrifice.

Idit is very different from her husband. Whereas Lot was willing to have his daughters raped to save the lives of the angels (who were never in danger in the first place), Idit was willing to sacrifice her life to save the lives of the cattle, and to do so in perpetuity, or as another midrash puts it, "until the day on which the dead will live again." In a sense Lot's wife is the Christ figure in this story, giving up her life to save the lives of the cattle.

Now on to Lot's unmarried daughters.

Remember that Lot begs the angels to allow him and his family to take refuge in Zoar. The Hebrew word *Zoar* means a "place of insignificance." When Lot arrives there, however, he suddenly decides he cannot stay there (Gen 19:30). Why? Because he could not bear to live a life of insignificance. So he takes his daughters to live alone in the mountains.

His daughters imagine that the three of them are the last people on earth and conceive a plan (pun intended) to save the human race by having sex with their father and getting pregnant by him. Like mother, like daughter. Idit saves the cattle by becoming salt, and her daughters save humanity by becoming pregnant.

Clearly, Lot's daughters aren't the brightest bulbs on the tree (if you'll pardon the Christmas reference). How could they be the only people on earth? Even if they shared their father's antipathy to the insignificant folk of Zoar, there was always their cousin Abraham and his family—they could have found husbands there. Whatever their reasoning, our rabbis determine that their motives were moral, and we find no fault with them. Lot, however, doesn't fare as well.

Torah tells us that Lot's daughters got their father so drunk that he didn't know when they came to have sex with him or when they left (Gen 19:33, 35). In Tractate *Horiot* of the Babylonian Talmud, the rabbis note that the word *b'kumah* ("when she rose" from Lot's bed) is spelled differently with regard to each daughter (Gen 19:33, 35). They read into this difference the teaching that while Lot didn't know when his elder daughter entered his bed, he did know when she left it. Lot knew what had happened between them, but since it had already happened, he pretended to be asleep so as to cause his daughter no shame.

Knowing what had happened with his eldest daughter, our rabbis taught that Lot suspected the same would happen with his youngest daughter. This is why the spelling is different. While Lot was innocent of incest the first night, he was guilty of incest the second night.

So what are we to make of all this? Honestly, I don't know. There are so many elements to this story that I cannot weave them into a single cloth. I will rely on your reading for that and be content to simply read on.

Chapter 11

The Binding of Isaac

Genesis 22:1-19

Mike: Christians divide over the story of the binding of Isaac. They argue whether the God they knew in Christ is capable of commanding that a father sacrifice his son. Both sides tend to interpret the story in terms of their already determined concept of God. One school of thought argues that God gave the command; the other insists Abraham misunderstood God or perhaps went a bit off the deep end and imagined God to have ordered the sacrifice of Isaac.

I think it best to start with the story on its own terms, consider its place in the larger Abraham and Genesis narrative, and only then draw some conclusions.

"God tested Abraham," goes the story. What does that mean? Perhaps it means God chose to test Abraham to see who came first with him: his only son Isaac or God. If so, the test anticipates the first of the commandments: "You shall have no other gods before me." Abraham no doubt idolized (term intended) Isaac. Perhaps the aging patriarch was in danger of confusing the gift (Isaac) with the giver (God). The "test" is a kind of shock therapy designed to free Abraham from incipient idolatry. When I allow myself to try to imagine the deep feelings Abraham must have held for Isaac, I can almost buy into this interpretation.

To my way of thinking, a better approach places the story in the context of a larger tale: God at work to call out, shape, and launch a people who know and serve a God who is different from the already familiar gods of the area. A number of the other religions in the region required child sacrifice on a seasonal basis in order to prompt fertility gods to ensure a good harvest. Abraham lived surrounded by such religions. Under this approach, God's "test" of Abraham ultimately separates God from the other gods, revealing a deity whose character is quite different from theirs.

Abraham hears and obeys the voice of God. He sets out with Isaac, two servants, and a donkey to the mountain God will show him. Note the phrase "I will show you" (v. 2), which echoes God's earlier call to go to a land that God will show Abraham in due time. That's the first hint that the emerging story may play out differently than anyone in Abraham's time might have expected.

Abraham leaves the servants behind and goes on with Isaac. He lays the wood for the offering on Isaac's back, while he himself retains the knife and fire. In one of the most heartbreaking scenes found in the Bible, Isaac asks Abraham, "Where is the lamb for the burnt offering?" Abraham's answers, "God himself will provide the lamb for the burnt offering, my son." The answer may be understood in a number of ways: "God has already provided the lamb—it's you, Isaac," a desperate hope or emerging trust that God indeed will provide an alternative, or simple evasion of the question.

Upon arrival, Abraham prepares the altar and wood, binds Isaac, and lays the boy on the wood. By now, Isaac surely realizes he is the sacrifice. What are we to make of his seeming acceptance of his fate? Is he too dull to imagine his own death? Does he trust his father so deeply that he believes Abraham will not harm him? Is the ethos of child sacrifice so pervasive that Isaac, realizing what is about to happen, simply accepts impending death as his proper role? I think any of the options believable.

Abraham takes the knife to kill his son. At this point, I think Abraham no longer hopes for deliverance. He actually intends to slay Isaac, believing his God requires such a sacrifice. Then, and only then, God speaks again to Abraham through a messenger. The angel forbids Isaac's sacrifice and proclaims that Abraham's obedience proves his reverence for God. When Abraham dares lift his eyes, he sees a ram snared in a nearby thicket. Abraham takes and sacrifices the ram to God, and he gives a name to the place of Isaac's near death: "the LORD will provide." The angel of the Lord speaks again to reaffirm God's promises to Abraham, and the old man and his son return home to continue to live into the future God is shaping.

"The Lord will provide" is the theme of the story. Learning to accept and live as if this is true, as if the covenant is real and trustworthy, has been the challenge confronting Abraham throughout his journey with God. Those who come after Abraham will face the same challenge through the various "tests" that come their way.

Rami: I have to say, Mike, I'm surprised to hear you say Christians are divided over whether God could command a father to sacrifice his son. Isn't that the core of the Christian message? God the Father sacrifices his Son to ransom people from sin. Abraham's near sacrifice of Isaac, who, according to Jewish tradition, is thirty-seven years old at the time, is a foreshadowing of God's sacrificing of Jesus, who was thirty-three years old.

In any case, my reading of the *Akeida*, the Binding of Isaac, is, as you might expect, a bit different from your own.

To understand this story we have to remember that we're talking about the same Abraham who stood up to God in defense of the innocent in Sodom, saying, "Shouldn't the judge of all the world act justly?" (Gen 18:25). How can this Abraham not do the same in defense of his son?

I don't see the "test" here as God testing Abraham to see whom Abraham loved best, God or Isaac, but a test to see if Abraham was still willing to stand up to God. God wants to make sure that Abraham is still the right person to carry the new religion of justice into the world. There are hints of this throughout the story:

1. God says to Abraham, *Kakh-nah et binkha*, "Please take your son" (Gen 22:2). What kind of command contains the word *please*? God isn't commanding Abraham, but inviting him to test the strength of his convictions.
2. When telling Abraham where to travel, God uses the same phrase he used in commanding Abram and Sarai to leave home: *lech lecha*/to walk (*lech*) toward yourself (*lekha*) (Gen 12:1). The real journey is an inner one: a pilgrimage to the self whose faith doesn't require the slaughter of innocents (humans or animals), but justice, compassion, and humility instead (Mic 6:8).
3. When Abraham, Isaac, and the two servants arrive at the base of Mount Moriah, Abraham tells his servants to wait while he and Isaac ascend the mountain: "We will bow down there, and then return to you" (Gen 22:5). Abraham never speaks of an offering up of a gift (*olah*) or a sacrifice (*korban*), only a bowing down (*hishtakhavah*), and he affirms that both he and Isaac will ascend the mountain and both he and Isaac will come down the mountain. Abraham has no intention of killing Isaac at all. His intent is to teach his son to bow down and place his life in service of this new God of justice, compassion, and humility.
4. As father and son climb the mountain, Isaac speaks for the first time: "Here is the fire and the wood, but where is the lamb for the offering

[*olah*]?" (Gen 22:5). Isaac lacks his father's spiritual maturity and still imagines a God who needs to be placated with the raising up of gifts. Where Abraham sees faith in lowering oneself, Isaac sees faith in lifting something up to God. Abraham's response? "Let God take care of his own offering!" (Gen 22:8). We are going to bow down to God, to place ourselves in service to God's justice. If there is to be a sacrifice, we have the fire and the wood, but God will have to provide the sacrifice itself.

This is a subversive teaching. God is to provide his own sacrifice? That defeats the entire point of sacrifice as far as Isaac understands it. Abraham is instructing his son in the new faith, a faith that doesn't require the worship of God through the death of another, but devotion to God through giving one's life over to godliness.

As the story reaches its climax, the real test is revealed: not whether Abraham is willing to kill his son—he isn't—but whether God is the old god of sacrifice or the new God of justice. This is why, when Abraham raises his knife over a bound Isaac and prepares to kill him, the angel has to call to Abraham twice: *Avraham! Avraham!* (Gen 22:11) Abraham ignores the first call, as if to say, "Are you sure you are done with human sacrifice? Are you sure You wouldn't rather I kill my son?" God is, in effect, saying, "No! Stop! I'm sure! I'm sure!"

It is then that Abraham sees the ram caught in a thicket. He frees Isaac and offers the ram up as a *korban*, a sacrifice (Gen 22:13), honoring Isaac's level of understanding and yet making it clear to him that if you are going to sacrifice, at least never let it be a human sacrifice.

Our story ends with Abraham naming the place "God sees" (Gen 22:14). What does God see? God sees that the new faith of justice and that the new worship of laying oneself down in service to justice is superior to the old faith of sacrifice.

So the test here is two-sided. God tests Abraham to see if he will stand up to God once again, and Abraham tests God to see if he will live up to Abraham's understanding of what a just God should be. They both pass.

Mike: Our different perspectives on the nature of God and the plight of humanity probably lead to our distinctive takes on the story. We seem to share at least one conclusion: the God of Abraham is going to differ from those gods in surrounding cultures who demand human sacrifice. We disagree, unless I misunderstand you, over why this is so.

With regard to God, to my eyes the larger story revolves around God selecting a person through whom to found a people, a people who in due time will prove a blessing to the world at large. God is already a God characterized by love and justice, the only real God in a world filled with humanity-made gods, a God who provides without requiring the ego satisfaction of a human sacrifice. Humanity, fallen into alienation and fear, can no longer conceive of such a God, so God sets out to teach one person (Abraham) that—among other things—God might well be spoken of as trustworthy love. God instructs Abraham in a variety of ways, but one method is a kind of shock therapy, the call to sacrifice Isaac, which ends in God staying Abraham's hand and providing a highly unfortunate ram. Abraham becomes the first person to grasp, at least in part, that God is steadfast love. Like a bit of yeast in dough, the old man's new insight will slowly infiltrate and change the perception of God among many.

Your scenario depicts Abraham as a person of profound insight who, in effect, shapes God. My approach makes God the shaper. That being said, our differences probably enrich our reading of the text, and they certainly provide varied entry points for other readers.

I'm intrigued by our translations. To the best of my knowledge, the NRSV text mirrors most modern English translations. Whereas you render Genesis 22:2 as "Please take your son," standard interpretations read, "Take your son." The difference in tone is obvious. Whereas most translations of Genesis 22:14 read (more or less), "The LORD will provide" or "God provides," you offer "God sees." Both of us know translation is as much art as science and that there is no such thing as a literal translation of any text, if by that one means finding one-to-one correspondence between two languages. Perhaps both the standard and the Rami versions owe a substantial debt to the theological assumptions of the translators!

One last point: both of our approaches lead to the abolition of human sacrifice. That marks a significant departure point in human history. From this point onward, human sacrifice is off the table (pardon the expression) for the people of God. Perhaps the story also lays the groundwork for rejecting all forms of religion that require the obliteration of individuality in order to know and serve God.

Rami: Let me respond first to your questions of translation. While I too rely on the NRSV and find it to be the academic standard, it often streamlines the Hebrew to produce a clearer English. The Hebrew in Genesis 22:1 is

Kakh-nah, "take (*kakh*) please (*nah*)." The phrase in Genesis 22:14 is *YHVH Yireh,* "God (*YHVH*) sees or will see (*yireh*)." I don't know why the NRSV leaves out the Hebrew *nah* or how it comes up with "provides" from the Hebrew *yireh.*

The larger issue is our different notions of God. For me the God of Torah, indeed the God of any Scripture, is the product of its author. If you believe that God is somehow the author of Torah, then the images of God offered in the narrative actually tell us something about God. He is, as he says, jealous (Exod 34:14), a man of war (Exod 15:3), and for all his compassion he is equally vindictive, violent, and even genocidal (Deut 20:16-18). This is not a God I can believe in. Nor is it the God of the Gospels, which seem to reflect a far later and more sophisticated notion of God than that found in much of Torah.

If, on the other hand, you believe, as I do, that sacred texts are of purely human origin, then the God of Torah tells us nothing about God per se and lots about the various authors of Torah. To put it plainly, I think there are two sources for Scriptures of any kind. The first and most prevalent is the ego of the human author who creates a god in his own image and uses that god to propel his own agenda. This god wants power, territory, and promotes a class system where the wealthy exploit the poor and the priests dominate the people. The second and more rare material comes from authors who glimpse the God beyond human imagining: the God who manifests all reality. The experience awakens us to the interdependence of all life and evokes in us a sense of caring and compassion and a commitment to justice and equality.

I think the author of the Binding of Isaac is trying to promote a new relationship between humanity and a God of compassion. The author is not yet ready to abandon all sacrifice and restricts his compassion to humanity, but it is a step toward a more loving God, who requires the death of no one and nothing.

I see Christianity as part of this progression. God the Father only requires the death of his Son, and in so doing spares the millions of animals that would otherwise have been offered to him. The next stage in spiritual evolution will be a new reading of Jesus, where sacrifice is no longer the point and the crucifixion is read (as it was enacted) not as a spiritual sacrifice but as state-sanctioned political murder. This new and perhaps emerging Christianity will refocus its attention on the kingdom in this world rather than getting into heaven after we die.

This brings me back to an issue I raised earlier, which I think you passed on. So let me ask again: What kind of God is it that requires the death of anyone or anything in order to forgive? It seems to me that Christianity is an abrogation of the Binding of Isaac story with God doing the very thing Abraham was told not to do: kill his son. What is your take on this?

Mike: All I can add to the translation question is that the New American Standard Bible, which is often regarded as the most strictly accurate of English translations, takes the same approach as the NRSV. I would love to pose the question to someone versed in the history of translations, but since I can't, I'll move on to take up the other matters you raise.

The two of us have long recognized we hold different concepts of God. Our notions of God drive our interpretation of Scripture. I've always found it rather remarkable that we arrive at similar interpretations with regard to behavior!

You seem to posit two views of God's relationship to Scripture: either God is the author or God is the product of the various authors. I prefer a third alternative: Scripture as the record of an ongoing interaction between a quite real God and equally real humans. The Scriptures tell us mostly about the perceptions of God by various individuals and/or groups at different times in history, but those perceptions are rooted in their experience of God. From my perspective, God has always been God's self. God was never a tribal god given to human sacrifice, genocide, the death penalty for disobedient children and such. Those who experienced the true God, though, saw him— to borrow Paul's phrase—through a glass dimly.

I suspect we find it almost impossible to imagine how far a person reared in a child-sacrifice culture would have to travel intellectually and emotionally to conceive of a God who provides without requiring or needing a sacrifice. Having spent most of my life trying to wean women and men from their cultural assumptions about God and others so that they might embrace a bigger and kinder God, I attest to the difficulty of the project. Take the example of the flourishing "health and wealth" gospel in the United States. We are born into a culture habituated to think of blessing in terms of personal finances and physical health. Generations of Christian theologians have hammered at this assumption, pointing to the God we know through Christ as a God who loves the poor, advocates modest contentment rather than conspicuous consumption, and calls us to sacrifice seeming security in favor of faith-based service. At best, a minority of Christians has gotten this message. Humans, even those who have a sense of deep connection to God, naturally try to align God with what they regard as tradition, a worthy purpose, a necessity, or simply self-interest.

Scriptures, then, become a means through which we may learn from our spiritual and/or actual ancestors. Some of what they wrote has turned out to be prescriptive. Others of their conclusions have proven to be distortions of God's intent. All of what we find in Scripture cautions us as to the dangers and difficulties of rightly perceiving God, even as we accept the call to try.

Frankly, all of the above conditions inform my answer to your other question: "What kind of God is it that requires the death of anyone or anything in order to forgive?" I understand the question, and I can see why you ask it, but I do not think in such categories. Starting (at least) with the story of Isaac's near sacrifice, we see a God who provides whatever is required to make, keep, and extend God's covenant. In this case, God provides what is needed to save Isaac and the future bound up in the boy. As the larger story in the Hebrew Scriptures and the New Testament unfolds, we discover that the one thing actually required is that God be constant, that *hesed* be operative.

From my perspective Jesus may be said to be the incarnation of *hesed*, God's sure love. Jesus' teachings and life call us to let down our guard, lay aside our fears, and live securely in such love. Massive changes in perception, human relations, one's sense of self, and the like follow. The death of Jesus, while certainly politically driven in one sense, takes on a larger significance. I would say "the world" tried to kill Jesus and thereby discredit *hesed*. Jesus died, thereby acknowledging the reality of suffering and death for those who embrace *hesed* in the world as it is. The resurrection, in this scenario, becomes the announcement that *hesed* cannot be conquered even by the greatest power the world may bring to bear against it and the promise that *hesed* shall prevail.

Rami: One of the things I love about our conversations is that we push each other right up to the point where we either make room for and respect our differences or cease talking altogether. We have been carrying on this dialogue for many years, and I'm only too happy to say that we value the conversation more than "winning the argument" and hence always step back from the silence of the brink. We live to talk another day. And this seems to be one of those days.

I cannot convince you of the rightness of my theology or my view of Scripture, but I doubt we are really that far apart when it comes to the latter. What you call seeing God "through a glass dimly" (1 Cor 13:12), I call creating God in our own image. While I recognize that we are not saying exactly the same thing, we are admitting to exactly the same problem: Scripture reflects cultural assumptions, and our task is to wean people from them.

You used personal finances as an example. This morning as I walked on the treadmill at the gym, I watched a televangelist expound her theology. She taught that Jesus' death on the cross and Abraham's willingness to sacrifice Isaac on the altar were meant to teach us that unless and until we are willing to give up what we have, God is not willing to give us more. But if we are willing to give up what we have—and by this she meant give it up to her by sending her money—God will return our gift seven-fold. It is all about getting more! Try to fit that idea into your far more spiritual notion of Jesus as *hesed*, God's unending and steadfast love!

I recognize that we are moving from my historical analysis to your more theological one, but I find your understanding of Jesus as *hesed* compelling. How can one doubt that the world—then and now—tries to murder love? Almost every headline in the daily newspaper, on the Internet, and on cable news screams the death of love. Love is dead: stand your ground! Love is dead: shoot to kill. Love is dead: get what you can regardless of the cost to others. Love is dead.

And then there is the resurrection.

I'm not a Christian, and I have nothing to say regarding the risen Christ, but you don't have to be a Christian to be grateful for and heartened by the message that you can't kill love.

On to the next story?

Chapter 12

Jacob and Esau

Genesis 25:19–27:40

Mike: The story of Esau and Jacob opens with a familiar theme: barrenness. While modern science suggests Abraham and Isaac probably were infertile, the biblical account holds Sarai and Rebekah to blame. Hence, we find Isaac praying to God that Rebekah might conceive.

God grants the request, and Rebekah becomes pregnant with twins. The twins struggle within her. Rebekah laments, "If it is to be this way, why do I live?" When she poses the question to God, God responds by saying that each child will spawn a nation, each of which shall be at odds with the other. In the end, "the elder shall serve the younger."

During their birth, the twins' struggle continues. Esau arrives first, but Jacob is close behind and is born gripping Esau's heel. The name Jacob, I'm told, means "heel" or "usurper." The boys grow to adulthood and take different paths. Esau becomes a hunter and is beloved by Isaac. Jacob is a different sort of person, quiet, a bit of a homebody, and Rebekah's favorite.

To my mind, several themes emerge.

First, God continues to act upon the family of Abraham in unexpected ways. God gives no explanation for reversing the cultural practice of the first-born receiving the inheritance. Instead, the decision is simply announced. Note that Rebekah alone receives the message. Contrary to the common theory and practice of the day, the woman hears the voice of God and thereby is invited to join God in what God is doing. Both elements are quite subversive.

Second, Jacob is marked for conflict. He and his brother will be in conflict most of their lives. Jacob will struggle to take, hold, and play out the blessing normally due to the oldest son. He will contest with his uncle. He will battle God each time the chance presents itself. Trust will not come easily to Jacob, nor will others trust him. Yet Jacob carries the hopes of God within his life.

Rami: As always, Mike, you introduce and frame these stories well and with the broad brush such introductions require. Now that you have done so, we can go into the story in greater detail.

Let me start with the barrenness of Rebekah. Rebekah—like her mother-in-law, Sarah, and Rachel, her future daughter-in-law—is barren. I don't think biology is the issue. By making these women barren, the story-teller is reminding us that we are about to meet a hero who is touched by God from the very moment of conception. We see the same thing in the Greek myths where heroes like Heracles (the son of Zeus and Alcmene) are the offspring of a human mother and a divine father.

I think the same mythic element is present in the story of Jesus' birth. Unlike Isaac, Joseph doesn't pray to God to help Mary conceive; like Zeus, the Holy Spirit takes the initiative and impregnates Mary on his own (Matt 1:18). In either case, however, the meaning is the same: something new, special, and holy is coming into the world.

The relationship of the twins even in the womb is a cantankerous one. The English word *struggle* is very bland compared to the Hebrew original (*yitrotzatzu*). In the Hebrew, the twins are literally running back and forth in Rebekah's womb, racing against each other to see which will be born first. One rabbinic commentary tells us that when Rebekah would pass by a pagan temple, Esau would run ahead of Jacob in the womb, and when she would pass by a Torah academy (clearly the rabbis weren't concerned with historical accuracy in their commentary), Jacob would race ahead.

Another more universal commentary says that we are all Rebekah, with two capacities warring inside of us: *Yetzer ha Tov*, our inclination for wholeness, and *Yetzer ha Rah*, our inclination for separateness. When Rebekah asks what may be THE existential question, "Why do I live?" the rabbis suggest the reason we live is to bind our capacity for separation to our capacity for wholeness so that we might honor differences without making them absolute.

Here are a couple additional details we mustn't overlook. First, Esau emerges from the womb "red and hairy." Red in this case means that the baby was healthy, ruddy, while hairy implies that he was powerful even as a newborn. This was a strong baby, who, one could tell just by looking at him, was a doer. Hence his name, *Esau*, from the Hebrew *asah*, "to do."

Esau captured everyone's attention. Torah says, "They named him Esau" (Gen 25:25). "They" could be Isaac and Rebekah or all those who were attending the birth. When Jacob emerges, however, we are told nothing of

how he looks, and when it comes to naming the baby, only Isaac does so—
"So he called his name Jacob (*Ya'akov*)" (Gen 25:26), because the boy was
clinging to the heel (*ekev*) of his brother. It's like Jacob emerged as an afterthought while everyone's attention was focused on Esau.

The differences between the two boys become evident as they mature.
Esau is a doer, a skilled hunter, and an *ish sadeh*, a man of the field, an out-
doorsman (Gen 25:27). Jacob, on the other hand, is an *ish tam*, which the
NRSV translates as a "quiet man," but which is better translated as a "man of
integrity" who dwells in tents (*yoshayv ohalim*) (Gen 25:27).

The Hebrew word for tents, *ohalim*, is composed of the same letters as
the Hebrew word for God, *Elohim* (in case the English transliteration should
mislead you, remember, there are no vowels in the Hebrew script of the
Torah). From the rabbinic point of view, this similarity cannot be accidental,
and we are to find some meaning in it. Perhaps the tents in which Jacob
dwelt were the tents of piety, study, and godliness.

With this in mind, let's look into the question of why Isaac loved Esau
best. Isaac was a passive man. As we mentioned just a short while ago, Isaac
never resists his own sacrifice. Indeed, if Isaac has any importance at all, it is
merely in being the father of Jacob. So it isn't surprising that Isaac would love
Esau the doer over the retiring Jacob. Isaac was living vicariously through his
eldest son.

The question will arise later, when we take up the tricking of Isaac by
Jacob and his mother Rebekah, whether or not Isaac was fooled or whether
Isaac knew that while Esau was his preferred son, the future of the tribe
would be better served by Jacob.

We will come to that soon enough. First, back to you.

Mike: I appreciate your detailed descriptions of various approaches to
aspects of the twins' birth story, Rami. The images of the yet unborn twins
"running back and forth" in Rebekah's womb and Jacob as an afterthought
are worth the price of admission. The possible play on the Hebrew terms for
tents (*olihim*) and God (*Elohim*) helps me further grasp the rabbinic point of
view.

Let's move to the subsequent story to see what each of us might do with
the themes we've identified. The story jumps ahead to when the twins are in
adolescence or early adulthood. Both are well established in their roles: Esau,
the doer, the hunter, the obviously vigorous man; Jacob, the quiet man in the
making who stays near the tents and pursues other interests. Esau returns

from one of his outings, tired and famished. Jacob, meanwhile, has prepared and cooked a stew. Esau takes the initiative and asks to eat some of the "red stuff" (NRSV). Jacob withholds the stew, pending an agreement: "First, sell me your birthright."

Esau makes an incredible statement: "I am about to die; of what use is my birthright to me." No doubt, he is hungry and tired, but it seems most unlikely he is about to die! Still, he agrees to the bargain, giving his word to Jacob. At that point, Jacob ladles up the stew and gives him bread. Esau eats and drinks his fill, then goes his way. The story ends with the statement, "Thus Esau despised his birthright."

From my perspective, both twins exhibit serious flaws. Esau focuses only on the immediate. In our day, we might describe Esau as someone who functions on the basis on immediate gratification. That's most likely unfair, but I think it likely Esau is a person trapped in the present moment as he perceives it. He lacks imagination enough to see himself in light of the history of Abraham and Isaac or to project himself into the future as the heir of the promise. I do not think Esau actively despised or devalued his birthright. Instead, he was incapable of grasping its worth.

Another possible interpretation might be that Esau did not take Jacob seriously. Esau the doer, the one who enjoyed his father's favor, perhaps could not imagine Jacob as a threat. What did it matter if he sold his birthright to Jacob for a bit of stew and bread? Who would take the word of Jacob over that of Esau? Would Jacob even dare try to act on the bargain? And if Jacob made such an attempt, who could conceive of Jacob vanquishing Esau in a fight of any kind? Turning again to modern terminology, I think Esau thought of himself as invincible in much the same way as many a teenager or young adult in our time.

Based on what you've shared so far, I would expect rabbinic lore to portray Jacob as a man of piety, study, and godliness even at this point in his life. My own take is that the story depicts Jacob as shrewd, self-serving, and willing to take advantage of his brother. That his actions might help advance God's intentions (that the younger shall rule the older, etc.) does not let Jacob off the hook. Instead, it reinforces a theme we've seen emerge again and again in Genesis: God works with flawed persons. In the slice of time occupied by the story, Jacob's success serves largely to reinforce his reliance upon cleverness.

Taken in this manner, the little story about the brothers' bargain finds its place in the larger story of God's patient effort to forge a new kind of people in the midst of humanity.

Rami: We're pretty much in agreement here, Mike, so let me explore some additional rabbinic commentary you may find interesting.

According to Jewish tradition, the day Esau returned empty-handed from the hunt was the very day on which his grandfather, Abraham, died. The stew that Jacob was cooking was the traditional mourner's meal intended for his father Isaac (Talmud, tractate *Bava Batra* 16b). This is a nice bit of parallelism with Jacob's mother preparing Isaac's final meal and having Jacob pretend to be Esau when delivering it. Feeding dad seems to be central to Esau's problems with his brother.

So when Esau demanded the mourner's stew for himself, Jacob realized his brother's total lack of concern for family. In this one act, Esau disrespected both Abraham and Isaac, and if he were to lead the people, all links to the past would be lost and with them the wisdom the past contained. Hence, Jacob's desire for Esau's birthright.

In another commentary, the color red plays an important role. Esau emerged red from his mother's womb (Gen 25:24) while the stew he wants poured down his throat is said to be "red red" (Gen 25:30)—the doubling of "red" is usually dropped in English translations—and Esau even calls himself *Edom*, "the red one" (Gen 25:30). Red is the color of both passion and shame. When speaking about the law against murder, our sages said that it referred to both actual murder and to shaming others and making them blush. Both acts caused blood to rise to the surface and people to turn red. The conclusion is that Esau is not just a man of action but a man of passion as well, and that his passions (of which his desire for stew is only symbolic) brought shame upon him and his family.

But what of Jacob? Is he blameless? As you say, Mike, the rabbis certainly hold him so. One way they do this is to note that the Hebrew usually translated as "Jacob gave Esau bread and lentil stew" is better translated as "Jacob had already given Esau bread and lentil stew" (Gen 25:34), suggesting that Esau didn't sell his birthright to Jacob for stew but simply abandoned it as worthless (the word *m'kor* in this verse can mean both "sell" and "abandon"; see Deut 32:30). So, again, Jacob is blameless.

Another commentator notes that at the time of this encounter, Esau and Jacob were only fifteen years old and too young to enter into any binding agreement. So this was just brotherly bickering and jockeying for power, and the birthright stayed with Esau, which is why Jacob had to trick his father into giving him the blessing belonging to the holder of the birthright (Gen 27).

Jacob's reputation aside, however, I think you're right regarding Jacob's cleverness: Jacob is no fool and is set on a self-serving course of action that pits him against his brother, his father, and later his uncle. Both Esau and Jacob are flawed, and both have to overcome their flaws if they are to reach their holy potential or, better, their potential for holiness (living compassionately and justly). The genius of the complete Jacob and Esau story cycle is that both boys do achieve this goal. More on that when we get to Jabbok's Ford (Gen 32–33).

Mike: The story of how Isaac came to bless Jacob builds on established themes: God's intent that the "promise" pass to the younger of the twins, the rivalry of the twins, Isaac and Rebekah's relationship to each of the boys, and the character of Esau and Jacob.

Frankly, I don't know whether to think of the tale as tragedy, high comedy, or a bit of both. Perhaps the nearest modern equivalent is a sitcom in which the father is well intentioned but rather clueless, the mother keeps the family on course, and the children enjoy the benefits of and pay the price for the family culture.

The tale comprises four scenes. In scene one, Isaac makes plans to bless Esau. Scene two unfolds the deception of Isaac by Rebekah and Jacob, ending with Jacob receiving the blessing, which by custom should have gone to Esau. The third scene stars Isaac and Esau as they discover the deception, start to comprehend the consequences, and fashion an alternative blessing. Scene four sets the stage for subsequent stories. Esau plots to kill Jacob. Rebekah discovers his plans and sends Jacob to her brother Laban in Haran, where she assumes he will be safe.

I'm going to resist the temptation to treat the story as a case study in dysfunctional family dynamics (though I'll gladly go that direction if you feel so inclined). Instead, I want to note a few matters, then see what you have to say.

Start with the power of the words. The story assumes that words shape reality. Isaac's act of speaking the words of blessing actually conveys the promise given Abraham to Jacob, and once spoken they cannot be recalled. In a similar fashion, the blessing Isaac fashions for the disappointed Esau shapes his oldest son's future and the future of his descendants. In Genesis, God speaks and thereby shapes the creation. Humans, made in God's image, share a bit of God's ability to create by means of words. Taken seriously, such ability calls for wisdom and care in the use of words.

I'm also struck by how God's intention that Jacob inherit the promise given to Abraham comes to pass through the actions of fearful, ambitious, clever humans. Rebekah is a master schemer. She overrides Jacob's fear that Isaac may penetrate the disguise and curse him, gathers together all the ingredients needed to pull off the caper, and coaches Jacob. In the aftermath, she not only tells Jacob to flee to Laban, but also fools Isaac into thinking Jacob's flight is his own idea.

Rebekah is the hero of the story, by which I mean she drives the story. She is not the first or the last strong, resourceful woman to play a major role in the unfolding story of God's people. Would it be going too far to say that in Rebekah we find the original template for the "Jewish mother" so often invoked by comedians?

Esau and Jacob, in contrast, seem caught in currents that run stronger and deeper than they comprehend. I suspect that's important for us to notice, though I'm not certain what to do with the insight. Perhaps, at the least, we're reminded that all of us are born into and live in a world moved by forces we scarcely comprehend. We remain responsible for ourselves and our decisions, but at our wisest we cannot foresee how what we say and do will interface with and affect the larger world over the long term.

Rami: Let's avoid the family dynamics issue, Mike. It's too easy. Torah reflects real families, if not historical ones, and real families are all dysfunctional. You offer a number of avenues leading into this story, and I am happy to grapple with each of them, beginning with your observation about the power of words.

The bedrock of the Jewish worldview is linguistic. God speaks the world into existence. The ancient rabbis took this literally. God spoke Hebrew, and when he did, the words became things. In fact, the Hebrew words for *word*, *speak*, and *thing* all share the same root. Words have the power to create multiple realities: physical, emotional, political, religious, cultural, etc. Isaac's words to Jacob alter the very hierarchy of the tribe and the future of the people.

I am not sure about your notion that God intends Jacob rather than Esau to carry forward the lineage of Abraham and Sarah. Are you reading this into the text we have, or am I missing the verse where God states his intent? It seems to me that there is no story, no drama, if we already know what God intends. And if this is what God intends, why attack Jacob at Jabbok's Ford? I think it is Rebekah who sees that the people are better led by a tent dweller than a hunter and plots to make this a reality without ever consulting with or being aided by God. The implications of this for Jewish civilization are enormous.

The rabbis understand Jacob's tent dwelling to mean that he was a scholar who devoted himself to study in the tents of the learned. For thousands of years, the scholar was the pinnacle of Jewish life. Jacob the scholar becomes a shepherd under the tutelage and exploitation of his maternal uncle, Laban, and ultimately becomes a God-wrestler (the meaning of *Yisra-El*) as the story comes to a close, but it is important to note that the scholarly God-wrestler is still the central archetype of Jewish culture.

It is this scholar ideal that creates what ultimately becomes the stereotypical American Jewish mother. For millennia the ideal was for men to study and women to go into business. Just look at the ideal woman described in Proverbs 31. She manages her household, runs an import/export business, makes and sells textiles, and counsels her husband in matters of social and political import. When Jews came to America in large numbers, we brought this dynamic with us but found that the ideals of America were the inverse of the ideals of Judaism.

Women were to stay out of work, and men were to work rather than study. Women, who for centuries had been trained to run their own businesses, were suddenly stripped of their role. All the energy that had been focused on worldly success turned toward the family with mothers now living vicariously through the success of their children. I don't think it was an accident that so many of the pioneers of twentieth-century feminism—Betty Friedan, Gloria Steinem, and Bella Abzug to name but three—were Jewish. They were reclaiming their Jewish heritage by breaking out of the home.

I agree with you that Rebekah is the hero of this story. I also agree that all the characters in this story are caught in currents they cannot comprehend. This is true of all of us.

Let me add a couple things. First, was Isaac really fooled by Jacob's ruse? He recognizes Jacob's voice even as he says the hands feel like Esau's (Gen 27:22). I think he knew what was going on and collaborated with the subversion of power. After all, it was his mother, Sarah, who made certain that Isaac would supplant his older brother Ishmael. In a sense, Jacob and Esau are pawns in a game their mother and father are playing against the norms of their own time.

This theme of the weaker triumphing over the stronger is a central one not only in the Bible but also in Jewish civilization as a whole. Again, the scholar is superior to the hunter (indeed, hunting even for food is prohibited to Jews since the only animals we can eat are those that are ritually slaughtered), and the prophet's power trumps even that of the king. Later, the rabbis triumph over the priests. I wonder if we can even see this dynamic in Jesus' notion that the meek shall inherit the earth and that, in the kingdom of heaven, those who would be last (in this world) will be first. Judaism is a culture of reversal, with traditional power structures overturned in pursuit of divine justice and compassion.

Mike: The theme that God intends the inheritance to pass to the younger rather than the older is set in Genesis 25:22-23, where God speaks with Rebekah.

I like your notion that old Isaac sees through and goes along with Rebekah's scheme. The great stories, including those found in the Scriptures, cannot be tamed so as to lead to but one possible interpretation. In this case, Isaac as the one deceived or as the one practicing a necessary deception engages the imagination. If I go with your approach, I find Isaac and Rebekah teaming up to do what is needed for the sake of the larger family, though each realizes their actions will lead to stress and conflict in the family. Their actions also accord with God's announced intentions. The drama of the story is multilayered. Will Rebekah choose to work with God, and will Isaac join her when all is said and done, to overturn cultural convention for the sake of the promise? Will the family survive or degenerate into civil war? Will either of the boys prove worth the risk?

"God-wrestler" describes anyone who takes life and God seriously. The stories of Abraham, Sarah, Isaac, and Rebekah—let alone the yet-to-be-discussed Jabbok's Ford tale—reveal this is so. Christians sometimes like to describe the life of faith in terms of serenity or assurance. I don't dispute that both qualities exist in the Christian experience. More often, though, I find we wrestle with God.

My own story includes a number of such episodes, ranging from the classic concerns of theodicy to the most mundane matters imaginable. I wrestled with God over my life's work. Given my temperament and interests, the world of the Christian minister did not seem a likely place for me. In a sense, God said to me, "And that's precisely why I want you to go and dwell there. You will never get to settle down or feel as if everything has a place and is safely in its place. You will never be allowed to retreat from engagement with people. You will confound many who think they know what ministry is, even as you wonder why in the world I sent you into ministry!" To put it mildly, God and I contended with one another, and we still do. Most of the time, the struggle ends when I'm worn out or God breaks away. At such times, it is as if God looks at me and says, "That's enough for now. Get back to work. And, remember, I think the ministry is good for you, and you're good for the ministry."

All this makes for an interesting if sometimes uncomfortable life!

Rami: I suspect Jews like to imagine that *Yisrael*, one who wrestles (*yisra*) with God (*El*), refers to Jews alone. That may have been the case once upon a time, but in our time we are moving toward a post-ethnic identity that is action-oriented rather than blood-fixated. So, with you, I say that anyone who wrestles with God, however defined, is a God-wrestler and can benefit from the wisdom of the Bible. And for what it's worth, I agree that you are good for the ministry. Whether the ministry is good for you, only you, your doctor, and your family can say for sure.

Chapter 13

Jacob's Dream

Genesis 28:10-22

Mike: Pardon me, Rami, if I become distracted as we discuss Genesis 28:10-22. Anyone reared in a Baptist church in the South in the mid-twentieth century cannot help hearing a children's song in their minds when they read the passage: "We are climbing Jacob's ladder. We are climbing Jacob's ladder. We are climbing Jacob's ladder. Children of the Lord." I remember wondering what the song could possibly mean and trying mightily to line it up with the actual story, in which neither Jacob nor any other human climbs the ladder! Songwriters and children's teachers can scarcely imagine what goes through the mind of a child.

Okay, on to the story. Jacob leaves his home and heads toward Haran. Somewhere along the way, he stops for the night. He appears to be in a relative wilderness since he makes his bed on the ground and uses a stone for his pillow. Jacob falls asleep and dreams. In his dream, he sees a ladder or ramp set upon the earth and reaching to heaven. The messengers or angels of God climb up and down the ladder. In his dream, the Lord suddenly stands beside him. God identifies himself and gives the promise once given by Abraham to Jacob. The promise includes the standard features: God will give to Jacob the land and numerous descendants through whom all the people of earth shall be blessed. God adds two elements that speak directly to Jacob's personal situation: presence and provision. Regardless of where Jacob travels, God will be there too. No matter the circumstances he may encounter, God will be with him, see him through, and return him to the promised land.

Jacob wakes from sleep. He exclaims, "Surely the LORD is in this place—and I did not know it" (Gen 28:16). Religious awe strikes, and he realizes he is on holy ground. Later, when morning arrives, he takes the pillow stone, sets it up as an altar, and names the place *Bethel*, or "house of God." Then he gives a response to the presence and words of God: "The LORD shall be my

God, this place shall be God's house, and I will give God one tenth of my livelihood, provided God keeps his promise" (Gen 28:20-22).

As I reflect on the text, several possible insights come to mind. First, Jacob is between places. He is neither home nor at the refuge of his uncle's territory. Leaving aside speculation about his mental and emotional state, I think it fair to say the story implies we often encounter God or the divine when we find ourselves in the "in between" places.

Second, Jacob's response suggests to me that while he knew the stories of the God of Abraham and Isaac, he had not had much sense of God's reality or presence prior to the dream. That, of course, is speculation on my part. Still, I think it a common human phenomenon. Something starts to change for Jacob that night, and I believe his sudden awareness that God is more than a family tradition is at the heart of the matter.

Third, Jacob responds with words and ritual. The story, insofar as I can tell, accepts his response as appropriate. Words and ritual are not all there is to human response to God, but we cannot seem to do well without them for very long.

Fourth, Jacob is still the Jacob we know. His words of response amount to a personal interpretation of the promise God gave to him. Note how he adds specifics about God providing bread and clothing. And, being who he is, Jacob attaches the word "if" to the promise, making it a kind of contract. If, indeed, God does all that he has promised, then Jacob will take the Lord as his God and treat God accordingly. At this point in his story, Jacob's world has changed to add God as a living player in his life. However, Jacob, if possible, would still like to control the game.

Rami: We Jews are not called the people of Abraham or the people of Isaac, but *Yisrael* (Israel, "one who wrestles with God"), the name given to Jacob by God at Jabbok's Ford (Gen 35:10). The Jacob saga names us and in so doing defines us as a people. We Jews don't surrender to God, the truest meaning of the word *Muslim*, nor do we follow God as the Second Person of the Holy Trinity, which, as I understand it, is what it is to be a Christian. We wrestle with God, we argue with God, we debate with God, and we challenge God. We are taught that argument and doubt are central to Judaism and that only when we wrestle with God in the name of godliness (universal justice and compassion) as Abraham did (Gen 18:16-33) are we living up to what it means to be a Jew.

In order to argue with God, one has to learn to stand one's ground. Jacob has yet to learn this. Living under the protective wing of his mother, he lives by exploiting the weaknesses of others rather than by his own strength. This he will learn to overcome. He is not pushed into this, however, but pulled toward it. His night vision shows him what is possible if he is willing and able to move forward on his own.

What is this vision? Jacob's dream has three distinct parts, yielding three distinct and yet overlapping messages. First, he sees a ladder uniting earth and heaven. Second, he sees messengers of God rising from the earth to heaven and then returning to earth again. Third, he sees God standing by his side.

The ladder belies any thought of separation between heaven and earth. As Jesus will remind us centuries later, the kingdom of God is within us and around us (Luke 17:20-21; *Gos. Thom.* 77b). Jacob is shown that this world is where God's will is to be lived. And what is that will? Do justly, love mercy, and walk humbly (Mic 6:8).

Also, in ancient rabbinic literature, the ladder is actually rising up out of Jacob's head, and the angels rising up from earth to heaven are symbolic of Jacob's capacity to lift his consciousness from the material to the spiritual and then to return to the material and infuse it with the spiritual (you can read all about this in my book *The Angelic Way*).

Jacob's vision of God, the third of the three revelations given in this story, is usually translated so that God is either above the ladder looking down on Jacob or actually standing beside Jacob on the earth. The Hebrew is a bit more provocative, suggesting not that God occupies a specific space, but that God is seen whenever and wherever we are alert to the *Shekhinah*, God's presence. In other words, Jacob's thoughts are purified as they rise heavenward so that when they return to the material world, they see God present in it and as it.

This is what each of us is to strive for: realizing the unity of earth and heaven ("Your will be done as earth as it is in heaven" [Matt 6:10]; "the kingdom of God is within you and around you" [*Gos. Thom.* 77b]) by lifting our thoughts from the selfish to the godly and then realizing that God is present every*where* and every*when*.

None of this is a matter of cause and effect, of course. God isn't present *because* Jacob sees the ladder and the angels; God is always present. What is missing is us. God is present in this place and every place, but "we do not know it!" (Gen 28:16, paraphrase). Knowing is the deep spiritual work of the Bible: "Be still and know I am God; I will be exalted in the nations, I will be exalted in the earth" (Ps 46:10).

We usually read this psalm to mean that all peoples will acknowledge God, but again the Hebrew is more slippery. The verse could be read, "Be still and know that I am God exalted in each person, exalted in all of nature." That is to say that when we are awake to the *Shekhinah*, we awaken to the holiness of every person, every being, and every thing.

I think this is how God fulfills the promise to make Jacob's people as the dust of the earth, spread out everywhere (Gen 28:14). It isn't Jews God is talking about, but the realization that Jacob and those who achieve what Jacob will eventually achieve will have the capacity to see God in and as everyone and everything. And those who see God present in and as all things will engage with all life in a manner that is a blessing to all life (Gen 28:14)—the same promise given to Jacob's grandfather, Abraham (Gen 12:3).

Bear with me a bit longer, Mike. I know I'm going on, but this story is so vital to me, my people, and all people that I can't let it go.

When Jacob awakes, he realizes that "this is a gate to heaven" (Gen 28:17). What is the "this" to which he's referring? Is it the patch of dirt on which he slept or the rocks that surrounded his head? No, it is the human capacity to lift our consciousness to heaven and return to make heaven on earth.

This is why I don't understand or appreciate the notion that we humans should be "in the world but not of the world" (John 17:16). From the Torah's point of view, we *are* the world (Gen 2:7), created for the sole purpose of midwifing life and transforming a lifeless rock into a garden (Gen 2:5). In Jacob's vision we see that we are to rise to heaven not to escape the earth, but to remember our true calling and to return and transform the earth into the paradise it was meant to be.

And yet with all this, Jacob hesitates. As you say, Mike, he qualifies everything with an "if": "If God will be with me and keep me on this path on which I am going, and will give me bread to eat and clothes to wear; and I return in peace to my father's house—then YHVH will be God to me" (Gen 28:20-21). He has just seen God in all as all and yet doesn't trust what he saw.

This theme is repeated over and over in the Hebrew Bible not because Jews are especially thick-headed, but because humans are forever seeing the truth and then blinding themselves to it. Indeed, we even have a phrase for this: "blinded by the light." We see the light, and at the very moment we do, we don't!

Jacob is not yet ready to embrace God. He is not yet ready to wrestle with God, but only to bargain with God. But he is not the first to do so, for Abraham bargained with God. If there are fifty innocents in Sodom, God must spare the city. But what if there are only forty . . . how about thirty . . . how about twenty . . . how about ten? (Gen 18:16-33). But Jacob's bargaining is selfish, whereas Abraham's is selfless.

Mike: Rami, your take on the story serves to remind me of the depth of the tradition on which you draw, the interesting differences between your perspective and that typical of many Christians, and some significant points of agreement.

With regard to the first matter, Christians also have a rich and long history of interpretation of the Hebrew Bible and the New Testament. Protestant Christians, though, seldom access the tradition, and when they do, they most often plumb primarily their particular theological current rather than the river. When you write, it feels to me as if rabbis across the ages live within your imagination so that you partake in a conversation that began long before your time and will continue long after you are gone. Some Christian scholars, clerics, and writers achieve such a state, but it is relatively rare. I deeply appreciate this facet of your life and work, and I wish more Christians sought something similar.

Turning to one difference of perspective, I'll start with your own words: "The Jacob saga names us and in so doing defines us as a people." Christians, I think, in practice tend to place more weight on the Abraham and Joseph stories. The Abraham story features the launch and defining of elements important to us: calling, unlearning old ways of thought and action, the promise of descendants through whom God will bless all peoples, and the notion of a life as a portion of the longer, larger story being written by God. Jacob's story fascinates us because of its drama and humor, but most Christians see Jacob's primary importance in terms of how his life sets up the life of Joseph. I'll leave the matter of Joseph for later, except to say that Christians see him as the one who, in eventual cooperation with God, saves his people and prepares the way for the greatest defining event in the Hebrew Bible, the exodus event.

We're closer with regard to other matters than one might think at first. You write that you understand the Christian identity to be bound up in the image of followers of God as the Second Person of the Trinity. That's one element in our identity. "Follower" may be the most common metaphor in use in America at this time. Still, we think of ourselves in any number of ways. We can even speak of ourselves as wrestlers with God. Other self-descriptive terms or phrases include but are not limited to worshipers of God, disciples, children, apprentices, ambassadors, temples, yeast, and the like. To be a follower of Christ is to enter into a lifelong journey in which we may live into many roles. Each of the roles, ideally, continually shapes us more nearly into persons who trust God enough to be honest with God, practice self-giving love toward all others, and lay down the burden of trying to be God in favor of taking up our God-given humanity.

Certainly you and I agree the ladder belies any thought of separation between heaven and earth. God is here with us, and we are with God. Like you, I think we tend to blind ourselves to this truth, even after we have seen it. Our blindness, though, does not change reality: God is always here with us, and we are always with God.

I want to comment on the phrase "in the world but not of the world." Christians are guilty of misusing the phrase to justify withdrawal from surrounding cultures into what I consider Christian ghettos: places where Christians can worship, eat, play, educate, and work without having to interface with people different from themselves. I almost regard the phrase as too damaged to remain in use. Properly understood, though, the idea is that in Christ we begin to be transformed into the kind of humans who realize God's dream for humanity. That dream includes our entering into a grace-filled relationship with God, loving and serving one another, and taking up responsibility for stewardship of the creation. Such an understanding, I think, is close to what you suggest.

Rami: I like your notion of Judaism as an ongoing conversation among Jews—some rational, some mystical—across the ages. It is absolutely that, though sadly most Jews, including rabbis, have fallen silent. Fewer and fewer Jews have the knowledge base and skill set to follow the conversation, let alone enter into it. This is the fault of us rabbis.

There was a time, Mike, when the goal of a rabbi was to teach Jews how to enter the conversation. Today, however, most of us are content simply to indoctrinate young Jews into what has been said by long-dead Jews in order to settle the arguments rather than deepen and perpetuate them. This shift, I suspect, will spell the end of Judaism as a dynamic civilization.

In traditional Jewish educational settings, students sit across from one another at long tables—a setting that encourages dialogue—and are taught to argue and debate, to plunge into book after book of Jewish literary history to find ways of sharpening their questions and their investigations. In liberal classrooms, we find students sitting in rows facing the teacher, a setting that only disempowers the student, reinforces the authority of the teacher, and shuts down dialogue. Students are taught "what Jews believe and do" as if there were a set of ideas and practices to which all Jews adhere. What Jews believe is that there are multiple ways of believing and things to believe in; what Jews do is argue about what we believe. But that is being lost. I cannot tell you how much this pains me.

While one can argue that Jews have given the world a vast body of literature—the Hebrew Bible, New Testament, Apocrypha, Mishnah, Talmud, Zohar, Kafka—all of this depended upon the Jewish mindset, a mindset that is being abandoned by the very people who are entrusted to promote it. If I'm right about this and the trend is not reversed, Judaism may well survive, but doing so will be largely irrelevant to most Jews and to the world.

I was taken with your notion of Christians being more drawn to Abraham than Jacob/Israel. I can see that. Isaac too, I would imagine, since his near sacrifice by his father can be seen as a foreshadowing of Jesus' real sacrifice by his Father. And your notion of Christians as followers of Christ highlights a difference between us, and not just the obvious one that I am not a Christian.

While no rational Christian would say "I am the Christ," all Jews would say "I am Israel." But in the end it may not be all that different. You seek to be Christ-like, to put on the mind of Christ and live as he lived, and I seek to be *Yisrael*, the God-wrestler, to live into the mindset of God-wrestling by cultivating the mindset that has defined Jews for the past 3,000-plus years. I imagine that as a pastor you seek to help others do the same. And that is certainly the task I set myself as a rabbi.

Chapter 14

Joseph and His Brothers

Genesis 37–38

Mike: The story of Joseph takes center stage for the final chapters of Genesis. God plays a muted public role in the larger story. The narrator occasionally but significantly notes, "God was with Joseph." At the climax of the tale, Joseph perceives that God has been at work through his personal history to preserve the people of Israel. God, though, does not step on stage as in earlier stories. I don't know if the development is significant, but I suspect it captures the reality of how God's people most often experience God: we live our lives, and only in due season might we look and see in retrospect some of God's handiwork.

Joseph's tale begins at home, where he is the favorite son of Jacob and a pain to his brothers. Jacob keeps him out of the fields. He gives him a special coat as a mark of favor. Not only do his older brothers have to work harder than Joseph, they also must endure the sight of a younger brother receiving an honor that normally might be due the eldest brother. No doubt, the older sons, knowing their father's history, worry that the younger brother may take their rightful inheritance from them. They view Joseph as a threat to their futures and the futures of their descendants.

The young man dreams too. Insofar as he or anyone else knows, the dreams are his alone. The story makes no mention of God sending the dreams. In his first dream, he and his brothers are binding sheaves in the field. Suddenly, his sheaf stands upright, and the sheaves of his brothers bow to it. Joseph tells his brothers of the dream, and they are not amused. "Are you then to rule over us?" they ask. A reader can almost feel the menace in their question. Joseph's second dream is even more outrageous. In it, the sun, moon, and eleven stars bow to him. When he shares the dream with his father and brothers, both rebuke him. Jacob, though, continues to ponder the matter. He, more than most, knows something of the power of dreams, not to mention the possibility of the youngest supplanting the oldest.

Jacob sends the older brothers away to shepherd the family flocks. At first, they seek water and grass near Shechem, but they later move on to Dothan. Jacob sends Joseph to check on them and bring back a report. Joseph goes first to Shechem, but his brothers are no longer there. A rather mysterious man (is this an echo of the story of "the man" who wrestled with Jacob?) tells him where they may be found. Jacob sets out to find them.

His brothers spot him at a distance, and they conspire to kill him. Their initial plan is to take his life, dispose of the body in a pit, and later claim that a wild animal must have devoured him. The story becomes a bit confused at this point, as at least one of the older brothers persuades them not to take Joseph's life but instead to content themselves with simply throwing him in the pit. In the end, they spot a caravan of Midianite traders, who deal in slaves in Egypt. The brothers sell their brother to the Midianites for twenty pieces of silver. They take their brother's coat, rip it, dip it in the blood of a goat, and take it to their father. The brothers ask Jacob, "Is this your son's robe or not?" Old Jacob identifies the robe and enters into mourning. In the meantime, Joseph is taken to Egypt and sold to a man named Potiphar, the captain of Pharaoh's guard.

If God is at work through the story, it's not evident to Joseph, Jacob, or the brothers. Only time and more of the longer story will provide an opportunity to discern the possibility of God's backstage efforts. On the surface and as experienced, the story is one of a tragic family dysfunction, one so severe that the older brothers cannot bring themselves to speak of Joseph as their brother, let alone treat him as one.

The story prompts me to ask some questions: Do I actually think God works through even the tragedy of human brokenness, alienation, and loss? If so, can I look back and start to see how God might have used a situation in which I saw nothing but tragedy at the time? On a larger canvas, might it be possible to discern something similar in the broad currents of human history?

Rami: Before I get into the Joseph saga, Mike, let me comment a moment on your notion that we notice "God's handiwork" only in hindsight. I don't disagree, but I would be remiss if I didn't point out that this "noticing" could be pure imagining as well. I suspect we bring order out of the chaos of our lives by looking back, sifting through the past for key moments, and weaving a story from those moments that gives our lives a sense of purpose and meaning. Meaning and purpose, however, are imposed upon rather than intrinsic to the events themselves.

At the close of the Joseph story, his brothers worry that when their father dies, Joseph will inflict terrible revenge upon them for having sold him into slavery. Joseph puts them at ease saying: "Fear not. . . . Although you intended me harm, God used you for good. Because of you a great people was saved—this is as clear as day" (Gen 50:20). In other words, everything turned out the way it should because God was in charge. As you said, God isn't a major player in the story, so it is Joseph who is seeing God's hand in the twists and turns of his life. But he does so only in hindsight, suggesting that Joseph may be seeing only what he wants to see and not what is literally true.

We humans are storytelling animals. Story is how we make meaning out of life. If you are correct that God's people most often experience God only in retrospect, it may be that the God we experience is simply a *deus ex machina*, a literary device used to solve seemingly insolvable situations or explain away otherwise unexplainable events. This God removes the mystery from life and flattens the yeastiness of reality. This God always wants what has already been, whereas I wonder if God really wants what we have yet to achieve.

I look forward to hearing your take on this, but for now let me get into the story.

It's sad that Jacob, himself a product of a father playing favorites between his sons (Gen 25:28), does exactly that with his own sons. You'd think he would know better. Or maybe the message is that sons learn to father from their fathers and more often than not replicate the mistakes of their fathers, visiting the sins of the fathers upon the children (Exod 34:7). How often do I find myself imitating my father and doing to my son the very things I wish my father had not done to me? Too often, I admit.

Our story opens with the line, lost in the NRSV translation, "Jacob settled in the land of his father's wanderings" (Gen 37:1). Wandering is essential to spiritual maturation; settling is its antithesis. God is *Ehyeh asher Ehyeh*, the Forever Becoming (Exod 3:14), and we humans, being the image of God (Gen 1:27), are also forever becoming, forever maturing, forever deepening our capacity to see God in, with, and as all reality. To achieve this forever becoming, we cannot settle, in either sense of the word. We cannot settle down and cease to journey on, and we cannot settle for anything less than full spiritual maturity.

Jacob's brother Esau approximated wandering by hunting in the fields, while Jacob himself didn't even do that much but stayed in the tents (Gen 25:27). If Jacob was to mature into Israel, he had to leave the settled life and wander, which he did up to a point. Once he falls in love with Rachel and marries both Leah and Rachel, Jacob again settles among the tents of Laban, his maternal uncle and father-in-law. Only when forced to wander does Jacob meet God—first in a dream at Beth-El (Gen 28:13) and then again at Jabbok's Ford (Gen 32:24).

Wandering is a metaphor for God's command to Abraham and Sarah (and through them to each of us) in Genesis 12:1 to *lech lecha* (literally, walk to yourself, or walk toward your truest self as the image of God). When we settle (in both senses of the word), our journey ends, and the promise of spiritual maturation remains unfulfilled.

Remember, *lech lecha* requires us to leave home, to let go the conditioning of nationality, ethnicity, culture, gender, religion, and parental bias, and to wander to a place we can only see when we are free from all conditioning. It is there that we become powerful and learn to use our power to become "a blessing to all the families of the earth" (Gen 12:3). Jacob the heel-clinger, even after becoming Israel the God-wrestler, reverts to clinging and settles. And because he does, he falls into old patterns of parenting and sets his older sons against Joseph.

It is important that Torah speaks of "Jacob" and not "Israel." It tells us that meeting God isn't enough to keep us from falling back into old patterns of thought and behavior. We have to internalize that meeting and become godly ourselves if we are to fulfill our potential as the image of God. Becoming Israel the God-wrestler means we have to continue wrestling to bring the world into alignment with godliness. We can never settle. And if we do, all our gains are lost.

Torah makes this clear when we learn that it was Israel who "loved Joseph more than all his sons" (Gen 37:3). Israel, not Jacob. What might this mean? To me it says that having settled back into being Jacob, even his experience of being Israel is corrupted. As soon as we settle, as soon as we abandon the challenge of *lech lecha*, we misuse whatever wisdom we have gained and, despite claims to the contrary, live our lives as Jacob—clinging to this and that—rather than as Israel—wrestling with God.

Mike: I want to interact with several of your insights. Let's start with the matter of hindsight, the human tendency to create stories in order to assign meaning to our lives. I strongly agree that we do so. Humans find patterns in all things, and we're not content until we do so. I suspect our brains are hard-wired to seek and notice patterns. Joseph, of course, is conditioned by his heritage to look for God at work in all things.

One of your sentences particularly intrigues me: "Meaning and purpose, however, are imposed upon rather than intrinsic to the events themselves." No doubt, this is often the case. Still, I fail to see how we can say this is *always* the case. How would we prove such a statement? Is it not possible that the patterns we discern in a given event or sequence of events might correlate with reality? I think so.

What you say is true. Joseph may be wrong. On the other hand, Joseph may be right. From my perspective, God chooses to leave such decisions to us, in part to guard our freedom and in part to challenge and hone our pattern-seeking minds. Such a God leaves plenty of room for the mystery of life, decision-making, and the possibility that any of us may come to see God in the stories of our lives and the lives of others.

I wonder if such questions lead us away from the deepest value of the story. More and more, I think the most useful thing to do with a story is to enter the story via the imagination, feel and think with the characters, and see their worlds and lives through their eyes. We immerse ourselves in the story. The world we know fades away for a while, and we live an alternative life. When we emerge from such an experience, we see things differently, at least for a little while. In this case, we see that God might be found at work in the unfolding of our lives. The possibility that this is so alters our decision-making, actions, and response to the good and hard times of life.

Turning to Jacob/Israel and the matter of wandering versus settling, I find you quite persuasive. To settle down and cleave to one place is to court spiritual stagnation or regression. We, indeed, must wander if we are to encounter God in various ways and find our truest selves along the way. For these reasons, the image of the ever-traveling pilgrim is often embraced by Christians as a symbol of the way to spiritual maturity.

We may differ slightly on one point. I agree that we are called to leave home and the various kinds of conditioning common to humanity. I am not certain, though, that we ever become free from all conditioning or that such complete freedom must precede our becoming a blessing to others. Rather, my experience (both personal and with others) is that we become progressively more able to bless others as we continue along the way. This happens not because we attain a state of unconditioned perfection but because we learn to see how we've been conditioned, acknowledge such conditioning's effects, and act counter to our conditioning.

I'll look forward to any response you care to give, and I invite you to take up the dreams of young Joseph as well.

Rami: What? I have to prove the statements I make? When did we decide that? I just make statements; if I knew I had to prove them, I would make fewer of them, and then I would be out of a job! Proof? Huh.

Okay, let me take a breath and admit that of course I can't prove that there's no meaning or purpose intrinsic to reality and that what meaning and purpose we find is the meaning and purpose we create for ourselves. Then again, there is no way to prove I'm wrong either. So this is a statement of faith on my part, I suppose. But let's go into this a bit.

Your notion that the patterns we discern may match the sequence of events seems true enough to me. I'm not saying we make up stuff out of whole cloth. We draw on our observations and then extrapolate meaning and purpose from them. The question is this: does God imbue reality with meaning and purpose, or do we?

We humans are meaning-making and purpose-building animals. We evolved naturally from the world, and as such we are the way the world makes meaning and purpose. The world is intrinsically meaningful and purposeful to the extent that we humans make meaning and purpose.

I know this is not what you believe, but I find it compelling. It allows me to avoid saying that the world is meaningless and without purpose, while at the same time allowing me to say that God doesn't implant meaning and purpose for us to discover. Rather, God creates the universe in such a way that eventually meaning and purpose making happens. And on this planet, this eventuality is achieved through, and in, us.

Joseph is a case in point. As you say, he is conditioned by his heritage to see God working in and through all things, but this is nothing but conditioning, and conditioning of a certain kind. Joseph never sees the Egyptian gods controlling reality, though the Egyptians among whom he lives cannot help but see their gods doing so. So Joseph sees what he is conditioned to see, and the Egyptians see what they are conditioned to see. But what might we see if we were free from conditioning?

This takes me back to Genesis 12:1-3, where God calls Abram and Sarai to leave behind all the conditioning of country, kin, and parents to go to a place that God can show them only after they have dropped all conditioning. This is the promised land—not the state of Israel per se, but the land beneath your feet when you can see it without the blinders of conditioning. This is the kingdom of God that is within and without. And what do we do with this realization? We act in ways that make us a blessing to all the families of the earth!

As usual, I'm not sure we really disagree as much as we have differing ways of articulating these ideas. When you say God leaves us free to make meaning as best we can and leaves plenty of room for mystery, I hear this as saying that we are nature's meaning makers and mystery is the stuff out of which we make it.

Now on to "wandering." While Judaism emerged within the context of wandering, the idea of settling the promised land is never far from our psyche. I wonder if there is a tension implicit in the Jewish psyche between wandering and settling. I wonder if our periodic exiles are the result of our having abandoned our wandering. When we are too comfortable, we are uprooted and forced to move on. Yet our yearning to return to Zion is thousands of years old, and our support of Zionism and the modern State of Israel is in response to the horrors that our wanderings led to over the last 2,000 years.

There is no way to resolve this; it is a tension we Jews have to live with. Or maybe not. Maybe the wandering is spiritual, internal, *lech lecha* (walking toward oneself, Gen 12:1) rather than moving from country to country. Maybe we can be at home physically and wander intellectually and spiritually? I don't know.

I do know that my son Aaron thinks settling is antithetical to wandering. If we Jews are too comfortable, too safe, if we are not harried by being "other," the *Ostjuden*, the "outsider Jew," we settle intellectually and spiritually as well. Jews are at their best when the world keeps us from settling too long. We must settle somewhere just long enough to create something new—the Bible, the Talmud, the Zohar were all created in exile—and then move on to and create something newer still.

I do think that if forced to choose, I would choose wandering over settling. I love the idea of being an eternal pilgrim sauntering through the sacred—my positive spin on the anti-Semitic notion of the wandering Jew.

I realize I have been repeating myself a bit. But these are concerns central to my life. As for your doubt that we can ever be completely free from conditioning, I tend to agree. I think I have had moments of liberation, but

I fall back into conditioning soon after, perhaps seconds later. But I have had those moments, and their fragrance lingers.

Mike: You'll get no argument from me with regard to the tension between wandering and settling! Like you, if forced to choose between the two, I hope I would choose to keep moving.

Now, I want your take on the dreams of young Joseph. My own tradition tends to treat the dreams in a straightforward fashion. Though the text does not say so, we mostly assume the dreams are sent by God to foreshadow what is to come in the life of Joseph and his family. Their core message seems simple: a time will come when Joseph rules over his brothers and even his father.

Joseph and his family, of course, know nothing of what the future actually holds. They, like most of us, act as if the future will look like the past and present. Radical discontinuity is beyond the imagination of the brothers. Joseph's dreams seem to them to be the product of his overblown ego, his father's favoritism, or the beginnings of a plot to deprive them of their rightful places in the family. Jacob/Israel knows from experience that life takes unexpected turns, but even he chides Joseph for daring to speak of such dreams. Joseph himself knows nothing of any life other than the one he has known. No one so much as thinks of Egypt, famines, or the possibility of one of their family becoming part of the Egyptian power structure. To the brothers, the dreams are an irritant and a threat, the proverbial straw that breaks the camel's back and fuels their decision to get rid of Joseph.

Only the larger context of the Joseph saga, as you call it, enables us to see a greater role for his dreams. The young man's dreams start a string of events that work together to bring Joseph to the one place and station from which he might succor his family during a great famine. Seen in the even larger context of the subsequent exodus story, Joseph's dreams lead his people to the place where they might survive, be broken, rescued yet again, and rebuilt into God's community through whom the world will be blessed.

I suspect, Rami, that you have a much wider range of interpretive options with regard to the dreams of Joseph.

Rami: Let's just make it clear that we are assuming that Jacob is a real person with real dreams and that the story we are reading is in some sense history. I tend to see Torah as literature rather than history or biography, especially as we understand these terms today.

For me, Joseph's dreams are narrative devices designed to foreshadow the story to come. But even so, the author and final editor of this story choose their words carefully, and in their choices we can discern some interesting insights.

Let's start with Joseph's first dream, where the brothers' sheaves circle around and bow down to Joseph's sheaf (Gen 37:7). The most interesting thing about this dream is that it has Joseph and his brothers harvesting wheat when in fact they are shepherds. Why dream of sheaves rather than sheep? I think the answer is in the nature of farming, a communal effort, versus sheepherding, an individualistic one.

Joseph is feeling isolated from his brothers, yet he dreams of working side by side with them while harvesting wheat. Furthermore, Joseph's sheaf was to be piled up with those of his brothers (Gen 37:7), suggesting that he has no desire to be separate and apart. His sheaf took center stage of its own accord. His plea that his brothers listen to his dream (Gen 37:6) may have been a cry for acceptance and not a pompous celebration of his superiority. Perhaps the dream conveys his desire that his brothers overcome their dislike of him and work together with him, and the fact that they don't represents his doubt that this will ever happen.

We are not told when Joseph dreams his second dream, but clearly he hasn't learned anything from the experience of sharing his first. This second dream he shares not only with his brothers but with his father as well. Jacob has had his own dream encounter (Gen 28:12), which he would have shared with his sons. Perhaps Joseph thought his father could help interpret his second dream in a manner that would smooth things over with his brothers. Clearly this doesn't happen. His brothers only grow more angry and envious, leaving Joseph behind as they go off to graze their sheep in Shechem (Gen 36:12).

Joseph's first dream of the sheaves is very different from his second dream, where sun, moon, and eleven stars bow down to him (Gen 37:9). In the first dream Joseph is represented by a sheaf of wheat no different from those of his brothers. But in the second dream the heavenly bodies represent his family while Joseph seems to be himself. Why represent your family this way? Is Joseph admitting that any relationship with his family is beyond his reach? And what shall we make of him dreaming of his mother, Rachel, by now long dead, as the moon? Certainly this isn't a prophecy, unless his godlike status is to occur in some afterlife.

Is Joseph identifying with God? And if he is, is this hyperinflation of the ego or some deeper humanism that displaces God and, as the Greek philosopher Protagoras (480–411 BCE) taught, takes humanity to be the measure of all things? Of course, I could just be making far more of these dreams than they warrant. As I said, they may be nothing more than a clever narrative device to foreshadow for the reader/listener what is to come.

Joseph is either an egotistical fool or has no idea what his dreams mean. I suggest the latter. If the authors of the Joseph story cycle are any good— and I think they are very good—they are setting us up for a surprise. While Joseph, like his father, was a dreamer, he isn't a dream reader. Jacob knew what his dream meant (Gen 28:16), but Joseph hasn't a clue. Later, when he reads the dreams of his fellow inmates (Gen 40:8) and then of Pharaoh (Gen 41:15), he is probably as surprised as the reader is. Indeed, when reading the dreams of his fellow inmates and Pharaoh, Joseph credits God with interpretations and takes no credit for himself (Gen 40:8; 41:16).

So what shall we make of all of this? Let me offer one last comment. The issue in all of these dreams is dreaming rather than interpreting. Joseph doesn't interpret his own dreams and only shares them. His family interprets them for themselves. Nor does he interpret the dreams of the cupbearer or baker or even Pharaoh—God does. So what is Torah saying?

I suggest Torah is telling us that dreams matter, that dreams are somehow a message from God hinting at things to come or at things that might come if we don't listen to the dream. This is a fairly standard Jewish view. The Zohar, the "bible" of Jewish mystical teaching, says "a dream uninterpreted is like a letter unread" (1:183b). I believe dreams are often a way our unconscious mind processes data from our conscious mind and hints at insights of which our conscious mind may be unaware.

Chapter 15

Joseph in Egypt

Genesis 39–41

Mike: Genesis 39–41 features the descent and ascent of Joseph in Egypt. He falls into slavery and from there into prison, only to rise to a position of incredible authority. The story is complex, but I will try, in the next few paragraphs, to recount it in summary.

Potiphar, an officer of Pharaoh, purchases Joseph as a household slave. The evil deed of his brothers serves to plant Joseph among the powerful of Egypt. "The LORD was with Joseph," as the writer puts it. All that Joseph does in the service of his master prospers. Potiphar promotes Joseph so that the Hebrew slave quickly becomes the overseer of the household and all its enterprises. The one who owns Joseph places Joseph in charge of his economic life, and Joseph acts in a trustworthy manner. There's more than a touch of irony here, as the slave takes command of the life of his owner

Inevitably, with prosperity comes temptation. In this case, Potiphar's wife decides to try to take Joseph as her lover. She acts from her position of power and attempts to order Joseph to lie with her, and no doubt expects him to readily obey. What else would a powerless slave do? Yet Joseph refuses to betray Potiphar's trust and his own sense of morality.

Still, the story ends badly for Joseph, or so it seems. Potiphar's wife accuses him of attempted rape. Potiphar accepts her story and casts Joseph into Pharaoh's prison, from which few emerge alive.

"But the LORD was with Joseph" (39:21). The second occurrence of the phrase signals a twist of the story. Joseph descends into prison only to ascend to the functional peak of the prison system. The chief jailor, whom we should think of as a member of Egypt's ruling class charged with overall responsibility for the prison, takes a liking to Joseph and puts him in charge of daily operations. Like Potiphar, the chief jailor quickly comes to rely on Joseph and takes no further interest in the affairs of the prison.

Strangely enough, Joseph's fall into prison actually brings him closer to the time and place when his insight and skills will be needed by Egypt. Two fellow prisoners come to his attention: the chief cupbearer of Pharaoh and the baker of Pharaoh. Joseph notes they seem distressed. They tell him they have been troubled by dreams and that they have no one who can interpret their dreams for them.

Dream interpretation, I believe, was held in high regard in Egypt, and I suspect such interpretation was the special province of the magicians or wise men that advised Pharaoh. The two prisoners feel quite uneasy at being cut off from such resources. Joseph invites them to share their dreams with him, though he notes that interpretations belong to God. While he might mean to imply that he has no skills at dream interpretation, I think it more likely Joseph is claiming the territory of dream interpretation for God.

Both dreams draw on the dreamers' occupations for their central images. The cupbearer sees a vine with three branches, which quickly bud, blossom, and produce grapes. In his dream, he has Pharaoh's cup in his hand. He presses the grapes into the cup and then gives the cup to Pharaoh. The baker, meanwhile, dreams of bearing three cake baskets on his head, the topmost of which contains various baked goods for Pharaoh. Birds, however, come and eat the food intended for Pharaoh.

Joseph interprets each dream. He plays with the phrase "in three days Pharaoh will lift up your head." In the case of the cupbearer, Joseph says that Pharaoh will restore him to his role in the court. The baker, though, will be "lifted up" by being hanged, and the birds will eat his flesh. Both interpretations come to pass in three days when Pharaoh celebrates his birthday.

Joseph asks the cupbearer to speak a word on his behalf to Pharaoh. Once restored to his position, the cupbearer forgets Joseph. I tend to think he does so intentionally. What possible good might it do the cupbearer to remember and speak for Joseph? Is it not more likely to plunge the cupbearer into court politics and wind up placing him in danger? The end result is that Joseph spends two more years in prison.

Then Pharaoh starts to have dreams—two, in fact, on the same night. His dreams are most disturbing. The Nile River, the source of Egypt's agricultural security, produces seven fat cows, which in turn are followed by seven thin cows, which devour the fat ones. Pharaoh wakes up, then falls back asleep and dreams again. This time he sees seven plump ears of grain, followed by seven blighted ears. The blighted ears swallow up the good grain.

Pharaoh wakes deeply disturbed, for he takes dreams seriously as potential portents of the future. When summoned, all the magicians and wise men of Egypt are unable to interpret the dreams. Whether they actually cannot do so or simply are afraid to give Pharaoh bad news is unclear. Either way, they set the stage for the ascendance of Joseph.

It is the cupbearer who remembers Joseph. Whatever the reason behind his sudden recovery of memory, his actions also prepare the way for Joseph to step onto center stage in Egypt. The cupbearer tells Pharaoh about the dreams he and the deceased baker had, how Joseph interpreted those dreams, and how the Hebrew's interpretation came true.

Impressed or desperate, Pharaoh summons Joseph to appear before him. Joseph cleans up and comes to Pharaoh. Pharaoh shares his dreams with this most unlikely of listeners. Joseph, with no hesitation, declares the dreams are one and the same. Egypt is about to enjoy seven years of unprecedented good harvests followed by seven years of devastating famine. Nothing can be done to turn aside these developments, for they are "fixed by God."

Before Pharaoh or any of his court can react, Joseph strikes. He moves beyond interpretation to offer counsel. He advises Pharaoh to appoint overseers who will collect twenty percent of the produce during the good years, store it, and so create a grain reserve against the hard days to come. Only in such a way might Egypt be preserved.

Pharaoh is impressed, for he perceives the "spirit of God" is at work in Joseph. Accordingly, he appoints Joseph to oversee all his concerns—to be, in effect, his second-in-command. He gives Joseph his signet ring, dresses him in appropriate clothing and jewelry, gives him a chariot, and invests him formally with power. Pharaoh also gives Joseph an Egyptian name and an Egyptian wife. The Hebrew who was sold into slavery has now been adopted into the royal court of Egypt.

Joseph sets about his task and does it exceedingly well so that all is prepared by the time the famine strikes. Pharaoh, as planned, sends those seeking grain to Joseph, who sells the stored grain (note: he does not distribute it freely) not only to Egyptians, but also to others who come from the general, famine-stricken region hoping to purchase food.

Rami: Nice summary of the novella, Mike; now, let's take it apart a bit at a time. First, Joseph doesn't merely "fall" into slavery; he is sold into slavery. But the story starts a bit earlier than that, and I think it's worth rolling back the narrative so we can examine it as it unfolds. Flashback, then, to Joseph and his brothers.

After listening to Joseph's dreams and imagining themselves bowing before him, the brothers leave their home for Shechem. This demonstrates a rift in the family that Jacob hopes to mend by sending Joseph after his brothers. Clearly, neither Jacob nor Joseph has a clue as to how deeply the brothers despise Joseph.

When Joseph arrives in Shechem, his brothers are nowhere to be found. Torah says he was wandering around the fields when he meets an unnamed stranger. This may be the most important character in the entire Hebrew Bible. If Joseph had not met the man and the man had not set Joseph on the right track to find his brothers, he would never have been sold into Egyptian slavery or saved the Egyptian people from starvation. Further, the Hebrews would not have migrated to Egypt or have been enslaved or freed or received Torah at Sinai or settled in the promised land or exiled and returned or partnered with Rome or dominated by Rome. Hence, Jesus would not have not have been crucified, and Christianity never would have happened. Nothing would be the same without this fellow, and we have no idea who he is!

Some rabbis say he's an angel sent by God to make sure events unfold as they should, but Torah doesn't say this. We might imagine him simply to be a literary device to move the plot forward, but there is no reason for the narrator to have Joseph get lost in the first place, and so the detour seems conspicuous. What is the message here?

My own sense is this: Torah is telling us that seemingly insignificant events—like meeting a stranger who sets you off in one direction or another—can have profound implications on your life. I'm not talking about teachers, clergy, therapists, family members—people you know; I am talking about some seemingly chance encounter with a seemingly random person. There is nothing that happens that is without significance.

I don't believe in fate, but I do believe in consequences. Joseph isn't fated to meet this man, but his meeting with him has profound consequences not only for Joseph's life but the life of the entire Western world.

Whenever I read this story of the stranger, I look back to see where such strangers have stepped into my life. And I look to see if I can identify occurrences where I might have been the unnamed stranger in someone else's life, but I imagine there is no way of knowing this.

Mike: I agree with you that Joseph did not merely fall into slavery but instead was sold into slavery by his own brothers. My choice of the term "fall" had to do with the structure of the larger Joseph story: He falls from his place as the beloved son into the place of a slave, which in turn prepares the way for his ascent in Egypt.

As for the unnamed stranger, I'm glad you backtracked to take up the matter of his role in the story. As you say, "Nothing would be the same without this fellow." Christians, much like the rabbis, differ as to who or what he might have been. Some see him as a messenger (angel) from God, others as a literary device, and still others as simply an unnamed historical person. I'm not certain the story implies Joseph got lost on the way to find his brothers. My reading of the story is that the brothers had moved on and were no longer where Jacob and Joseph thought them to be. Either way, though, the stranger enables Joseph to go and find his brothers.

Regardless of the unnamed stranger's identity, I agree with you that he reminds us of how seemingly small (I'm not too fond of the term "insignificant") persons or events redirect out steps so that we wind up heading in a direction different from the one we thought we would follow. For example, I remember sitting in a compartment of an English train long ago. I had come to London for a week while on my way to a summer of church-related work in Europe. I was nineteen years old and had never been outside the United States. Truth to tell, I had never been more than 500 miles away from home! I hoped I had gotten on the right train, could find my way around once I reached my destination, and would be able to catch the right train to bring me back at day's end. An English family asked if they could share the compartment. I nodded. Soon after they sat down, the father said, "You're American, aren't you? First time out and about on your own, I take it?" We talked a little, and he discovered we were headed to the same destination. "Tell you what," he said, "why don't you just come along with us for the day?" I accepted his invitation and frankly experienced my first peace of mind since boarding the plane to leave home.

Now, here's the thing: his unexpected intervention and kindness changed me. I had been taught to keep my distance from strangers and leave them to their own devices. The English father's actions forced me to rethink the entire matter and led to me forcing myself to learn to practice proactive kindness toward strangers.

Rami, all of this sounds like a small thing, but the results led me to meet and engage others in ways my family conditioning did not encourage. Such encounters resulted in conversations, friendships, and other connections I would not have known otherwise. Who knows? Because of the course adjustment prompted in my life by an English stranger, I may well have become the unnamed stranger in the lives of others.

Rami: Getting back into a close reading of our story, it's important to note that Joseph's brothers see him coming and call him not "our brother" but the "master of dreams"! The phrase tells us two things. First, his brothers have not gotten over their anger with Joseph because of his dreams. Second, they now take the dreams as revelations of his intentions toward them. The phrase "master of dreams" doesn't mean that Joseph controls dreams, but rather that he is using his dreams to determine his future. This is what Joseph does when reading the dreams of Pharaoh; he uses Pharaoh's dreams as a means of elevating himself in Egyptian society. His brothers expect him to act in a manner that will elevate him above them, and they want him dead because of it.

This is reinforced by their plan to murder him, toss his corpse into a pit, and then cover up the murder by claiming he was killed by a wild animal (Gen 37:20). Reuben, the eldest brother, puts an end to that idea. He commands the others to imprison Joseph in a pit with the intention of rescuing him and returning him to their father.

Reuben then disappears from our story. When Joseph arrives, the remaining brothers take his coat from him and toss him into a dry well. Then they sit down to eat. In the next scene, a caravan of Ishmaelites passes by. Ishmaelites, children of Abraham's firstborn, Ishmael, are cousins to these Hebrews. The brothers, now under the leadership of the second eldest, Judah, plan to sell Joseph to their cousins and make some money without actually endangering his life since he was still family to the Ishmaelites.

While the brothers are negotiating with their Ishmaelite cousins over the sale of Joseph, a group of Midianites stumble upon him, and they sell him to the Ishmaelites for twenty pieces of silver (shades of Judas!), leaving the brothers without their hoped-for profit.

After all of this, Reuben returns, from where we don't know, and goes to the pit to rescue Joseph, but finds him gone. With no other plan presenting itself, Reuben joins with his brothers in the coverup, taking their brother's coat, dipping it in blood, and presenting it to their father as proof of Joseph's death at the claws of some wild animal.

Jacob is heartbroken and refuses to be comforted. By the way, this short observation that Jacob refuses the consolation offered him by his sons and their wives (Gen 37:35) is the proof-text we Jews use to argue that no one can console another. When Jews enter the home of the bereaved, we are to be silent and not initiate conversation, though we can respond to the mourners if they want to talk, of course. In this way, or so we are taught, we allow the bereaved to open themselves to the consolation of our presence and not to any platitude we might utter. But back to the story.

While Jacob laments the supposed death of Joseph, the Midianites take Joseph into Egypt and sell him to Potiphar, one of Pharaoh's chief officials (Gen 37: 36). What? Didn't Torah just say the Midianites sold Joseph to the Ishmaelites (Gen 37:28)? Our rabbis say that this implies Joseph was sold and resold back and forth between different Midianite and Ishmaelite traders until all trace of him was lost. If his brothers, knowing as they did that he was not dead, ever wanted to find out what happened to their brother, they would have no easy trail to follow.

I love this interpretation because it suggests to me the story of each of our lives: we are tossed around and back and forth so often that we can't figure out where we are or where the heck we are supposed to be going. We have no control over our own destinies. We must surrender to the unknowing and simply make the best of what we find.

Mike: Rami, I think we take a similar approach with regard to how the brothers perceive Joseph's potential use of his dreams and their resultant desire to see him dead or at least removed from the scene. As for the story of their plots, the Ishmaelites and the Midianites, and just who got the money, the account is confused enough to allow for a number of different readings.

For me, the brothers labeling Joseph "master of dreams" rather than "our brother" strikes home. They distance themselves from Joseph, which makes it possible for them to treat him as a problem to be solved rather than a family member or even a fellow human. A follower of Jesus can scarcely read the sentence without thinking of the parable of the prodigal son. The elder brother refuses to see his younger brother as his brother. When he speaks to his father about his brother, he calls his brother "this son of yours." Without discounting all the factors fueling his feelings toward the younger brother, the elder brother's key error is to deny their kinship.

Mind you, we humans are fully capable of hurting even those we call brother or sister, but we are more apt to inflict intentional, harsh damage on anyone we treat as less than a brother or sister. Denying them the status of kin is often the first step down the road to murder, enslavement, deportation, or exploitation. The story of the brothers' treatment of Joseph casts this sad truth in the package of a story.

In my line of work, I deal with Christians who find it all too easy to rail against what they call welfare cheats, people who "work the system," and the like. Most of the time, though, when they find themselves dealing with a particular person, learn his or her name, and pay attention to her or his specific story, their tune changes. I think I know why. When we treat another person as someone with a name and a story, we take a long stride toward recognizing them as kinfolk. When that happens, we're more apt to refrain from labeling or harming them and, perhaps, more likely to help them too.

Rami: I agree completely. Within Jewish culture we don't use our last names as much as the names of our parents. In a ritual setting I'm not Rami Shapiro, but Yirachmiel ben Yisrael v'Sarah, Yirachmiel (the long form of *Rami*), son of Israel (my dad's Hebrew name) and Sarah (my mother's Hebrew name). In this way, when I share my name, I share my lineage as well. When people convert into Judaism, when they become a part of the tribe, they choose a Hebrew name and then are given the following lineage as bar or bat (son or daughter) of *Avraham v'Sarah* (Abraham and Sarah). The lineage of a convert is directly linked to the founders of the faith and people: Abraham and Sarah. In this way strangers become kin.

Returning to our story, Joseph's life with Potiphar opens with the affirmation "YHVH was with him" (Gen 39:2) and is quickly followed in the next verse by the observation that Potiphar knew YHVH was with Joseph. This is important. Egypt had many Gods, but YHVH was not one of them. How does Potiphar come to know YHVH is with Joseph? Because of the success that followed Joseph in whatever he did.

From Potiphar's perspective, having a God translates into worldly success. Slaves are not known for their success and therefore are not thought to be accompanied by any God. Yet here was this Hebrew slave thriving in Potiphar's court. Indeed, the more power Potiphar bestows on Joseph, the more God rewards Potiphar (Gen 39:5). Over time, Potiphar puts his entire estate under Joseph's care, to the extent that the only thing of which he was aware was the bread he happened to be eating at any given moment (Gen 39:6). In other words, by empowering Joseph, Potiphar is working in sync with YHVH and benefits from doing so. While I don't share the belief that aligning with God leads to material success, I have heard a number of prosperity gospel preachers on TV use this story of Joseph as evidence it is so.

It is interesting to note that it is only after Joseph's success with Potiphar's estate that we learn that Joseph is physically beautiful (Gen 39:6). We usually take this observation to explain Potiphar's wife's desire to have sex with Joseph, but this may be too simple a reading. After all, if we were

referring to Joseph's physical beauty, we would have learned of it much earlier. What makes Joseph attractive to Mrs. Potiphar is Joseph's success and
the success her husband gleans from empowering Joseph. Everything Joseph
touches "turns to gold," and Potiphar's wife wants in on the action. When
Joseph remains loyal to Potiphar, Mrs. Potiphar charges him with attempted
rape. Given what we know of the life of slaves in Egypt, any slave who
attempted to rape the wife of his master would have been killed immediately.
Why doesn't Potiphar do this?

The Jewish view is this: as a chief agent of Pharaoh, Potiphar was in
charge of the prison system and benefited financially from it. Seeing the
blessings Joseph brought on his other estates, Potiphar wasn't willing to lose
such a valuable resource. Instead, he turned the situation to his advantage
and sent Joseph into Pharaoh's dungeon, where he might bring benefit to
Potiphar once again.

Indeed, we learn that just as God had been with Joseph in Potiphar's
house, now God was with Joseph in Pharaoh's dungeon (Gen 39:21), and
with the same result: Joseph brought success to the dungeon. We learn that
the chief of the prison, who we are taught worked for Potiphar, did exactly
what Potiphar had done, turning the entire prison operation over to Joseph
(Gen 39:22) and leaving him alone to run the place as he saw fit (Gen
39:43). And everything Joseph did was a success.

Mike: I find myself agreeing with you with in regard to Potiphar: He comes
to believe a god accompanies Joseph on the basis of Joseph's golden touch.
Power recognizes power, and Potiphar is happy to exploit what he sees as a
resource: the god who has arrived with the slave Joseph.

We perhaps disagree over the significance of the phrase "God was with
him." God is mentioned so seldom in the Joseph story that I find each
occurrence significant. In this case, I think the phrase serves as a reminder to
those listening that Joseph's story does not take place in a vacuum but
instead in the presence of the God who journeys with Joseph. The story, in
my view, affirms the presence of God with Joseph regardless of how keenly
aware Joseph may be of that presence.

As for Joseph and Potiphar's wife, I do not doubt your interpretation,
but I think the story also comments on the nature of slavery. Potiphar's wife
operates from a position of power, the power of the slave-owning class.
While she may well want to benefit from Joseph's good fortune, she intends
to do so from a position of power. She would command Joseph, and hence

Joseph's god. In her own small way, Potiphar's wife represents all those who hold power and who would constrain God to validate and solidify their power. Both Joseph and Joseph's God elude her grasp, though Joseph loses a cloak in the process!

As you can see, the story holds quite a bit of meaning for me.

Rami: Focusing on the power issue is interesting, Mike. If I am understanding you correctly, both Potiphar and his wife are using their power at the expense of Joseph. Fair enough; that is what slaveholders always do to their slaves. In fact, as we shall see, when Joseph is empowered by Pharaoh, he too abuses his power and enslaves almost all of Egypt.

Pharaoh's power is absolute, as his imprisoning of his cupbearer and baker seems to suggest. And the encounter of these two with Joseph in prison reconnects Joseph and dreams and makes it clear that God alone reveals the truth of our dreams, and not human dream readers (as most Egyptians believed, Gen 40:8).

The cupbearer dreams of three vines bursting with grapes. Joseph focuses on the number "three" and says the dream is previewing what is about to happen. In three days the cupbearer will be recalled to Pharaoh's service. How does the dream tell us this? Because in his dream the cupbearer successfully hands the cup to Pharaoh, and Pharaoh drinks from it. Everything will be as it was.

The baker, hoping for a similar interpretation and restoration to his post, shares his dream with Joseph. Here, the number three comes into play via the three baskets stacked on the baker's head. Again, the three baskets represent three days. The top basket is filled with baked goods for Pharaoh, but birds are eating them. How does Joseph know this means the baker will be executed rather than simply fired or left to rot in jail? Because, according to our rabbis, birds would only get that close to a person if that person were dead.

And so it turns out!

Two years pass with Joseph still in the dungeon, though presumably doing quite well as God is still with him. Now it is Pharaoh's turn to dream: seven fat cows devoured by seven sick cows and seven fat and delicious ears of corn devoured by seven thin and inedible ears of corn (Gen 41:1-7). Pharaoh consults with his official dream interpreters, but nobody can make any sense of these dreams (Gen 41:8). Really? These are professionals whose very standing in society depends on their ability to come up with interpretations. Did they all really draw blanks?

Probably not. My guess is that they had lots of ideas but none of them suited Pharaoh. He sensed there was something more to these dreams than the official readers could discern. Enter the cupbearer who tells Pharaoh about Joseph.

Pharaoh has Joseph cleaned up and brought to him. When asked to interpret the dream, Joseph demurs, saying that it is God and not Joseph who interprets dreams (Gen 41:16). What is often lost in the English translation is that Joseph references *Elohim*, God, and not YHVH, the Hebrew God. Pharaoh has no idea who YHVH is, but *Elohim*, the more generic God or Gods works just fine. While Potiphar seems to have at least heard of YHVH, Pharaoh has not.

My son argues that using the name *Elohim* rather than the name of a rival and alien YHVH is Joseph's way of deftly sidestepping his own status as an alien. Perhaps so. In any case, Joseph's reading of Pharaoh's dream is simple enough, but his execution of the plan God reveals to him in the dream is not.

Joseph sees seven years of plenty followed by seven years of famine. His suggestion that Pharaoh find someone to run a food distribution program— Joseph's version of an Egyptian FEMA—may be self-serving, and it does turn out that he is chosen for the task, but it is interesting to note that Joseph insists that Pharaoh himself take responsibility for the program (Gen 41:34).

It's Pharaoh who is to appoint the officials who will administer the program, not the individual who is to oversee the program as a whole. And it is Pharaoh, and not the program head or his staff, who will impose a tax upon the land (Gen 41:34). Why? Perhaps because Joseph knows that this is going to be a very unpopular program and that any administrator who takes responsibility for it may suffer at the hands of people angry over the program.

Pharaoh picks Joseph to run the program and makes him the second most powerful man in Egypt (Gen 41:40). Pharaoh also gives Joseph a new name, just as God did with Joseph's father, Jacob. A new name reflects a new level of being: Jacob, "the heel," becomes Israel, the God-wrestler (Gen 32:29). Joseph, "he will add," becomes *Tzafnat Pahnayach*, "revealer of the hidden" (Gen 41:45). The name probably reflects the fact that Joseph revealed to Pharaoh what was hidden in Pharaoh's dreams. Along with this new name and status, Pharaoh marries Joseph— *Tzafnat Pahnayach*—to Asenas, Potiphar's daughter (Gen 41:45)!

I am assuming that Poti Fera, the priest of On, is also Potiphar, Pharaoh's chief agent. This is the assumption that Jewish tradition makes, explaining that Potiphar becomes a eunuch (*poti*, "mutilated") after his wife's false claim of rape and then becomes a priest.

I'm just filling in the details with rabbinic commentary, Mike. What do you make of them?

Mike: Let's start with what I find intriguing in your reading of the story: God alone reveals the meaning of dreams, Joseph's use of *Elohim* rather than YHVH, and Joseph's new name and wife. I think the three elements are subject to a range of interpretations, but the approach I find most useful is to see them all as part of the developing dance between Joseph (and, in the end, all of Israel) and Egypt.

What do I mean? Take the matter of the name of God. Joseph uses the more generic term *Elohim*. Is Joseph drifting into Egyptian ways, or is Joseph learning to accommodate his language to Egyptian culture? Might both possibilities be true? My hunch is that Joseph's story represents the story of the people of God in interaction with Egyptian culture. How far can accommodation go before one loses oneself in the dominant culture? Can the people of God carve out a place in Egyptian culture, serve the common good, and yet remain themselves? Such questions remain operative throughout the history of the people of God, even today.

Pharaoh, who is Egypt, moves to draw Joseph deeper into Egyptian life by giving him a new name and an Egyptian wife, which serves to associate Joseph with the ruling class of Egypt. Pharaoh is more than willing to have Joseph's generic god join the rest of the gods, if by doing so he can secure the services of Joseph and prepare for the coming famine. Pharaoh, though, remains the center of practical power.

Under such a scenario, Joseph's claim that only God (even the generic *Elohim*) provides the interpretation of dreams may serve to set a limit on the reach of Pharaoh and Egypt's claims and to serve notice that the God who travels with Joseph cannot easily be tamed. Even your note on "the priest of On" might be read as a clever device foreshadowing the day when Joseph's God will demonstrate that the gods of Egypt are no gods at all.

Of course, Rami, this is but one of several approaches I might take to the story. The story of Joseph's arrival in the court of Pharaoh almost begs us to indulge in theological play. I, for one, enjoy the game.

Rami: I am so appreciative of the fact that you refer to theology as play. I can see it as nothing else. But by "play" we don't mean something frivolous. Play is the way we access the imaginative level of consciousness that opens our intuition to insights that reason alone cannot uncover. It's not that I rank imagination above reason, but rather that they work together. Reason without imagination is often flat and lacking in meaning. Imagination without reason is often mindless and lacking in purpose. These stories playfully engaged can yield great meaning and purpose.

That said, let's get back to the main story. For seven years, Joseph enforces Pharaoh's twenty percent tax (Gen 41:34) and stores the produce of the people of Egypt. Then comes the famine.

When the people come to Joseph for food, he opens the storehouses containing the surplus produce they had grown. He had taken twenty percent of their harvest as a tax to be used for just this situation. But at no point did he suggest to anyone that he would *sell* the produce back to the people. After all, the food was theirs, collected so they might get it back during the famine. This is absurd and unjust. Imagine putting money in a savings account and then being charged to retrieve it! Of course, the people needed the food, and desperately, so they paid whatever Joseph asked, and what he asked must have been exorbitant since the people were made destitute within a single growing season (Gen 47:14-15).

Yet Joseph doesn't stop here. The famine grew worse (Gen 47:13), but the people had used all their money in the first round of food distribution. In lieu of money, Joseph forces the people to surrender their animals—horse, sheep, cattle, and donkeys—until all the animals of Egypt were owned by Pharaoh (Gen 47:17). Still, the famine continued. The people came to Joseph a third time, offering their ancestral lands and their own bodies, arguing that it is better to be a slave than to die. Joseph obliged them, reducing the entire population of Egypt, with the exception of the priests and the Hebrews living in Goshen, to slavery (Gen 47:22). All the land was Pharaoh's land (Gen 47:20) and all the people Pharaoh's slaves.

We Jews rarely notice the horror Joseph inflicts on the Egyptian people. He is our hero and we don't like to see him as less than perfect. But the authors of these stories are so much more honest than their readers. They do not flinch from showing us what happens when the former slave becomes the vice-Pharaoh. This is a morality tale, warning us of the evil that so often accompanies power, a lesson I suspect most Jews, especially those who turn a blind eye to the suffering of the Palestinians, have yet to learn. But the horror doesn't end with the enslavement of the people.

For no reason other than to break any hope of resistance, Joseph forces the newly enslaved off their ancestral lands and relocates them on the lands once owned by other newly enslaved families (Gen 47:21). This is a brutal act designed to break any ties one may have to ancestral lands in order to promote the perpetual serfdom of the Egyptian people. This was not part of Joseph's original plan, or at least not a part revealed to Pharaoh. All Joseph said he would do is store excess grain during the seven years of plenty and return it the people during the seven years of famine. Nothing was said of impoverishing the people and ending thousands of years of Egyptian agrarian civilization!

How do the Egyptian people respond to this atrocity? They welcome it! They are starving and praise Joseph for saving them. "We will gladly become Pharaoh's slaves" (Gen 47:25), they shout. Given the situation the people found themselves in, this is understandable. And it also explains Exodus 1:8, where a new Pharaoh arises in Egypt who "doesn't know Joseph."

How can anyone in Egypt not know Joseph? He was the second most powerful man of his day and singlehandedly transformed Egyptian civilization. What the phrase means, I suspect, is that a new Pharaoh arose who had no allegiance to Joseph, his policies, or his people—all of whom continued to flourish in the land of Goshen while the average Egyptian suffered. The new Pharaoh did nothing to liberate his people, but rather simply expanded the policies of Joseph to include the Hebrews themselves. Talk about karma!

Stepping too deeply into the exodus story is beyond the scope of this conversation, but as a Jew I think it is vital that we own our own Scripture and stop pretending that we were innocent victims of Egyptian tyranny. Unless and until we can own the shadow side of our history, both ancient and recent, we cannot hope to grow spiritually or culturally. Maturation requires owning one's shadow, and not continually projecting it on to others. The Jews have carried the shadow of Christian Europe for millennia. It may be that the Palestinians are carrying the Jewish shadow today. The result is never good for either party.

Mike: I can appreciate but not speak directly to the deeply personal component of your interpretation. For what it may be worth, I think Christians must work hard to own the totality of the Christian heritage. Our heritage includes the Scriptures we claim to cherish and the history our ancestors forged over the past 2,000 years. Taken seriously, our heritage forces us to deal with the good and the bad we've done in the name of Christ. We do not relish the experience, so we too often retreat into a narrative that paints us as victors or victims.

We're in agreement with regard to the outline of Joseph's deeds and the results. Rather than repeat the narrative, I offer three observations.

First, I suspect the storywriter intends us to take note of the irony implicit in the slave becoming the one who delivers nearly all of Egypt into slavery. As you note, the people of Egypt, desperate for food, cooperate in their own enslavement. The power of Pharaoh is enhanced, which, with reference to the subsequent exodus story, sets up a classic bout between the God of Israel and the god-king of Egypt.

Second, though the story seems to end well for Joseph and his family, the looming reality is that they also shall be enslaved. Once the machinery of slavery is set in place, no one is safe. I add one side note: Solutions forged to cope successfully with a given crisis often result in long-term negative consequences. The people survive, but they lose everything. Joseph thrives and saves his family, yet he lays the groundwork for the political/economic framework that will enslave them in the end.

Third, I suspect the story says something about the limits of any one person's vision, even one such as Joseph. Joseph acts to secure his own future and the future of the land in which, insofar as he knows, he must spend the rest of his life. As we shall see, he also manages to rescue his own family and make them as secure as possible in the land of Egypt. By almost any typical measure, Joseph proves to be a wise—if somewhat ruthless—person. Could he foresee the eventual enslavement of his own people? In my opinion, he could not. Joseph, to borrow a term from modern historians, is a "transformative" leader. Such leaders inevitably bring outsized blessings and curses to the people(s) they lead.

Rami: I'm intrigued, Mike, by your notion of Joseph as a "wise—if somewhat ruthless—person." Can one be wise *and* ruthless? My sense of wisdom doesn't allow for this linkage. I can get behind "clever and ruthless" but not "wise and ruthless."

Wisdom is the capacity to see the world within and without as an interrelated whole. It is the intuition that I can love both neighbor and stranger as my self, because both neighbor and stranger are part of my self—my true self, not my limited ego, but the cosmic self that is one with God.

Even if Joseph could not foresee the enslavement of his people, he could foresee the enslavement of the Egyptian people—in fact, he hardly had to "foresee" it; he was orchestrating it himself. Thus, his enslavement of them is an evil act. The foodstuffs he stored during the seven years of plenty belonged to the people, not to Pharaoh. I have no problem with Pharaoh charging the people a reasonable tax for storing their grain, but I cannot condone Joseph's extortionist practices.

I realize I am making Joseph into a villain where Judaism sees him as a hero, but I don't see a way out of this. Nor does it bother me as a Jew to admit that we have villains among us. On the contrary, what I worry about is when a people or religion sees itself as all good, all just, all loving. It is then that they can do the most horrible things, convinced that their actions are necessary and ultimately righteous. The Joseph saga that concludes the book of Genesis is a brutally honest, although mostly ignored, portrait of our shadow side. The story and Joseph don't have to be redeemed, only owned.

Chapter 16

Joseph Revealed

Genesis 42–45

Mike: Joseph's long story now reaches its climax. He rules Egypt in the name of Pharaoh, and he has, by stockpiling and reselling the people's grain, effectively enslaved most of the Egyptian population. Indeed, as noted, not only Egyptians but also people from the broader region come to Egypt to buy grain. The stage has been set for Joseph and his brothers to meet again.

Seeing that "there was food in Egypt" (Gen 42:1), Jacob sends Joseph's brothers to Pharaoh's court to buy grain. However, he keeps his youngest son, Benjamin, at home, for he cannot bear to risk losing him. The brothers are brought before Joseph, and they bow to him, acting out the very dreams that fed their fear and hatred of the young Joseph. Joseph recognizes them, but he treats them as strangers. They do not realize the Egyptian official before them is Joseph. Joseph has aged, adopted the dress of Egyptians, and speaks to them in the Egyptian tongue. In addition, they cannot imagine Joseph might be the person in front of them. To their minds, Joseph is long gone, swallowed up in slavery somewhere or perhaps even dead.

Joseph does not identify himself. Instead, he tests his brothers. He accuses them of being spies. The brothers, who once held power enough to sell Joseph into slavery, are now powerless before him. He casts them into prison for three days, thus giving them a taste of the life he once knew in Egypt and forcing them to experience what it is like to be defenseless in the face of power. On a side note, while the period of three days may have no significance at all, listeners or readers who also know the story of Jonah's three days in the belly of a sea monster and Christ's three days in the embrace of death may be excused for thinking a great deal can change over the course of three days.

Regardless, the brothers continue to insist that they have come on an errand to buy grain. They speak of their elderly father and their youngest brother. Joseph finally tells them that he "fears God" (Gen 42:18) and therefore will allow all but one of them to return home with grain. That one shall remain as a hostage in Egypt, until such time as they return with Benjamin in tow.

Now, the guilt the brothers feel over their treatment of Joseph breaks through, and they interpret their plight as punishment. They speak and debate among themselves. Though they do not know it, Joseph hears and understands all they say. Nothing, in the end, is hidden. His own long-suppressed feelings start to emerge; he turns away, and he weeps. Simeon stays in Egypt as the hostage. Joseph arranges for the brothers' sacks to be filled with grain and for their money to be slipped into the bags as well.

The brothers start for home, discover the money, and despair. They ask, "What is this God has done to us?" When they arrive home, they share the story with Jacob, including the demand that Benjamin journey to Egypt. Jacob, seeing the money, loses hope. He is long bereaved of Joseph. Now Simeon is lost as well. He will not risk sending Benjamin to Egypt.

The famine deepens. The grain runs low. Jacob finally bows to the pressure of reality and tells his sons to return to Egypt. Judah refuses to go unless Jacob agrees to send Benjamin, and Judah promises he will ensure Benjamin's safety. Jacob relents, prays that God grant them mercy in the presence of the Egyptian official, and sends them on their way.

Upon their arrival, Joseph has the brothers brought to his house. They are afraid, thinking he intends to arrest them and make them slaves (yes, there is more than a bit of irony here!). They tell the story of the money and note that they've brought it back and doubled it in order to square the books. Joseph tells them God must have put money in their sacks, for he had received their payment. He brings Simeon to them. They take a meal together, and Joseph inquires about the health of Jacob. Once again, the brothers bow to Joseph. Joseph, overcome by emotion, leaves the room for a time.

When the brothers depart for home, Joseph once again has their money placed in their bags. He has his own silver cup put in the bag of Benjamin. He sends his steward and men after the brothers to accuse them of the theft of the cup. The brothers insist they are honest men and rashly declare that if one of them has stolen the cup, that one should die and the rest of them be sold into slavery. The steward searches their bags and finds the cup in Benjamin's bag. He takes them all before Joseph, who continues the play by berating them for the supposed theft. Judah interprets their plight as God's punishment for what they did to Joseph long ago. Joseph insists Benjamin must remain in Egypt as his slave. Judah honors his pledge to Jacob and offers himself in place of Benjamin.

Joseph's control cracks. He sends away all his retainers and servants and, weeping loudly, confesses, "I am Joseph. Is my father still alive?" (Gen 45:3).

The brothers fall into deeper dismay. The most powerful person in Egypt other than Pharaoh is the person they nearly murdered and actually sold into slavery! Surely now they are doomed.

Joseph calms them, telling them they need not fear. Joseph insists that he now sees that God took all they did and used it to make provision for the days of famine. In short, from Joseph's perspective, God used the evil deeds of his brothers to bring about good. God sent Joseph to Egypt and made him ruler over the Egypt, all so that many might be preserved in the time of famine.

The notion that God takes even the evil that humans do and uses it to create unexpected, salvific realities is deeply engrained in Christian thought, Rami. The story of Joseph and his brothers informs the perspective. As you may well imagine, Christians interpret the suffering and death of Jesus along such lines.

Joseph tells his brothers to bring Jacob and all his people and goods to Egypt, where they will take up residence in the land of Goshen and live under his protection. Pharaoh endorses Joseph's plans. The brothers return to Jacob and tell him the news. Jacob exclaims, "Enough! My son Joseph is still alive. I must go and see him before I die."

Rami: It's a lot to summarize, Mike, and you did it well. Despite the length of the story, it is fairly straightforward and leaves us with only a few questions to ponder. Lucky for us, the questions are less straightforward than the story.

One of the questions raised by the early rabbis was the notion that Jacob "saw" that there was food (*shever*) in Egypt. Clearly, Joseph couldn't see hundreds of miles into Egypt, and so the rabbis said that he didn't see *shever*, "food," but *sever*, "hope." Jacob saw that Egypt held hope for the survival of his family, which is why he sends them there. This kind of Hebrew wordplay is an essential part of how we Jews read Torah. But what does it mean that Jacob saw hope in Egypt yet didn't see the horror that followed it? Did God deliberately hide it from him?

The rabbis say no. In fact, by playing with Hebrew numerology (*Gematria*), the rabbis try to show that God at least attempts to reveal the coming horror to Jacob. As the rabbis point out, Jacob commands his sons to "go down" (*radu*) to Egypt rather than to simply "go" (*lech*) to Egypt. The numerological value of *radu* equals 210: the precise number of years the Hebrew people would be enslaved (r/200 + d/4 + u/6 = 210). So perhaps God did reveal to Jacob what was to come, even if Jacob didn't understand the revelation.

I spoke with Aaron, our erstwhile editor, about this, and he had an interesting take. If we assume that Jacob didn't foresee his people's enslavement, then we must confront the question of the dark side of hope—that is, the unknown consequences of our actions. We make the best choices we can with the limited knowledge and foresight we have, but because our knowledge is always incomplete, we may—as Joseph does, as Jacob does—set in motion terrible realities beyond our ken. Or if we imagine that Jacob actually understood God's numerological hint, then we are forced to recognize the awful difficulty of his decision: go to Egypt and be enslaved or stay home and die, but die free.

Read this way, Jacob's choice prefigures that of Nachshon ben Aminadav—who, if you recall, led the Jews into the Reed Sea to escape the Egyptian army, even though it seemed like suicide to do so. Jacob, however, makes the opposite choice. For him, it is better to live enslaved than to die. So are we to see this as an error?

Aaron doesn't think so. The question is not whether to live or die or even whether to be enslaved or free, but rather whether by living or dying, by choosing one path or another, one might best serve the needs of godliness. Consider this: if Jacob chooses freedom and death over slavery, then, as far as he knows, his people will vanish from the earth—and their assigned role to be a blessing to all the families or the earth (Gen 12:3) or, put another way, to be a light unto the nations (Isa 49:6) will fail.

We're merely playing with possibilities here, Mike. What do you think about this connection between hope and horror?

Mike: The connection between hope and horror, as you put it, intrigues me. While I appreciate the insight suggested by *Gematria*, I think the story suggests Jacob did not envision the enslavement of the Hebrew people.

Similarly, as I may have noted, I don't think Joseph could have foreseen the disaster he was creating. Joseph shaped the political system into which he brought his people. We've already noted how his plans saved the lives of many during the years of famine and led to an increase in Pharaoh's, and thus his own, power. Now Joseph, with Pharaoh's blessing, brings his family to Goshen—the only part of Egypt untouched by famine—arranges for them to enjoy a relatively free status, and simply assumes such a situation can be maintained. Frankly, given his record of success in Egypt, I rather doubt Joseph could envision the possibility of his people ever being reduced from this extraordinary height to the equally extraordinary low of slavery.

Yes, watching from a distance and with the benefit of hindsight, we find it relatively easy to see the potential for long-term disaster in Joseph's decisions. Joseph, though, lives inside the story. He sees Egypt as *his* Egypt, a place to which he has been sent providentially to prepare a safe haven for his family. I think he does the best he knows how to do within the context of what he knows. Joseph, at least, makes a decision and acts upon it. The future holds what the future may hold, but in the present moment Joseph, like Jacob, chooses life over death for his people, and thus is able to continue God's plan for them.

Be that as it may, I think you are right to say that even our best choices can set terrible things in motion. As a result, and speaking for myself, I do not see how hope and sorrow can be separated. Each situation carries both possibilities within it. The horror of Joseph's own slavery holds within it the hope of Israel's survival. The hope Israel finds in Goshen holds within it the potential horror of the day when a pharaoh arises who knows not Joseph and sees in the Israelites only another pool of slave labor. Are our lives so different? I think all our decisions hold potential for hope and horror. Are we to allow the possibility of horror to paralyze us? I think not.

A friend of mine used to say that his job was to make decisions. As he put it, "I will make a decision. If needed later, I will make another decision." He understood that even well-informed decisions might eventually bring unintended consequences that required another set of decisions. Experience leads me to believe he was right.

Rami: Moving on to a later point in the narrative, here is another question this story raises for me: why did Joseph test his brothers? The common answer is that he wanted to see if they had become righteous adults, but framing them for theft when he had no reason to think them thieves makes no sense to me.

Rabbi Samson Raphael Hirsch, one of the great nineteenth-century Torah commentators, suggests that Joseph's concern focused on his brother's relationship to Benjamin. Joseph and Benjamin were the only sons of

Rachel, and Joseph wondered if his brothers' hatred of him was due to their hatred of his mother. If that were so, they might transfer that hatred to Benjamin as they had done to Joseph, and the young boy's life might be in danger. The test was Joseph's way of seeing if his brother was safe.

Again, this is a stretch. Nothing in the story leads us to believe that his brothers' ill will was caused by anything other than Joseph's narcissism. What the test says to me is this: Joseph is still Joseph, and he still takes delight in torturing his brothers and, by insisting that they return with Benjamin, his father as well.

I suspect you are more tolerant of Joseph than I am. So what do you make of this testing?

Mike: I am not sure I am more tolerant of Joseph than you, but I probably read his motives and the family dynamic differently.

Joseph's brothers might well be labeled thieves in that they took Joseph's normal life from him and did much the same to Jacob. The essence of a thief's character is that he or she takes something from others. The brothers fit the profile.

That being the case, I tend to see Joseph's scheme as an elaborate test of his brothers' character. Framing them for theft puts them in danger of being enslaved should they return to Egypt. Will they run such a risk for the sake of their father and youngest brother? Setting a trap for Benjamin threatens the boy with enslavement in Egypt and so poses a risk to the boy and to Jacob's happiness and life. Will the brothers risk loss in order to save their youngest brother and father? If not, perhaps they remain the kind of people who would sell someone into slavery simply because they feel annoyed or threatened by him. On the other hand, if they act sacrificially for the sake of their brother and family, perhaps they have grown.

I agree with you that the young Joseph took some delight in tormenting his older brothers, but the price they made him pay far exceeded his crime. By testing the brothers, Joseph discovers that they are not the people they had been, but instead have learned—in some measure—to sacrifice their own welfare for the sake of those they love.

Joseph, too, has grown. The wonder of the story is that he refrains from enslaving his brothers when they arrive helpless on his doorstep. His response is measured, at least by the standards of the time, and the results ultimately bridge the gulf between Joseph and his brothers.

Rami: I'm just going through a litany of questions this story raises, and the next one has to do with the fact that Joseph "fears God" (Gen 42:18). What does this mean in the context of the story? Joseph uses the phrase in the midst of holding one half-brother hostage and tying his release to the condition that the others return with Benjamin, Joseph's full brother. What God condones hostage-taking?

The word Joseph uses for God here is *Elohim*. Earlier in the story we are told over and over that is it YHVH who is securing Joseph's success and that even Potiphar perceived this (Gen 39:3). Yet whenever Joseph speaks of God, he speaks of *Elohim* rather than YHVH. Why?

From an academic perspective we might argue that we are seeing the blending of two versions of the saga, one common to the southern Israelites who speak of God as YHVH and the other common to the northern Israelites who speak of God as *Elohim*. The narrator, seeking to unite the tribes into a single people, uses both YHVH and *Elohim* to tell the tale.

While I am happy to accept this hypothesis, it doesn't add anything to our reading. As I mentioned a while ago, I suggest Joseph refers to God as *Elohim* to avoid having to remind the Egyptians that he is a foreigner with no ties to their gods. To avoid this faux pas and the dangerous consequences to which it might lead, Joseph restricts himself to the generic term *Elohim* and thereby allows his listeners to imagine whichever God they please. In addition, I suggest that Joseph uses the generic *Elohim* with his brothers so as not to give away his true identity. Only an Israelite would use YHVH when referring to God, and Joseph is trying to pass as an Egyptian.

Mike: By this point in the story, Joseph has become Egyptian, at least in the eyes of the Egyptians. His dress, marriage, language, politics, and position are thoroughly Egyptian. He has lived a long time without benefit of Hebrew company. My hunch is that Joseph, at least to the eye, sometimes acts more Egyptian than native-born Egyptians. He does so in part as a survival strategy. As you point out, there's no advantage in Joseph reminding the Egyptians that he is not one of them by birth. I suspect assimilation is also in play. By this time in his life, Joseph held no dream of returning to the family of Jacob. Though powerful, he was not free to leave the service of Pharaoh and chart his own course. He was on the edge of becoming Egyptian, including the language he habitually used and perhaps had come to think in as well.

If this is the case, the brothers' arrival leads not only to the salvation of Jacob and crew, but to the salvation of Joseph as well. The encounter draws him slowly back into Jacob's world, the world of the people of God in the making. Even as Joseph gives his family hope of survival, they restore him to his birthright as well.

Rami: This is my last problem with this story, Mike, and it is a huge one.

When Joseph's brothers, led by Judah, beg him to release Benjamin and allow him to return to his father, Joseph at last breaks into tears and reveals himself to his brothers. More importantly, he reveals to them the secret of God's working in history: it wasn't the brothers but God who sent Joseph to Egypt, and in this way God used Joseph to ensure the survival of his father and brothers (Gen 45:7).

God's will, not human choice, is at the heart of history. The brothers thought they did what they did for reasons of their own—jealousy, anger, etc.—but Joseph tells them it is God who decides what happens to us. It was God who caused Joseph to dream and to share his dreams with his brothers. It was God who caused his brothers to sell him into slavery. It was God who caused Potiphar to purchase him, and his wife to falsely accuse him of attempted rape. It was God who brought Pharaoh's cupbearer and baker to the dungeon, and it was God who caused Pharaoh to dream dreams his dream readers could not read. No one acts out of free will, but does only what God wills.

Yes, we feel like we are choosing, but feelings are deceptive. Could Joseph and his brothers really have chosen otherwise? We can't say for certain why they did what they did, but for me, they did what they did because conditions allowed them to do nothing else. This is what "God's will be done" means to me: we have no free will.

I suggest Jesus reveals something similar when he begs God to "take this cup from me" (Luke 22:42). In the end he says, "Not my will, but yours be done." Could Jesus have simply refused to be crucified? Could he have slipped away to safety before the soldiers arrived to arrest him? Not if God willed otherwise. Jesus was not free to be anyone but Jesus, and to be Jesus meant and means to be crucified and resurrected on the third day. He had no choice in any of it. And neither do we.

I am not happy with this position, but I can't see a way around it. I'm hoping you can show me one.

Mike: Rami, if you think me capable of resolving an issue that has plagued Christian thinkers since Christian thinkers first appeared, I'm flattered but doomed to disappoint you. That being said, I'll share how I deal with the matter as a contribution to the larger conversation.

The great biblical stories portray God as determined to reconcile us unto God—that is, to reshape us into persons who are at home with God, in tune with God, in love with God, and able to cooperate with God. In order to do so, God chooses to work through a long and messy process with the goal of creating a community in which such humans may be nurtured. From a Christian perspective, Jesus is the culmination of the story and the catalytic personality who launches yet another story of community-building that may come to involve all peoples.

Why take such a hard and long way, if God could just as easily force humans to be the kind of humans God wishes them to be? Maybe God just loves a lengthy, involved story! Some Christian thinkers tend to say, "God is sovereign. We cannot fathom the reasons behind his decisions. Bow before God and dutifully accept what he does." I think something else is in play, something that looks back to our conversations about the stories of the creation of humankind. God makes humanity in the image of God, and therein lies the challenge, which God confronts. To be made in the image of God is to possess, in some measure, the freedom of God. The will of God may be as fate to all creation for all we know, but humanity is gifted with the ability to defy even the will of God, though at great cost. God is bound by God's decision to endow humanity with such freedom, unless he chooses to shatter us and make us into something other than human.

Let's apply my perspective to the stories you mention. God's will is that Jacob's family become God's kind of community. Had they done so, the story of how God brought such a family through the great famine would be a different tale than the one we have. The family's dynamics and choices took them on a different journey. God proves to be a master improviser, more than able to take even the bad decisions of the family and fashion a future that preserves them as God's community. Did the brothers have to sell Jacob? No. Since they did so, though, God responds like a master chess player and charts a new course toward checkmate.

With regard to Jesus, my perspective is that Jesus made real decisions. The wilderness temptations, for example, offer him real alternatives to suffering. After all, there are well-proven roads to effective power. As I sometimes say, Jesus could have bought, wowed, or bludgeoned others into allegiance. He chooses to cleave only to God, to love the world and all within it as God loves the world, and to pay the price of suffering that comes with such love.

In similar fashion, in the garden, Jesus chooses once again to be the Messiah he believes God wants him to be. The prayer you mention is spoken in the context of utter freedom. Jesus is free to flee, if he so chooses, but instead he stays the course he believes God would have him follow. In this case, God does not have to improvise but instead may continue with Jesus toward the cross, the resurrection, and the community yet to come.

What might God have done had Jesus chosen another way? Who knows? That's a story untold because it turned out not to need telling.

Rami: I appreciate your notion of God's "long and messy" process for leading humanity toward holiness, and I realize that as a Christian you find Jesus to be the culmination of this process, and I would be tempted to agree if Jesus were fully human only and not fully divine as well. The problem is this: because Jesus is God incarnate, God is basically saying there is no way for humanity to ever achieve the goals God has in mind; because they can't, God will have to become human himself in order to have those goals realized. So while Jesus can end the story, he cannot *fulfill* the story; we cannot do what Jesus does because we are not God as Jesus is.

Still, I find the notion intriguing and love your idea of God as the grand improviser. Now I can see why God wants humanity to be free—it's more fun for God. Rather than being a playwright and having actors follow his script, God is participating in improvisational theater, never knowing where the other actors will take the scene and having to stay on his toes to keep nudging the story along the way he wants it to go.

Think of Jesus in this light. The story is veering dangerously close to another disaster. Noah failed, Abraham failed, Moses failed, the Hasmoneans failed, the Sadducees failed, the Pharisees failed. God has got to come up with a plot-shifting device that will save the day (pun intended). In literature this is called a *deus ex machina*, the god in the machine: a device pulled in from left field that "solves" the plot problems and puts the story on track to its intended conclusion. Jesus, theologically and narratively, is the *deus ex machina*; he is literally the God in the machine. God himself steps onto the stage of history, intervening in the action; he becomes human and operates metaphysically thorough his death and resurrection to ransom humanity, something humanity cannot do for itself.

There is no precedent for this in Judaism, no idea that God could become human or that the death of God is somehow necessary for the salvation of our souls. Indeed, the salvation of souls idea itself is alien to Jews in Jesus' time. So when Paul reveals the purpose of Jesus as *deus ex machina*, it is a plot twist so outside the box that most Jews—then and now—reject it. But it works nonetheless. Jesus' death and resurrection gets the story back on track, and now all God has to do is get people to accept Jesus as God and Savior. Back to nudging, I suspect.

I'd love to hear your thoughts on this. And then take us into the next story if you would.

Chapter 17

The End of the Beginning

Genesis 46–50

Mike: One of the things I enjoy about our conversations is that they help me get a feel for how someone else might view humanity, God, and Jesus. We Christians spend most of our energy talking with (or at) one another. I'm grateful for the way you invite me into your perspective.

I do not view Jesus as a *deus ex machina* in any fashion, though I certainly see how it is possible to do so. If I thought God and humanity to be utterly separate from one another, I might do so, but I think God and humanity are bound together. Jesus is the realization of this: he is *fully* human and *fully* divine—which is why I have no problem with his stepping into the story. While many Christians fall prey to the temptation to try to figure out just how this works, a goodly number know that words such as incarnation, Trinity, and the like are simply ways of talking about the great mystery that is the God/human connection.

Taking this approach, I do not think of the human story in Genesis as a long line of failures or of God having to do something humanity cannot do alone. Such categories do not apply. Neither God nor humanity acts in isolation from one other, whether we are dealing with a broad story or the tale of an individual. Both God and the people with whom God is working improvise each step of the way. God, it's true, is the better improviser, the one whose skill and wisdom ensure that in the end the long story will resolve itself in humanity becoming as it was intended to be—that is, reconciled with God. This is, in fact, what I think is meant by atonement. The Greek term translated as atonement historically carries the idea of reconciliation, of return; the notion of "at-one-ment" is an apt, if somewhat quaint, way of getting at the idea.

Rami: What is true of Christians is true of most of us: we talk with people who confirm our own biases and allow us to maintain the conceit that we aren't biased at all. What I love about talking with you, Mike, is that we both know we are biased and find our differences far more interesting and valuable than our agreements.

As for Jesus being fully human and fully divine—I agree. But I think the same is true of you and me as well, and of everyone else for that matter. We are all human and divine—at once, since this is what it means to be human, to be alive, to be part of the oneness of all life in/as an expression of God's unity. The difference between Jesus and me is that he knows and actualizes this at a level I cannot imagine.

I love your reading of atonement as at-one-ment. I do the same thing with *Yom Kippur*, the Jewish Day of Atonement. But it only works in English, a language that neither God nor Jesus spoke. Does atonement as "at-one-ment" work in Greek?

Okay, enough of "being nice." You know you can't talk about "mystery" without pushing my buttons, so here goes: when we say that words "such as incarnation, Trinity, and the like" cannot be defined and that they have something to do with the God/human connection that is itself a mystery, I can't help but wonder if we are really saying that none of this makes any sense and that rather than admit that it makes no sense, we pretend that the word "mystery" makes some kind of extrasensory sense.

This is true—in my anything but humble opinion—regardless of which religion is taking refuge in mystery. When we say that life is a mystery or that God works in mysterious ways, we are only saying that at the moment we can't answer some of the questions we are asking. We used to think thunder was a mystery and ascribed lightening bolts to Zeus. Then we invented meteorology. We used to think snakes crawled on their bellies because the first snake convinced the first woman to eat from the tree of knowledge. Then we invented biology. So if we can't define the terms we use, I suggest we don't use them until we can. Of course, I'm as guilty of this as anyone, and I understand how hard it is to do, but we ought to try.

Another thing I love about talking with you, Mike, is that after years of my trying to change your mind, you still think of God as a self-conscious, willful being, separate from the universe, who has a plan for humankind. For me, God is the universe and hasn't got a clue that humanity exists or matters. We are to God what a wave is to the ocean that waves it—a natural extension (in material and consciousness) of God's oceanic waviness. But stipulating for a moment that God does have some kind of plan for humanity, I want to know, as a science-fiction buff, what do you think about God's concern with beings on other planets? Does God care for Klingons (to choose one metaphorical possibility) the way God cares for humans? Is there a Christ for every planet that has ensouled beings on it? Do beings other than humans have souls?

Mike: Now, Rami, hang on a minute. Let me go back to where we started before I get into life on other worlds. First, the word atonement: yes, it works in Greek—though obviously the wordplay doesn't. The Greek word is *kattalage*, which translates more or less as reconciliation. The point being that even in Greek, the word connotes return or reunification. Second, I did not say that terms such as incarnation, Trinity, and the like *cannot* be defined. Instead, I gently reminded us of the limits of language. Theological terms attempt a description of the human experience of God, but wise theologians acknowledge that the fullness of God remains beyond full description. I am not taking refuge in mystery. Instead, I am simply acknowledging the reality of mystery. My approach does not preclude the possibility that we shall discover more about God and so revise our concepts of God. In fact, I assume this will prove to be the case. Still, since I live with the assumption of an infinite God, I find that humility requires that I accept the limits of our ability to plumb the depths of God.

As for the matter of changing my mind, coming over to your way of thinking, and the like, I have changed my mind many times with regard to the implications of the human experience of God. You've helped me refine my thinking in ways I realize and no doubt in ways I've not yet recognized. For example, our conversations and friendship consistently expose me to someone who holds your view of God and attempts to fashion an ethical life on that basis. This is important. Some Christian circles tend to argue that other approaches to God cannot provide the basis for an ethical framework that values both creation and human life. You, my friend, are living proof that this is not so. We remarked over the course of our conversation on the fact that though we hold differing opinions as to the nature of God, we often reach similar ethical conclusions. I hope you're comfortable being one of my poster children for how other views of God may provide adequate foundations for healthy ethics!

As to your question about extraterrestrial beings, I haven't a clue as to how God might relate to life throughout the universe, intelligent or otherwise! My guess, though, is that all intelligent life might be made in the image of God. What life might have done or is doing with such an opportunity elsewhere in the universe remains to be discovered.

Well, so much for sci-fi and for this introductory detour. Let's try to wind up Joseph's story. In Genesis 46–50 the story of Israel's transplantation to Egypt draws to a conclusion. Along the way, the story suggests that God approves of the move, depicts the relocation's details, features meetings between Jacob and Joseph and Jacob and Pharaoh, and foreshadows the story yet to be told in Exodus.

Jacob makes sacrifices and seeks the counsel of God, who then tells Jacob not to be afraid to go down to Egypt. In response, Jacob gathers all his people and goods and brings them to Egypt. When Jacob at last arrives in Goshen, Joseph goes to meet him. Joseph weeps, and Jacob declares that now at last he can die, for he has seen for himself that Joseph lives. I find it interesting that Jacob appears in no hurry to die. In fact, he lives seventeen more years. I cannot help but think that the writer intends us to smile a bit.

Of course, Egypt and Israel are not the same. Knowing this is so, Joseph advises Jacob's household on how to deal with Pharaoh. For example, they are told not to mention that they are shepherds, perhaps because Egyptians hold shepherds in low esteem. Joseph's advice seems to be, "You're in Egypt now. Act accordingly." When Pharaoh meets with the brothers, though, they call themselves shepherds and request Pharaoh's permission to settle in the land as such. My hunch is that the storyteller is trying to make a point: Israel is itself, a people set apart or different from the Egyptians; while they may dwell in Egypt, they are to remain Israelites. If this is correct, the story sets up what will become a running theme in the stories to follow: Israel's struggle with the temptations of assimilation. At any rate, Pharaoh—no doubt acting out decisions already taken in counsel with Joseph—grants their request.

Joseph introduces Jacob to Pharaoh. Jacob identifies himself as a sojourner-shepherd, notes that his own life has been brief compared to his forefathers, and then does an astounding thing; he blesses Pharaoh. I suspect this is the storyteller's way of saying that while Israel may dwell in Egypt, Israel remains the people of God and the ones in the position to bless.

Rami: You certainly touch a nerve with Jews when you take the Joseph story into the realm of assimilation, Mike. As you said, Joseph basically tells his family to try to "pass" as Gentile. This is something I had to deal with as a kid.

As a Jew in a Gentile world, I was different, and the desire to "pass" was strong. Belonging to an Orthodox synagogue made "passing" all the more difficult. But as a kid you want to fit in. My parents made no effort to water down our Jewishness, and I simply had to learn how to handle being "other."

Of course, I grew up at a time when anti-Semitism was more prevalent than it is today, but much less than it was for my parents and grandparents when they were kids. For example, the only country club in our town was closed to Jews and African Americans. When the law changed and such discrimination was illegal, the club invited one family of each to join. My family wasn't that one.

For most Jewish leaders, things haven't changed much since Joseph's time. Assimilation is still a major issue. Not for me, though. I like assimilating American values (the MSNBC version, anyway) into my Judaism. Indeed, I think American Judaism is a new kind of Judaism, one that blends liberal, egalitarian, democratic values into what was an autocratic, patriarchal, illiberal way of life.

On a slightly different note, it bothers me, though it doesn't seem to bother you, that God makes this hard and fast distinction between Jews and Egyptians. I can't do this. I find the notion of God choosing a people—even my own people—offensive. Why couldn't God raise up prophets among all peoples? Why isn't there an Abraham, Moses, Jesus, or Mohammad in every culture in every generation? And why do these prophets have to be men?

Mike: Sorry if I hit a nerve! Still, I think the matter of assimilation—as in being fully engulfed by a strong, surrounding culture so as to completely lose all distinctions—is a major theme in the story of Egypt and Israel, not to mention large segments of the Hebrew Bible. For what it is worth, pre-Constantine Christians wrestled with a similar challenge, and my strong hunch is that postmodern Christians are going to have to do so too.

As to your suggestion that I am unbothered that God seems to make a hard and fast distinction between Jews and Egyptians, I plead not guilty! The matter simply did not occur to me as I dealt with the story. The story before us is told from the perspective of Jewish writers (or, at least, the religious ancestors of Jewish writers). From their perspective, God is acting to call out and shape a particular people for a particular purpose: to prove a blessing to all the peoples. That perspective is important to Christians as well, for we—in various ways—see ourselves as grafted into the story of Abraham's family.

However, one must never presume to know the story of what God may have done or be doing in the context of other cultures. Jesus, in fact, cautions his disciples not to assume they are the whole story of what God is doing when he tells them he has followers about whom they do not know. My hunch is that God works within all cultures in ways that may speak to each culture, tugging and prodding them toward God's vision for humanity. I like to think that if we knew more of the full stories of each culture, we might be able to spot those prophets or spiritual leaders who play such a role within their history.

And speaking of stories, let's get back to ours. As we noted in an earlier chapter, the final sections of Genesis detail the movement of the Egyptian people, with the exception of the priests, into a state of virtual, if not quite literal, slavery. The famine continues, and Joseph continues to sell grain to the Egyptians. In the end, having previously sold their livestock, they now offer their land and very bodies in exchange for food. Joseph makes the deal, in effect making nearly all Egyptians sharecroppers living on Pharaoh's land. As I mentioned the first time this story came up (in a previous chapter), I think that at the very least, the storyteller means us to see the irony of a Hebrew enslaving others to Pharaoh, especially in light of the later story in which the Hebrews themselves become enslaved to a pharaoh who knows not Joseph but certainly uses the system Joseph devised.

Rami: Doesn't it bother you that the Egyptian priests escape the famine? If Ra were still god, we would say that he is showing the world that the Egyptian priests were favored, and those of us who believed in Ra would point to this story to prove that we worship the one true God.

I understand your notion about the irony of the soon-to-be-enslaved Hebrews enslaving the Egyptians, but I find it far more offensive than that. We Jews open our Passover story—the central story of our people—bewailing our enslavement in Egypt without ever mentioning the fact that Joseph enslaved the Egyptians to Pharaoh. Enslaving the Hebrews in Exodus is simply, to borrow a phrase from Malcolm X, the chickens coming home to roost. The fact that Joseph is the inventor of this horror is something that we Jews ought to own, but we prefer to hide behind the moral high ground of always be the victim. This is no less true today than in Joseph's time. Too many of us imagine that the Holocaust, anti-Semitism, and anti-Zionism somehow exempt us from living up to our own moral standards.

Nonsense. If we are to be a light unto the nations and a blessing to all the families of the earth, we have to learn how to embody the ethic of justice, mercy, and humility despite the horrors inflicted upon us—or, rejecting that, at least admit that we are no less capable of evil than anyone else and say something along these lines: "Life isn't fair, just, or compassionate, and if we are to survive, it is going to be at the expense of others. So while we aren't proud of what we do in order to survive, we do it nonetheless."

Of course, this would apply to all peoples. Either life is a zero-sum game with winners and losers, and each people is on its own when trying to be winners; or life is a non-zero sum game, where the only way to win is to see that everyone wins. The non-zero sum model is the prophet hope held out by Micah and Isaiah, where war is no longer studied and everyone sits fearlessly beneath her or his vine and fig tree. The zero-sum model is what we see in the news day after day and in history books chronicling millennia. I opt for hope.

Mike: Yes, the fact that the priests (not to mention Pharaoh and the nobility) not only escape but profit in various ways from the famine bothers me. That they do so, though, makes the story ring true for me. Take even a cursory look through human history, and I think you'll find that those who already have power and wealth usually come out on top during times of economic stress. Like you, I think Jews, Christians, and other religions do well to recognize and confess that we often contribute to such an outcome rather than challenge it.

That being said (and meant!), the wonder of the story as told is that God finds a way toward a future in the context of such an admittedly brutal cultural reality. What would we have God do? If God plays by the rules God seems to be establishing (humans made in the image of God, humans free enough to make meaningful decisions, God's promise never again to simply destroy the human race, etc.), what choice has God left himself other than to play the game as the great improviser?

If we accept this, we are still left with the problem of our own tendency to turn a blind eye to the evil we do. The possibility always exists, though, that some of us in any given time might choose otherwise, take actions and live into the consequences. When we do so, history takes a different turn. I think of the anti-slavery movement in England, the anti-child labor movement in England and beyond, the strong efforts of many today to confront human trafficking, the seemingly never-ending effort to reform structures that condemn large segments of humanity to chronic hunger and disease. I do not know what might have happened if Joseph had attempted to structure another way to deal with the famine. I do know that any number of

Jewish and Christian persons over the centuries have chosen to articulate and work toward a world in which human life and dignity are valued.

I sometimes wonder, Rami, what drives each of us to look at the same world yet see first its opposite sides. Frankly, I doubt we ever could discover all the factors that have shaped us into the persons we are. Still, I appreciate that you keep me honest about the dark side of religion and human nature!

Rami: Yes, the story rings true for me also. Not historically accurate, perhaps, but true nonetheless. That is what is so powerful about the Bible—if we are not forced to read it as history or science, we can discover great wisdom in it.

I like your notion that religion ought to challenge the excesses of power rather than contribute to them. I think this is what the prophets seek to do, at least when they are at their best. And I think this is what Jesus tried to do as well. This is why I find the challenge to "take up your cross and follow me" (Matt 16:24) so compelling. Taking up the cross in Jesus' day meant confronting the powers that be in the name of justice and compassion. And this was more often than not rewarded with execution. How far we religious folks have fallen. Today, it is too often we who are most likely to do the executing, or at least condone it.

But you are right to challenge my pessimism. There are many religiously motivated people working tirelessly for justice. I often forget that. So if I keep you honest about the dark side of religion and humanity, you keep me honest about the light side. A good match, you and I.

Mike: Agreed. But back to the story! At last, Jacob's days draw to a close. He calls Joseph to him, has him swear to take Jacob's body back to Canaan for burial, retells the story of God's appearance to him and the promise of God, blesses the Egyptian-born sons of Joseph (though he appears to reverse the proper order of the blessing), and declares once again that he is about to die.

Again, the humor of the story strikes me, for Jacob takes his time dying. In fact, he lingers long enough to tell Joseph that God will be with him and will in time bring even Joseph home to be buried alongside his forefathers. Then the old man speaks a poem or prophecy or song (take your choice). He tells of the destinies of the descendants of his sons. In the process, he clearly elevates the roles of the descendants of Judah, Joseph, and Benjamin.

When Jacob finally dies, Pharaoh grants Joseph's request to take his remains back to Canaan for burial. The story says that all the servants of Pharaoh and even the elders of Egypt accompany the brothers to Canaan in order to honor Jacob. Afterward, with their father now dead and buried, the old fears of the brothers resurface. They fall down before Joseph and, in unconscious imitation of the Egyptians and perhaps conscious fulfillment of Joseph's dreams, declare themselves to be his slaves. Joseph comforts them. He reminds them that he is not God and that God took their intended harm and used it to preserve the family. He promises to provide for them and their descendants.

Rami: Having Jacob live so long is a good plot device, Mike, though the humor is lost on me. The central element of this part of the story is Joseph's brothers' fear that with the death of their father, Joseph will exact his revenge (Gen 50:15). Given his treatment of the Egyptians as well as his emotional torturing of his brothers themselves when they first came to Egypt, their fear is warranted.

I know rabbis who believe the Holocaust was part of God's plan and the good that came from it was the rebirth of the State of Israel, but this makes no sense to me. First, if God is all-powerful, why did he need the death of six million Jews—not to mention the millions upon millions of others who died in WWII—to bring about the State of Israel? Second, we Jews would probably be better off if those six million had not died but had lived and had families. In short, if God is the all-powerful controller of history, why does God need the horrors of slavery, genocide, global epidemics, etc., to carry out his will?

The question of theodicy—why does a good God permit or even commit evil—is ancient and, for all practical purposes, unanswerable. I find the suffering of the innocent reason enough to deny the existence of this version of God (though not of God in general). It seems senseless to me. And the fact that God himself becomes human in order to suffer as well makes even less sense. If God came to end human suffering by taking it upon himself, then that would be different. But suffering is no less, and perhaps even more, since the time of Christ, which is why, I suspect, the notion of a second coming and eternal reward in heaven was necessary.

I'm not expecting you to answer this, Mike, and you might have to take refuge in the "mystery" argument, but if you have some insight, I'm all ears.

Mike: You're quite right. I have no answer to the problem of human suffering or theodicy that can be proven to be right. Of course, when has such a limitation ever kept either of us from holding and stating an opinion?

It seems to me that humans who hold to the existence of a loving God have three options. One is to attribute all suffering to the sinfulness of humanity, declare that the world can only get worse over the long haul, and hope for some kind of redemption in a new heaven and earth (to use traditional language). The second is to declare that the loving God has some kind of master plan that requires human suffering in order to play out according to God's intentions. The third option is to posit a loving God who works within self-imposed limitations in order to honor the freedom, creativity, and responsibility with which he has endowed humans. This is the option I prefer, and it also helps to explain the question you raise regarding the necessity of Jesus' suffering as a human. From my particular Christian perspective, the God of the third option must do more than the God envisioned in the other two possibilities. He cannot stand outside of the world as its judge and redeemer, because to do so would negate his gifts to humanity as well as humanity's very purpose. So rather than stand outside the world, he enters it to labor and suffer alongside us in the work of redemption—that is, the work of healing, of making right the world.

All three streams of thought, I think, run through the Christian Scriptures. I think something like the third option is implicit in Joseph's declaration regarding God's use of the brothers' wickedness. Thus, the long Genesis tale winds to a close, focusing finally on forgiveness and on the hope of the fulfillment of God's promise to a particular people.

Of course, Genesis leaves some questions hanging: Will the Israelites survive as God's people or be assimilated into Egyptian culture? Will they listen if and when God finally calls them to return to Canaan? Will they even know how to listen for God? And even if they listen, will God be able to bring them up out of Egypt should Egypt choose to resist the move?

Those, of course, are questions that find their answers in another book.

Rami: The promise you mention, Mike, that godliness and salvation will come to the world through the Jewish people, is the promise at the heart of Judaism. Indeed, Jesus himself says as much in John 4:22: "Salvation is of the Jews." I was raised to believe it. But I can't.

I love my people, but I don't see us as "chosen," or special, in any way. We have our unique traits—especially our love of argument and doubt—and I am proud of those and wouldn't want to be without them, but other peoples have other traits that I value no less.

Similarly, I love Torah, and I never tire of delving into the stories of Genesis, but I am not a believer in the sense that I take story for history. The more I engage with these texts, the more meaning I can derive from them, but it is always me doing the heavy lifting. I engage in eisegesis rather than exegesis; I read into the text rather than find revelation in the text.

For me, reading into the text, using my imagination to build new meanings out of ancient stories, is a spiritual practice. Indeed, it is probably my major spiritual practice. While it is true that I chant, pray, and meditate, most of my life is spent in the reading and deliberate misreading of Torah and other Jewish texts. I became a rabbi to learn how to do just that, and I see that practice—we call it making midrash—as the genius of rabbinic Judaism. This continued reinvention of our story is how we have survived the past 2,000 years and more.

Salvation is freeing ourselves—all humans, not just Jews—from the conditions that bind us to zero-sum thinking and behavior and that prevent us from living in the non-zero sum manner necessary for us to be a blessing to all the families of the earth. One major aspect of this conditioning is rooted in story and language, and Judaism revels in reinventing the former by playing wildly with the latter. So to the extent that people suffer from oppression by story and word, Judaism has a mission in the world. To play with John's Gospel, in the beginning was the word. Right after that came the Jews mucking around with it.

I'm also curious as to how you, as a Christian, see the fate of the Jews. I have evangelical friends who assure me that the Jews have been rejected by God and replaced by Christians, though not all Christians, only those Christians who are Christians like themselves. I'm not insulted by this notion. It's just a Christian version of the Jewish idea. I no more believe in the one than the other.

For me, Torah is a great anthology of myth and parable that, like much ancient literature, is a playground for the human imagination, more a Rorschach test than divine testament. I study it not as a scholar but as a seeker, in a way that is uniquely Jewish, a way that welcomes imaginative flights of fancy, that encourages deliberate misreading of the text to yield meanings the authors themselves could not have imagined. The entire history of Judaism is rooted in this act of misreading, and as long as we do this, the book is alive and enlivening.

Genesis is a huge saga, and this has been our longest conversation yet, but I find that, like working with the Torah, it never exhausts either itself or me. The book and the conversation both are endlessly enervating, endlessly self-renewing. And that, of course, is why we turn to them.

Mike: With regard to your question about the fate or status of the Jews, my answer is bound up with the larger question of what I think God is attempting to accomplish. My hope is that God is working—admittedly on a time frame that challenges our imagination—to fashion all of humanity into chosen people—that is, people of God. In the meantime, by which I mean the time I'm given to live, I do my best to treat all others as persons made in the image of God, loved by God, and filled with potential to serve God by working for the health of the creation and of humanity.

As always, we differ on the nature of Scripture in that I allow for a historical basis to the stories even as I treat their final form as stories worked and reworked to better reveal at least bits and pieces about what God is trying to do with the world and us. I bring the tools of my own scholarship to my study, as do you, but in the end I think you and I both approach the texts as seekers. Our methods differ in some significant ways, for example the rabbinic use of deliberate misreading in order to throw up unexpected meanings versus my tendency to try to live first within the structure of the story. Both of us, though, value the use of the imagination in producing new insights, questions, and applications from the stories.

Genesis, I think, provides most of the great themes with which our respective traditions wrestle. As such, the text remains alive and capable of sparking the kind of conversation we've enjoyed.

I use the term "conversation" quite intentionally. No longer can the world afford the luxury of religious traditions treating their sacred texts in isolation from one another. Instead, we must choose to converse with one another. Formal exchanges at academic conferences and councils certainly might help, but I see greater hope in thousands of conversations between practicing individuals, conversations in which potential friendship is assumed and actual friendships develop. I fear if we do not learn to talk with one another, we may well wind up destroying one another. Pardon the informality of my phrasing, but I rather think God will be very disappointed if we choose such self-destruction. Far better, I think, to pull out chairs, share meals, and talk with one another for as long as it takes to become friends.

Other available titles from SMYTH& HELWYS

#Connect
Reaching Youth Across the Digital Divide
Brian Foreman

Reaching our youth across the digital divide is a struggle for parents, ministers, and other adults who work with Generation Z— today's teenagers. *#Connect* leads readers into the technological landscape, encourages conversations with teenagers, and reminds us all to be the presence of Christ in every facet of our lives. *978-1-57312-693-9 120 pages/pb* **$13.00**

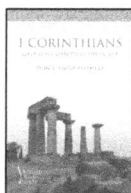

1 Corinthians (Smyth & Helwys Annual Bible Study series)
Growing through Diversity
Don & Anita Flowers

Don and Anita Flowers present this comprehensive study of 1 Corinthians, filled with scholarly insight and dealing with such varied topics as marriage and sexuality, spiritual gifts and love, and diversity and unity. The authors examine Paul's relationship with the church in Corinth as well as the culture of that city to give context to topics that can seem far removed from Christian life today. *Teaching Guide 978-1-57312-701-1 122 pages/pb* **$14.00**
Study Guide 978-1-57312-705-9 52 pages/pb **$6.00**

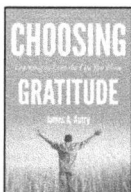

Choosing Gratitude
Learning to Love the Life You Have
James A. Autry

Autry reminds us that gratitude is a choice, a spiritual—not social—process. He suggests that if we cultivate gratitude as a way of being, we may not change the world and its ills, but we can change our response to the world. If we fill our lives with moments of gratitude, we will indeed love the life we have. *978-1-57312-614-4 144 pages/pb* **$15.00**

Choosing Gratitude 365 Days a Year
Your Daily Guide to Grateful Living
James A. Autry and Sally J. Pederson

Filled with quotes, poems, and the inspired voices of both Pederson and Autry, in a society consumed by fears of not having "enough"— money, possessions, security, and so on—this book suggests that if we cultivate gratitude as a way of being, we may not change the world and its ills, but we can change our response to the world. *978-1-57312-689-2 210 pages/pb* **$18.00**

To order call **1-800-747-3016** or visit **www.helwys.com**

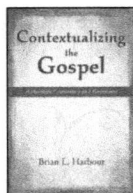

Contextualizing the Gospel
A Homiletic Commentary on 1 Corinthians
Brian L. Harbour

Harbour examines every part of Paul's letter, providing a rich resource for those who want to struggle with the difficult texts as well as the simple texts, who want to know how God's word—all of it—intersects with their lives today. *978-1-57312-589-5 240 pages/pb* **$19.00**

Dance Lessons
Moving to the Beat of God's Heart
Jeanie Miley

Miley shares her joys and struggles a she learns to "dance" with the Spirit of the Living God. *978-1-57312-622-9 240 pages/pb* **$19.00**

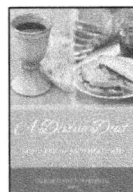

A Divine Duet
Ministry and Motherhood
Alicia Davis Porterfield, ed.

Each essay in this inspiring collection is as different as the mother-minister who wrote it, from theologians to chaplains, inner-city ministers to rural-poverty ministers, youth pastors to preachers, mothers who have adopted, birthed, and done both.

978-1-57312-676-2 146 pages/pb **$16.00**

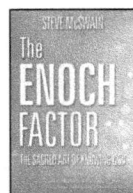

The Enoch Factor
The Sacred Art of Knowing God
Steve McSwain

The Enoch Factor is a persuasive argument for a more enlightened religious dialogue in America, one that affirms the goals of all religions—guiding followers in self-awareness, finding serenity and happiness, and discovering what the author describes as "the sacred art of knowing God." *978-1-57312-556-7 256 pages/pb* **$21.00**

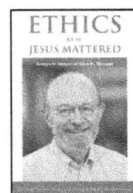

Ethics as if Jesus Mattered
Essays in Honor of Glen H. Stassen
Rick Axtell, Michelle Tooley, Michael L. Westmoreland-White, eds.

Ethics as if Jesus Mattered will introduce Stassen's work to a new generation, advance dialogue and debate in Christian ethics, and inspire more faithful discipleship just as it honors one whom the contributors consider a mentor. *978-1-57312-695-3 234 pages/pb* **$18.00**

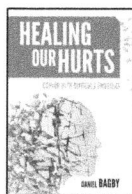

Healing Our Hurts
Coping with Difficult Emotions
Daniel Bagby

In *Healing Our Hurts*, Daniel Bagby identifies and explains all the dynamics at play in these complex emotions. Offering practical biblical insights to these feelings, he interprets faith-based responses to separate overly religious piety from true, natural human emotion. This book helps us learn how to deal with life's difficult emotions in a redemptive and responsible way.   978-1-57312-613-7 144 pages/pb **$15.00**

Marriage Ministry: A Guidebook
Bo Prosser and Charles Qualls

This book is equally helpful for ministers, for nearly/newlywed couples, and for thousands of couples across our land looking for fresh air in their marriages.   1-57312-432-X 160 pages/pb **$16.00**

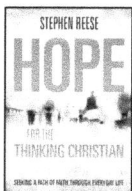

Hope for the Thinking Christian
Seeking a Path of Faith through Everyday Life
Stephen Reese

Readers who want to confront their faith more directly, to think it through and be open to God in an individual, authentic, spiritual encounter will find a resonant voice in Stephen Reese.

978-1-57312-553-6 160 pages/pb **$16.00**

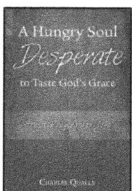

A Hungry Soul Desperate to Taste God's Grace
Honest Prayers for Life
Charles Qualls

Part of how we *see* God is determined by how we *listen* to God. There is so much noise and movement in the world that competes with images of God. This noise would drown out God's beckoning voice and distract us. Charles Qualls's newest book offers readers prayers for that journey toward the meaning and mystery of God.   978-1-57312-648-9 152 pages/pb **$14.00**

I'm Trying to Lead... Is Anybody Following?
The Challenge of Congregational Leadership in the Postmodern World
Charles B. Bugg

Bugg provides us with a view of leadership that has theological integrity, honors the diversity of church members, and reinforces the brave hearts of church leaders who offer vision and take risks in the service of Christ and the church.   978-1-57312-731-8 136 pages/pb **$13.00**

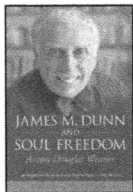

James M. Dunn and Soul Freedom

Aaron Douglas Weaver

James Milton Dunn, over the last fifty years, has been the most aggressive Baptist proponent for religious liberty in the United States. Soul freedom—voluntary, uncoerced faith and an unfettered individual conscience before God—is the basis of his understanding of church-state separation and the historic Baptist basis of religious liberty. *978-1-57312-590-1 224 pages/pb* **$18.00**

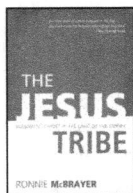

The Jesus Tribe
Following Christ in the Land of the Empire

Ronnie McBrayer

The Jesus Tribe fleshes out the implications, possibilities, contradictions, and complexities of what it means to live within the Jesus Tribe and in the shadow of the American Empire.

978-1-57312-592-5 208 pages/pb **$17.00**

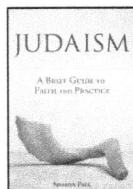

Judaism
A Brief Guide to Faith and Practice

Sharon Pace

Sharon Pace's newest book is a sensitive and comprehensive introduction to Judaism. What is it like to be born into the Jewish community? How does belief in the One God and a universal morality shape the way in which Jews see the world? How does one find meaning in life and the courage to endure suffering? How does one mark joy and forge community ties? *978-1-57312-644-1 144 pages/pb* **$16.00**

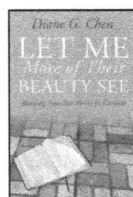

Let Me More of Their Beauty See
Reading Familiar Verses in Context

Diane G. Chen

Let Me More of Their Beauty See offers eight examples of how attention to the historical and literary settings can safeguard against taking a text out of context, bring out its transforming power in greater dimension, and help us apply Scripture appropriately in our daily lives.

978-1-57312-564-2 160 pages/pb **$17.00**

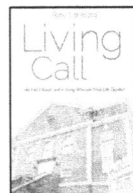

Living Call
An Old Church and a Young Minister Find Life Together

Tony Lankford

This light look at church and ministry highlights the dire need for fidelity to the vocation of church leadership. It also illustrates Lankford's conviction that the historic, local congregation has a beautiful, vibrant, and hopeful future. *978-1-57312-702-8 112 pages/pb* **$12.00**

Looking Around for God
The Strangely Reverent Observations of an Unconventional Christian
James A. Autry

Looking Around for God, Autry's tenth book, is in many ways his most personal. In it he considers his unique life of faith and belief in God. Autry is a former Fortune 500 executive, author, poet, and consultant whose work has had a significant influence on leadership thinking.

978-157312-484-3 144 pages/pb **$16.00**

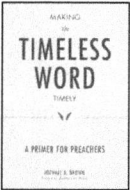

Making the Timeless Word Timely
A Primer for Preachers
Michael B. Brown

Michael Brown writes, "There is a simple formula for sermon preparation that creates messages that apply and engage whether your parish is rural or urban, young or old, rich or poor, five thousand members or fifty." The other part of the task, of course, involves being creative and insightful enough to know how to take the general formula for sermon preparation and make it particular in its impact on a specific congregation. Brown guides the reader through the formula and the skills to employ it with excellence and integrity.

978-1-57312-578-9 160 pages/pb **$16.00**

Meeting Jesus Today
For the Cautious, the Curious, and the Committed
Jeanie Miley

Meeting Jesus Today, ideal for both individual study and small groups, is intended to be used as a workbook. It is designed to move readers from studying the Scriptures and ideas within the chapters to recording their journey with the Living Christ.

978-1-57312-677-9 320 pages/pb **$19.00**

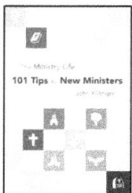

The Ministry Life
101 Tips for New Ministers
John Killinger

Sharing years of wisdom from more than fifty years in ministry and teaching, *The Ministry Life: 101 Tips for New Ministers* by John Killinger is filled with practical advice and wisdom for a minister's day-to-day tasks as well as advice on intellectual and spiritual habits to keep ministers of any age healthy and fulfilled.

978-1-57312-662-5 244 pages/pb **$19.00**

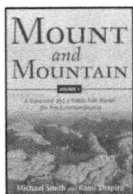

Mount and Mountain
Vol. 1: A Reverend and a Rabbi Talk About the Ten Commandments
Rami Shapiro and Michael Smith

Mount and Mountain represents the first half of an interfaith dialogue—a dialogue that neither preaches nor placates but challenges its participants to work both singly and together in the task of reinterpreting sacred texts. Mike and Rami discuss the nature of divinity, the power of faith, the beauty of myth and story, the necessity of doubt, the achievements, failings, and future of religion, and, above all, the struggle to live ethically and in harmony with the way of God.   978-1-57312-612-0 144 pages/pb **$15.00**

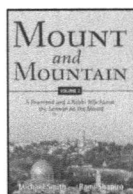

Mount and Mountain
Vol. 2: A Reverend and a Rabbi Talk About the Sermon on the Mount
Rami Shapiro and Michael Smith

This book, focused on the Sermon on the Mount, represents the second half of Mike and Rami's dialogue. In it, Mike and Rami explore the text of Jesus' sermon cooperatively, contributing perspectives drawn from their lives and religious traditions and seeking moments of illumination.   978-1-57312-654-0 254 pages/pb **$19.00**

Of Mice and Ministers
Musings and Conversations About Life, Death, Grace, and Everything
Bert Montgomery

With stories about pains, joys, and everyday life, *Of Mice and Ministers* finds Jesus in some unlikely places and challenges us to do the same. From tattooed women ministers to saying the "N"-word to the brotherly kiss, Bert Montgomery takes seriously the lesson from Psalm 139—where can one go that God is not already there?   978-1-57312-733-2 154 pages/pb **$14.00**

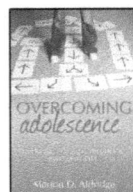

Overcoming Adolescence
Growing Beyond Childhood into Maturity
Marion D. Aldridge

In *Overcoming Adolescence*, Marion D. Aldridge poses questions for adults of all ages to consider. His challenge to readers is one he has personally worked to confront: to grow up *all the way*—mentally, physically, academically, socially, emotionally, and spiritually. The key involves not only knowing how to work through the process but also how to recognize what may be contributing to our perpetual adolescence.

978-1-57312-577-2 156 pages/pb **$17.00**

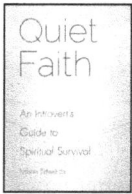

Quiet Faith
An Introvert's Guide to Spiritual Survival
Judson Edwards

In eight finely crafted chapters, Edwards looks at key issues like evangelism, interpreting the Bible, dealing with doubt, and surviving the church from the perspective of a confirmed, but sometimes reluctant, introvert. In the process, he offers some provocative insights that introverts will find helpful and reassuring. *978-1-57312-681-6 144 pages/pb* **$15.00**

Reading Ezekiel (Reading the Old Testament series)
A Literary and Theological Commentary
Marvin A. Sweeney

The book of Ezekiel points to the return of YHWH to the holy temple at the center of a reconstituted Israel and creation at large. As such, the book of Ezekiel portrays the purging of Jerusalem, the Temple, and the people, to reconstitute them as part of a new creation at the conclusion of the book. With Jerusalem, the Temple, and the people so purged, YHWH stands once again in the holy center of the created world.

978-1-57312-658-8 264 pages/pb **$22.00**

Reading Hosea–Micah
(Reading the Old Testament series)
A Literary and Theological Commentary
Terence E. Fretheim

Terence E. Fretheim explores themes of indictment, judgment, and salvation in Hosea–Micah. The indictment against the people of God especially involves issues of idolatry, as well as abuse of the poor and needy. The effects of such behaviors are often horrendous in their severity. While God is often the subject of such judgments, the consequences, like fruit, grow out of the deed itself. *978-1-57312-687-8 224 pages/pb* **$22.00**

Sessions with Genesis (Session Bible Studies series)
The Story Begins
Tony W. Cartledge

Immersing us in the book of Genesis, Tony W. Cartledge examines both its major stories and the smaller cycles of hope and failure, of promise and judgment. Genesis introduces these themes of divine faithfulness and human failure in unmistakable terms, tracing Israel's beginning to the creation of the world and professing a belief that Israel's particular history had universal significance. *978-1-57312-636-6 144 pages/pb* **$14.00**

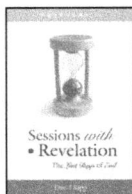

Sessions with Revelation (Session Bible Studies series)
The Final Days of Evil
David Sapp

David Sapp's careful guide through Revelation demonstrates that it is a letter of hope for believers; it is less about the last days of history than it is about the last days of evil. Without eliminating its mystery, Sapp unlocks Revelation's central truths so that its relevance becomes clear. *978-1-57312-706-6 166 pages/pb* **$14.00**

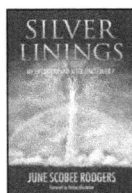

Silver Linings
My Life Before and After *Challenger 7*
June Scobee Rodgers

We know the public story of *Challenger 7*'s tragic destruction. That day, June's life took a new direction that ultimately led to the creation of the Challenger Center and to new life and new love. Her story of Christian faith and triumph over adversity will inspire readers of every age. *978-1-57312-570-3 352 pages/hc* **$28.00**
978-1-57312-694-6 352 pages/pb **$18.00**

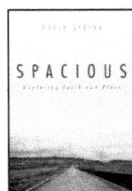

Spacious
Exploring Faith and Place
Holly Sprink

Exploring where we are and why that matters to God is an ongoing process. If we are present and attentive, God creatively and continuously widens our view of the world. *978-1-57312-649-6 156 pages/pb* **$16.00**

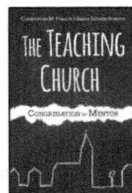

The Teaching Church
Congregation as Mentor
Christopher M. Hamlin / Sarah Jackson Shelton

Collected in *The Teaching Church: Congregation as Mentor* are the stories of the pastors who shared how congregations have shaped, nurtured, and, sometimes, broken their resolve to be faithful servants of God. *978-1-57312-682-3 112 pages/pb* **$13.00**

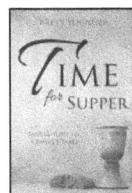

Time for Supper
Invitations to Christ's Table
Brett Younger

Some scholars suggest that every meal in literature is a communion scene. Could every meal in the Bible be a communion text? Could every passage be an invitation to God's grace? At the Lord's Table we experience sorrow, hope, friendship, and forgiveness. These meditations on the Lord's Supper help us listen to the myriad of ways God invites us to gratefully, reverently, and joyfully share the cup of Christ. *978-1-57312-720-2 246 pages/pb* **$18.00**

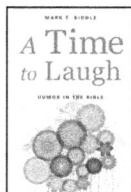

A Time to Laugh
Humor in the Bible

Mark E. Biddle

An extension of his well-loved seminary course on humor in the Bible, *A Time to Laugh* draws on Mark E. Biddle's command of Hebrew language and cultural subtleties to explore the ways humor was intentionally incorporated into Scripture. With characteristic liveliness, Biddle guides the reader through the stories of six biblical characters who did rather unexpected things.

978-1-57312-683-0 164 pages/pb **$14.00**

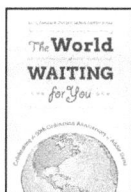

The World Is Waiting for You
Celebrating the 50th Ordination Anniversary of Addie Davis

Pamela R. Durso & LeAnn Gunter Johns, eds.

Hope for the church and the world is alive and well in the words of these gifted women. Keen insight, delightful observations, profound courage, and a gift for communicating the good news are woven throughout these sermons. The Spirit so evident in Addie's calling clearly continues in her legacy.

978-1-57312-732-5 224 pages/pb **$18.00**

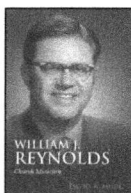

William J. Reynolds
Church Musician

David W. Music

William J. Reynolds is renowned among Baptist musicians, music ministers, song leaders, and hymnody students. In eminently readable style, David W. Music's comprehensive biography describes Reynolds's family and educational background, his career as a minister of music, denominational leader, and seminary professor.

978-1-57312-690-8 358 pages/pb **$23.00**

With Us in the Wilderness
Finding God's Story in Our Lives

Laura A. Barclay

What stories compose your spiritual biography? In *With Us in the Wilderness*, Laura Barclay shares her own stories of the intersection of the divine and the everyday, guiding readers toward identifying and embracing God's presence in their own narratives.

978-1-57312-721-9 120 pages/pb **$13.00**

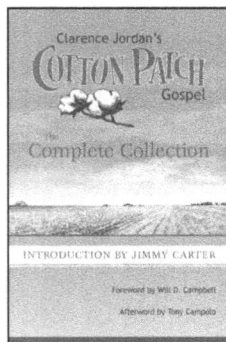

www.ingramcontent.com/pod-product-compliance
Lightning Source LLC
Chambersburg PA
CBHW062101080426
42734CB00012B/2718